Gorkhas in the Wilderness

About the Author

Dr. Khemraj Sharma (b. 1957), B.A. (Hons), M.A. Ph.D., P.D.F., Regional Director of the Central Board for Workers Education, Ministry of Labour and Employment. Government of India, Siliguri (West Bengal) has so for eleven books to his credit being published from various publishing houses of the country. His area of specialization is Industrial Sociology, Industrial Relation. The Gorkhas of North East India, Himalayan Society and Culture, Ethnicity and Social Structure, Labour Education, Tea Plantation Workers of North East India, Chinchona Plantation Workers of India and the Labour Relations in Indian Industries. Among his publications Plantation Sociology of North East India, Sociology of Indian Tea Industry, Marginalization of Gorkhas in India, Tea Industry in India, Socio-Economic Life of Cinchona Plantation Workers in India and The Nepalis of North Eastern Frontier of India are very prominent as well as scholarly publications. Presently, Dr. Sharma has been actively engaged in an empirical study on Tea Plantation Workers of Eastern Himalayas.

Gorkhas in the Wilderness

A Study in North East India

Dr. Khemraj Sharma

CONCEPT PUBLISHING COMPANY PVT. LTD.
NEW DELHI-110059

ISBN-13 : 978-81-8069-984-9

First Published 2013

Published and Printed by

Concept Publishing Company Pvt. Ltd.
A/15-16, Commercial Block, Mohan Garden
New Delhi-110059 (India)
T: 25351460, 25351794, *F*: 091-11-25357109
E: publishing@conceptpub.com, W: www.conceptpub.com
Editorial Office: H-13, Bali Nagar, New Delhi-110 015, India.

Cataloging in Publication Data--*Courtesy:* D.K. Agencies (P) Ltd. <docinfo@dkagencies.com>

Sharma, Khemraj, 1957-
Gorkhas in the wilderness : a study in North East India / Khemraj Sharma.
p. cm.
Includes bibliographical references (p.) and index.
ISBN 9788180699849

1. Gurkhas--India--Assam--Social conditions. 2. Gurkhas--India--Arun¯achal Pradesh--Social conditions. 3. Gurkhas--India--Assam--Economic conditions. 4. Gurkhas--India--Arun¯achal Pradesh--Economic conditions. 5. Tea plantation workers--India--Assam--Social conditions. 6. Tea plantation workers--India--Arun¯achal Pradesh--Social conditions. 7. Tea plantation workers--India--Assam--Economic conditions. 8. Tea plantation workers--India--Arun¯achal Pradesh--Economic conditions. I. Title.

DDC 305.8009541 23

Dedicated

to

LATE SHRI DHARMANANDHA SHARMA,

my beloved father who blessed me to pursue myself on the global academic journey

Preface

The Gorkhas are the masters of wilderness in terms of two pertinent dimensions, viz., Managing and Preserving wilderness. Historically, talking about the North Eastern Frontier wilderness as named by the British, made, managed and preserved the required level of wilderness by the Gorkhas. Having wilderness background of Pahar-Parvat (hills and mountains) of the Himalayas, the Gorkhas as dispatched to North Eastern Frontier wilderness, could easily adopt, adjust and love the region permanently. Sociology of wilderness, therefore, can best be proved to be the most useful resource to the government. In this way, the theory of Social Construction to study the North Eastern wilderness appears to be the most suited approach especially for the Gorkhas. Otherwise, the whole lot of wilderness had no meaning to the then people (tribals) living in the region. The theory of Social Construction of wilderness imparts manifold modalities of development such as social, cultural, economic and political. With the penetration of Gorkhas into the North Eastern Frontier wilderness, every resource there started calling for awarding human values and progress. The approach also helps us to comprehend the North Eastern wilderness from the historical perspective. The proponent of this theory, Daniel R. Williams (1993) stated that the approach "addresses the historical, cultural and political proceses by which humans seek out, create, evaluate and contest specific place meaning". Further, he stated that 'social construction refers to social, cultural and political processes by which groups of people create shared meanings and understanding of the place and how these shared meanings in turn structured social actions in and with respect to the place'.

Today, wilderness, Gorkhas and Globalization with particular reference to North Eastern Frontier wilderness in respect of Arunachal

Pradesh and frontier region of Assam (Sadiaya) proved to be the authenic fact that once wilderness as boon for Gorkhas has presently became bane for the local tribals that since two decades the wilderness invited contestation over the issue of ownership and non-ownership right on the land. The wilderness to the tribals was historically prior to British occupation of Upper Assam and hills of Assam (Arunachal Pradesh—known as the Prabhu Parvat in Vedic period) as most neglected place with neglected discourses but the meaningful amplifications by the Gorkhas through constructionist approach comprehended the region as the complete bliss in the sense that harnessing the wilderness provided subsequent contestations with the local tribals due to the state policy of tribalism and tribal development strategy. In fact, the North Eastern wilderness to the tribals was inclusive entity to be left at wilderness for ever by the government while to the Gorkhas, it is perfectly the exclusive entity for other nationalities of the country to come to the region by carrying national mainstream mission and vision in the light of sustainable economic development. The wilderness is both the means and ends of Gorkhas association for the last five hundred long odd years in the Indian mainland. The wilderness is the consequences of Gorkha sense of Social Constructionist Approach since early 1820 in the North Eastern Frontier wilderness. For the Gorkhas, wilderness is both the means and ends of their association. Go along with wilderness is being adequately supplemented by their culture of Basai Sarnu—shifting the habitation (Sharma: 2012) from one wilderness to another of the North Eastern frontiers. No other ethnic community had/has been able to translate the isolated wilderness into mainstream wilderness, from myth to reality, from tribal inclusiveness to national exclusiveness. In fact, considering the frontier situation, the wilderness is alpha and omega for the Gorkhas who love the wilderness, dear the wilderness, associate the wilderness and do manage the wilderness for common national cause. The Gorkhas are the harbinger of hill and foothill wilderness putting their benevolent efforts and positive attitude for the sustainable economic development mission of the government. The contestation brought about by the Globalization or market economy thesis between the Gorkhas and tribals over the ownership and non-ownership of landholding right, the whole sense of wilderness met with different connotations today in the North Eastern frontier wilderness that mainly includes the Arunachal Pradesh and hill region of present Assam (Sadiya). Both from the point of

Enlightenment and Recreational approaches or theories of social sciences again, the Gorkhas have managed the wilderness for the national cause to prove the region as tourist destination and thereby the centre for tourist recreation with their rich Gorkha cultural etiquette and manner. The whole lot of enlightenment and recreation theories emerged after connecting the basics of wilderness under the theory of Social Construction of the Gorkhas in the North Eastern wilderness. If the Gorkhas could not have penetrated deep into the dense jungles of the frontiers and managed the wilderness in the required and meaningful direction then the whole frontiers would by now be either as an unexplored entity for none or under the Myanmar or Chinese sovereignty. If the region would have been an unexplored entity, then again the present North Eastern frontiers would not have been given the name as North Eastern Wilderness for us today; provided the Gorkhas were not there at least officially from 1820 onward. Of course, in the beginning, the Gorkhas were lured, indentured and made captives in the wilderness of the North Eastern Frontiers of India. Thus, precisely enough, the Constructionist theory of wilderness is most appropriate approach for studying the Gorkhas in the wilderness.

The Theory of Social Construction of the North Eastern Frontier wilderness is for the first time being operationalized by this author in India while studying the Gorkhas living in Changlang, Lohit and Sadiya frontier-wilderness of Arunachal Pradesh and Assam respectively. The present wilderness theory of Social Construction of North Eastern frontier is a complete departure from the traditional anthropologist parlance of Verrier Elwin who had entirely dwelt with the inclusive tribal world of wilderness rather than the global orientations as have been interwoven by the Gorkhas to the tribals since time immemorial in the region. Pragmatically speaking, Sociology of North Eastern wilderness appears to have been a new endeavour of this author. So far, this approach has hardly been coined the day and operationalized in the parlance of Sociological study of the wilderness communities in India. The Gorkhas being borned, live and living in the wilderness Himalayas both environmentally and socio-culturally are accustomed to wilderness of entire east and North East India. Among the regions of North East India, the North Eastern Frontiers as in the British days are still officially or otherwise found to be conceptualized to be the North Eastern frontiers of complete wilderness. Who made the meaning of wilderness, who managed the wilderness, who profitably established the national orientation of the wilderness of North Eastern Frontiers? They were all Gorkhas and still are the Gorkhas. Both from the perspective of history and geography, the North Eastern Frontiers are still left into oblivion in terms of resource management of the wilderness and people thereof. In fact, studying the Gorkhas in the North Eastern Frontiers, I had at first a big hunch as to what, why and how the wilderness is a boon for the present Gorkhas and tribals under contestation, finally made a wonderful empirical study. Staying with the Gorkhas in place like Miao, Nampong and Chowkham of Arunachal Pradesh and Sadiya of Assam, the author managed himself to be completely assimilated, accustomed and integrated on their lifestyle leading to the wilderness—the wilderness located far away from the so-called civilized global society. In true sense, the Gorkhas since 500 long odd years of the North Eastern Indian history had complete absorption with North East wilderness as their home and hearth. The present contestation ever emerged since the last two decades is due to the political instability and disturbances in the region which has resulted into the emergence of terrorism that has been totally crippled the whole socio-economic fabrics of the North Eastern frontiers of the government. It is due to the casual approach of the governments towards insurgents both in Upper Assam and Arunachal Pradesh mainly in Changlang and Tirap districts.

The present study has encompassed the Gorkhas—their holistic orientations created in the North Eastern Frontier wilderness. May be the sectional interests with sectional approaches of the local tribals might have brought their momentous success but it is exclusively outturned by the integrated approach of the Central Government. However, the question of national tolerance, mainstreaming the local insurgent groups and appeasement policy of the government to the ultra organizations indicated through her Look East Policy, can do no longer sustain the vindictive, divisive and separatist attitudes of the tribals of North East frontier wilderness. Against this background, the Gorkhas are covertly appeared to be the useful populace in the region for the government, to establish sustainable national economy in the era of Globalization.

Working in the research project, I was out and out motivated and encouraged by my dear wife (Sarita Sharma) and beloved son (Abhinav Sharma). I would therefore extent my heartful thanks to them. Thanks are due to the moral support of Shri Narad Prasad

Sharma of Block Development Office, Matigara (Siliguri) Darjeeling of West Bengal. The Central Board for Workers Education, Ministry of Labour and Employment, Government of India, Siliguri chapter is the organization which directly or indirectly supplement my endeavour to constantly go ahead in this direction and therefore I am thankful to CBWE. I would also like to thank to Prof. Mohan Prasad Dahal of Nepali Department of University of North Bengal, Siliguri, for his academic support and suggestions. I would also like to thank Shri B.M. Ramudamu, Vice-President of All Sikkim Democratic Labour Front, Sikkim, Miss Nita Khawas (Ph.D. Scholar), Ranchi University (Jharkhand) and Shri Hari Prasad Khatiwasa, General Secretary of all Sikkim Democratic Labour Front for their untiring inspiration. Finally, I would also like to thank Shri A.K. Mittal of Concept Publishing Company Pvt. Ltd., New Delhi for showing keen interest on my research work and publish the same in recorded time.

The work will be a source material for the research scholars, professors, students and general readers who are interested to comprehend as to how the Gorkhas might have been surviving in the North Eastern frontier wilderness of the country.

Siliguri (W.B.) **Dr. Khemraj Sharma**
25.3.2013

Contents

I

Gorkhas in the Changlang Frontier Wilderness

There is hardly any study conducted on North Eastern frontier of India prior to the arrival of British in Assam during the Anglo-Burmese War from 1824 to 1826. The North Eastern Frontier of Assam was later on known as North East Frontier Agency (NEFA) in 1914. The North Eastern Frontier was administered from Sadiya (Assam) during 1914 to 1947. In fact, the British Government divided the NEFA into three parts, viz., Balipara Frontier Tract, Sadiya Frontier Tract and Lakhimpur Frontier Tract in 1914 (Mackenzie: 2011). The NEFA came under the administration of Union Government of India as a Union Territory in 1948. In 1948 again, the Union Government re-divided the NEFA into six frontier tracts, viz., Sadiya Frontier Tract, Lakhimpur Frontier Tract, Tirap Frontier Tract, Sela Sub-Agency, Subansiri Frontier Tract and Twensang Frontier Tract. The frontier tracts were renamed as NEFA in 1954 when it was re-divided into:

(a) Siyang Frontier Division.
(b) Lohit Frontier Division.
(c) Tirap Frontier Division.
(d) Twensang Frontier Division (This was included in Nagaland in 1964 while other divisions were made districts). The Sadiya came under the administration of Assam Government.

The Itanagar became the capital of NEFA in 1974. Prior to that, the name of NEFA was designated as Arunachal Pradesh (land of the rising sun) in 1972. Finally, in 1987, the Arunachal Pradesh became a full-fledged state of North East India (*Ibid.*).

Among the frontier divisions, Lohit and Tirap Frontier Tracts were located at the eastern most frontiers of Arunachal Pradesh adjoining the Myanmar (Burma). But if we see the history of Anglo-Burmese relations, since 1826, the Tirap Frontier Tract (earlier under the Sadiya Frontier Tract during the British period) and now the Changlang district of Arunachal Pradesh is very prominent from the point of the Gorkhas—their association with Northern Burma since 1826. In fact, from the present study, it is explored that the Gorkhas immigrated to present Changlang district and Upper Burma from 1826 onwards. The "Burma Ko Dhawa"—war with Burma and victory of the British Gorkhas enabled the Gorkhas to migrate from Nepal, Darjeeling, Sikkim and Bhutan Himalayas to the present hills and foothills of Changlang, Tirap as well as Lohit districts of Arunachal Pradesh and Upper Burma besides a few Gorkhas from Sadiya and other parts of Assam for agriculture and animal husbandry. Thus, it is found that the Gorkhas are in the Changlang district of Arunachal Pradesh from 1826 onwards when the whole areas of Assam and hills as well as foothills of Arunachal Pradesh and Upper Burma had been completely brought under the administration of British Colonial Government.

The Arunachal Wilderness

The whole area of Arunachal Pradesh especially frontier region can be called as the land of wilderness. The wilderness is characterized by the nature of land which is mostly consisting of forest land. The forest land requires thorough retrospection as the Gorkhas had been inducted in the forest land only. However, Maitree Choudhury (2009) reported that the land is a primary resource for Aruanchal agrarian economy. In Arunachal Pradesh, only 5 per cent of land is available for cultivation with more than 60 per cent of land under forest. While the existence of forest is seen as the most valuable asset from the point of view of environment and ecology, the same can be of little advantage as far as the agricultural development is concerned. Ownership of prime cultivable land and forest is important for the hundred odd tribes of the Arunachal Pradesh. There is no formal land tenure system in Arunachal Pradesh. The people exercise customary rights on land for Jhuming, hunting, fishing etc. They tend to exercise customary rights even in Unclassified State Forests. There is no *Patta* (land deed) system in Arunachal Pradesh. The only document the people receive from the state government in regard to land ownership is the Land Possession Certificate. The Land

Possession Certificate issued by the Deputy Commissioner for land up to 5 hectares very recently.

The Land Act of Arunachal Pradesh has been passed by the Arunachal Government. The tribes of Arunachal Pradesh are still governed by their customary laws and the land ownership right varies from tribe to tribe. While some tribes allow individual as well as family ownership of land, others are in favour of clan ownership and still others recognize their village or the community as the sole owner of land right. Thus, on the basis of ownership right, land in the state can be classified as follows:

1. land owned by an individual
2. land owned by a family
3. land owned by the clan
4. land owned by a village
5. land owned by the community

The state is consisted of total wilderness in terms of location of land mainly consisting of forests and the state has very thin population structure as found in difficult terrain conditions. The social solidarity of individual tribes necessitated communal farming and collective ownership of land. The abundance of land under forests prompted the tribes to adopt shifting cultivation which is called Jhum. Almost all the tribes except Apatanis, Khamtis, Sherdukpens and to some extent, the Monpas, practice shifting cultivation. As a principle, the entire land owned by a tribe belongs to the clan or of the village. The area of a village is determined according to traditional agreements with the neighbouring villages. The Jhum cultivators belonging to a particular tribe are not allowed to fell trees in the forested land beyond the jurisdiction of its own community. The practice of shifting cultivation makes the Arunachal tribals the semi-nomadic and their villages as the semi-permanent. The individual ownership of land is usually found in permanently settled villages. When a member of a particular clan puts in his efforts to make a piece of land operational and inhibits the area for a sufficiently long period, the ownership right of the land passes to him and to his descendents after his death. The outsiders in a village are not given land ownership right. A member from outside the clan may borrow the land from the village council and settle in the area but he cannot pass it to his descendents. In absence of any land tenure system in the state, for all practical purposes, the Unclassified State Forests are treated as community forests and in certain cases, as private forests where the people exercise their traditional rights of fishing, collection of fuel wood, small timbers, cattle fodder, cultivation and ritual hunting as well as collection of medicinal plants. The tribes of Arunachal Pradesh exercise their customary rights on forest areas for the purpose of protection as well as production. From this perspective, the Arunachal Pradesh forests can be classified into:

(a) Protected Forests
(b) Production Forests

All the tribes of North Eastern frontier like Tangsas, Mishmis, Khamtis, Singpoos, Noctes, Lisus, Wanchus etc. are having production forests. Under the production forests, the areas where the shifting cultivation is practiced by the tribesmen, come under the clan ownership. These forests are considered as common land or the community forest areas where the local tribesmen also exercise their traditional rights to the forests products. There are common lands of clan ownership or community ownership for practicing shifting cultivation. The production forests are demarcated by the natural features, chiefly by the water divides or valleys. Usually, the traditional village council deals the overall management issues of the production lands such as distribution of the forest land among the villagers. Opening of new land under cultivation, community hunting, and exploitation of the forest products on communal line and so on. The products from the common forest tracts is shared by every individual on the basis of respective needs. From the legal point of view, the forests of the state have been classified into Reserved Forests, Protected Forests, Wildlife Sanctuaries, National Park, Anchal Reserved Forests and Village Reserved Forests. Interestingly, almost all the Gorkhas have been stationed at Unclassified State Forests which are to be yet surveyed and demarcated. The Unclassified State Forests are under the ownership of tribal clans and community forests. Interestingly, in Changlang district, most of the land where Gorkhas are cultivating and grazing, generally fall under the clans ownership rather than community ownership because the tribes like Tangsas, Singpoos, Noctes of North Eastern Frontiers are by now have been influenced by the modernization process and concept of private property of market economy thesis. Whatever the forests are there in

Changlang district, they are under the private forests of the tribesmen which are leased out to the Gorkhas for cultivation and grazing. The Gorkhas are mainly engaged in wet rice cultivation in the district at low land called foothills. The wet rice agro-ecosystem though not as extensive as Jhum ecosystem is prevalent in comparatively low altitude areas. The wet rice cultivation is a complementary system to Jhum and is practiced on both man-made terraces and river valley flats. The system is restricted but crop yields are far better in the system due to higher soil fertility status of the soil. Unlike Jhum system, wet rice agro-ecosystem ensures crop yield year after year from the same plot of land and encourages the formation of permanent villages. It is a century old practice in river Noa-Dehing where Gorkhas are the wet rice cultivators. The observation made by Maitreyee Chakraborty (2009) is noteworthy especially from the point of view of Gorkha cultivators and grazers who are concentrated in both sides of the river Nao-Dehing of Changlang district since two centuries, i.e., from 1820 onwards. Both Miao and Nampong fall in the Changlang district located on the bank of river Nao-Dehing beyond which on the east one can enter the Namsai sub-division of Lohit district of Arunachal Pradesh and the river Nao-Dehing finally meet at the mighty Brahmaputra at Tengapani of Upper Assam.

The British Colonialism and Gorkhas in North Eastern Frontier Wilderness

In order to consolidate the entire hill areas of Arunachal Pradesh, mainly the Universe of the Study (Changlang district—the adjoining district of India to Myanmar), what the British Government did was as follows:

(a) Creating Gorkha force and posted at the Burmese borders of Changlang and Tirap districts as the buffer zones of North East India;
(b) British encouragement, of course unofficially, for the immigration of the Gorkhas especially to the hills and foothills of Changlang district of Arunachal Pradesh ever since 1826 as agriculturists and pastoralists (Subba: 2007).

Here, in this context, due to the non-cooperation of hill tribes to the British Government (Mackenzie: 2011), what the British administrators had intended to do was to encourage the Gorkhas to settle down in the unused land such as forest fringe, "Chars" (land around the river sites) and other Jhum (shifting) cultivated land of the tribals for agriculture and animal husbandry. The Gorkha force having absolute loyalty to the British Government as well as the stubborn Gorkhas (poor Gorkhas having Dukha-poverty, exploitation etc. in the Nepal Himalayas) settled in the hills and foothills of present Changlang, Tirap and Lohit districts and they made the colonial policy of expansionism of the British Government out and out successful in North Eastern Frontiers (Sinha:1990). This along with my personal observation in Changlang, Tirap and Lohit districts indicates that the Gorkhas had settled in and around 1820 in the eastern most frontiers. However, we will elaborately discuss this in the later chapters of the study. One of the interesting points to note here is that all the hill tribes of North Eastern Frontiers were asked to be there in hills only as nomadic tribes and later on all the tribals settled in hills only due to the Inner Line and Outer Line policy of the British Government since 1883 (Bose:1987). At that time, whosoever the Gorkhas were at the hills did not like to be there and came down to the foothills for better agriculture and animal husbandry. Earlier, these tribes had Ahoms of Assam as their slaves and thus they were fond of slavery system but later on after 1838, the tribals had to discontinue the slavery system with the pressure of the British Government. So, the hill tribes mainly the Singpoo and Khampti were not at all happy with the British Government on this aspect of their relationship. (Mackenzie: 2011). This continued till 1947. But as soon as the British left India, the tribe like Singpoo, Wancho, Nokte and Tangsa of the hills of Changlang district started coming down to the foothills and through their tribal councils they distributed all the foothill lands along with the forest fringe and other barren land and made the then Gorkhas of the land on cultivation as their tenants. However, at that juncture, they could not make the Gorkhas their slaves as they did it in case of the Ahoms of Assam in the pre-British days, due to the prohibition of slavery system in North-Eastern region of India. So, they all leased out their land to the Gorkhas at first on the rent system and today mostly they prefer to lease out their land on the "Bhagi" (share cropping) system.

Unfortunately, all the Gorkhas were forever taken for granted by the British as well as Indian Governments as immigrants in Arunachal

Pradesh as the special frontier zone dwellers during the British period and NEFA or Arunachal Pradesh after 1972 under the Inner Line Policy with the tribal development strategy for the tribal state of Arunachal Pradesh. In fact, today, the Arunachal Pradesh along with Nagaland, Mizoram and Meghalaya are purely considered as the tribal states of North East India. In this way, the Gorkhas are treated as non-tribals in the tribal land of Arunachal Pradesh of North East India forever.

The Gorkhas in Arunachal Pradesh Wilderness

Although the Gorkhas made the unclaimed barren land, forest fringe and "Chars" as potential economic resources, they are there where they were during the British period in so far as their socio-economic life is concerned. They are in the same stage of economic development as they were in the formative period of their settlement in Arunachal Pradesh. Still they are devoid of political, economic and other rights of the state. Even their cultural rights have been blurred and therefore cracked down to meaningless entity due to their religious conversion to Buddhism and Christianity and marriages with the local tribal women and being merged with the tribal way of life. In this context, I found about one hundred persons each from Gorkha community in Miao and Nampong of Changlang district of Arunachal Pradesh who due their marriages with the local tribal women have lost their Gorkha-ness in the sense that they do not even talk Nepali/Gorkha language properly. In fact, they have surrendered their ethnic identity at the feet of the tribals to simply survive in the most hostile as well as volatile environment of Changlang district of Arunachal Pradesh which was completely left into isolation till 1987 A.D. from the national mainstreams.

Coming to the question of Gorkha ex-soldier colony, Sadiya (Choonpura) was the frontier tract where they settled around 1826 A.D. It was again the Khonsa Gaon under the Tirap Frontier Tract where the ex-soldiers of Assam Rifles had settled down and pursued on agriculture and animal husbandry from 1826 onwards. It is found that as soon as the Gorkha soldiers were started to be recruited after the Treaty of Sogouli (1816) between Nepal and British Governments, in the Assam Rifles and Gorkha Regiments (later on named), they brought their families and settled their families in and around the places of their posting. Hardly, the Gorkha soldiers used to accompany their families with themselves in the army camps rather they due to the British encouragement, settled their families in the villages only. That was due to their cultural legacy of boastfully claiming themselves as "Lahurees" in their native villages. They had to do this as they had to be on mobile in North East frontiers. Interestingly, it is found that their numerical strength has hardly come under the consideration of the state demographic enumeration tables till the independence of the country in Arunachal Pradesh (NEFA). This has made the Gorkhas of Arunachal Pradesh as an unaccountable population of the tribal state of Arunachal Pradesh.

If we see the composition of Gorkhas in Arunachal Pradesh today, we find the following types:

(a) The Gorkhas of Burma (Myanmar) background.
(b) The Gorkhas of Assam Background.
(c) The Gorkhas of Assam Rifles Background.
(d) The Gorkhas of Nepal, Darjeeling-Sikkim and Bhutan Background.

The Burmese Gorkhas had settled down in Burma ever since 1826 but they were forcefully ousted from Burma after the Second World War (1939-1945) when the British Gorkhas defeated the Japanese force being nicely backed up by the then Burmese people (Shakespeare:1977). This shows that the Gorkhas of Arunachal Pradesh, mainly in the Changlang and Tirap districts had historical connectivity with Burma. Still today, there are over four lakh Gorkhas in Myanmar (Burma) as per the information quoted in Website (2011) while hardly the Gorkhas of North Eastern region had any kind of socio-economic relationship with China from the North-Eastern sides of the country. It is observed by Prof. Sinha (2009) that there were three important places where the ex-Gorkha soldiers were settled in the then NEFA, viz., Itanagar at first in 1826, still later on, the Sadiya in 1827 and Khonsa in 1828, the ex-Gorkha soldiers were also settled at Jairampur (1950) and Vijaynagar (1960) in the Changlang district of Arunachal Pradesh.

Let us see the demographic scenario of Gorkhas in Arunachal Pradesh from 1961 onwards.

Table 1.1 shows that Gorkha population increased from 10,610 to 94,919 in 2001 A.D. In spite of strict compliance ordained to the provisions of Inner Line Permit system in Arunachal Pradesh, the

Table 1.1: The Gorkhas in Arunachal Pradesh

Sl. No.	*Year.*	*Gorkha Population.*
1	1961	10,610
2	1971	30,912
3	1981	45,508
4	1991	81,176
5	2001	94,919

Source: Census of India: 2001, Jaisi: 1990, Dutta: 1981.

Gorkha population went on increasing may be due to the increasing demand structure of the local tribes for the Gorkhas in the state especially after 1987 in its agrarian sectors. Today, it is estimated that there are over one lakh Gorkhas in Arunachal Pradesh (Sharma: 2012). On the eastern frontiers of Changlang, there are over thirty thousand Gorkhas who are mostly engaged in agriculture, animal husbandry and floriculture. It is mainly found at Miao, Diyon and Nampong (adjoining Myanmar) that there is the concentration of Gorkhas in the Changlang villages. The Miao, Nampong and Diyon are the border areas of India besides Vijaynagar with Myanmar. According to the Census of India, 2001, following was the sex composition of Gorkhas in Arunachal Pradesh:

Male:	52,276
Female:	42,643
Total:	**94,919**

If we look the demographic scenario of Gorkhas of North East India, we find the following:—

Table 1.2: The Gorkhas in North-Eastern Region

Sl. No.	*State*	*Population*	*Percentage*
1	Assam	5,64,790	49.4%
2	Sikkim	3,38,606	29.6%
3	Arunachal Pradesh	94,919	8.3%
4	Meghalaya	53,155	6.1%
5	Manipur	45,998	4.1%
6	Nagaland	34,222	3.9%
7	Mizoram	8,948	0.8%
8	Tripura	3,377	0.2%
	Total	11,44,015	

Source: Census of India: 2001.

Table 1.2 shows that 8.3 per cent of the Gorkha populations of North East India are staying in Arunachal Pradesh. This is quite spectacular from the point of view of Gorkha demography of North Eastern region. They therefore might have been contributing a lot to the Arunachal economy. This will be very distinct if we see Tables 1.3 and 1.4.

Table 1.3: Rural/Urban distribution of the Gorkhas in North East India

Sl. No.	*State*	*Rural*	*Percentage*	*Urban*	*Percentage*
1	West Bengal	7,76,257	45.05	7,46,468	61.1
2	Sikkim	3,07,545	17.7	31,061	7.71
3	Arunachal Pradesh	70,186	4.1	32,590	8.1
4	Meghalaya	21,763	1.3	4,325	1.1
5	Nagaland	19,938	1.2	14,284	3.5
6	Tripura	828	0.1	851	0.2
7	Mizoram	1,210	0.1	7,738	2.0
8	Assam	5,03,057	29.4	61,733	15.35
9	Manipur	41,763	2.4	4,235	1.2
	Total	17,12,547			

Source: Census of India: 2001. Grand Total Nepali Population = 21,15,832.

Table 1.4: Settlement Pattern of the Gorkhas in North Eastern Region

	Male	*Female*
Rural	11,18,493	1012035
Urban	4,16,253	324968

Source: Ibid: 2001.

Tables 1.3 and 1.4 indicate that majority of the Gorkhas are staying in rural areas while majority of male and female Gorkhas are staying in rural areas. It is estimated in the Census Report of India, 2001 that altogether there are 21,15,832 Gorkha population in India. But Shri Nar Bahadur Bhandari, ex-Chief Minister of Sikkim estimated that there are over one crore and fifty lakhs Gorkhas in India (Subba *et al.*: 2009).

There are 335 villages in Changlang district of Arunachal Pradesh and the Gorkha population has been found in all these villages. In Vijaynagar, there are in fact, today nine villages viz., Fafarbari Gaon, Dara Gaon, Gairi Gaon, Budha Mandir Gaon, Topihill Gaon, Masu Gaon, Tohat Gaon, Santinagar Gaon and Ramnagar Gaon (Thapa: 2008).Population-wise, there are at least 3500 Gorkhas today who are mainly the ex-soldiers of the 7th Assam Rifles. There is no road connection to Vijaynagar from Miao Bajar or Namdapha National Tiger Reserve Park. Only there is air service from Mohanbari (Dibrugargh) of Assam to Vijaynagar of Changlang district of Arunachal Pradesh. Besides the Gorkhas there are Lusi, Yabin and Mizo tribes (*Ibid*). Shri Thapa has described the situation of Vijaynagar as the exploration of Gorkha like Hasta Bahadur Gurung, Lal Bahadur Cheetri, Vir Vikram Thapa etc. To go Vijaynagar by foot, there is a Gorkha Transit Camp at Miao Bajar of Changlang district which arranges everything for the people. Historically, they were the Sepoys (soldiers) of 7th Assam Rifles who helped Major General Gauraya under the leadership of Major Sumer Sing to explore Vijaynagar. When the Gorkhas of 7th Assam Rifles explored the place, the Gauraya came to the place and named the place in his son's name (Vijay) as Vijaynagar and another place called Pritnagar in the name of daughter of the Major General Gauraya. Another Gorkha who was involved in the process of finding the place later on known as Vijaynagar was Naik Shri Krishna Bahadur Rai of 7th Assam Rifles. The total areas in Vijaynagar including the Chokoon Valley adjoining Myanmar was 1200 acres (*Ibid.*). In this way, although the Gorkhas contributed a lot for the exploration of Vijaynagar, the different pockets of Vijaynagar were designated in the name of son and daughter of the Major General Gauraya. This indicates the marginalization of Gorkhas in Vijaynagar of Changlang district of Arunachal Pradesh. Presently, there are 6000 population consisting of Lisu tribe and Gorkhas in different villages like Gandhinanagr, Gairigaon, Ramnagar etc.(Website: 2012). In this context, Mr. Susanta Talukdar (2012) reported that the Gorkha residents of this once ungoverned territory are ex-servicemen of the 7th Assam Rifles and their families, settled there by the Government of India in early 1960s. An Assam Rifles Outpost was opened in 1962 and the first batch of ex-servicemen was flown there in 1963, three more batches were moved in by 1970-71. The Grokha settlers were given incentives in the form of cash, cattle, implements, houses, land and free air travel, besides jobs in the Assam Rifles. There are 13 recognized villages and one unrecognized in Vijaynagar. The Lisus concentrated in four villages and Gandhigram is being the largest Lisu village. Narrating the tales he heard from his grandfather, a local Lisu leader named Shri K.D. Yobin, said the Lisu tribe living in Putao in Myanmar used to make frequent visits to the jungles of Vijaynagar to hunt wild animals. Between 1935 and 1936, some Lisu families cleared some patches of jungle and settled there. In 1962, an Assam Rifles team, after a long march from Miao located Lisu families there. At that time, Vijaynagar used to be called as Daodi by the Lisus. It was named as Vijaynagar as mentioned above by Major General of Assam Rifles after the name of his only son known as Vijay who was in fact born there. Having lived in the same place, over the past four decades, the Lisus and the Gorkhas have started hiring each other's skills. The Lisu wooden pestle for grinding rice has been also adopted by the Gorkhas of the region. Except air service, there is no other means of transportation. The distance between the nearest town named Miao and Vijaynagar is 157 Kilometers. The residents hire Chakma refugees to carry grocery items and other household goods from Miao. The porters charge Rs. 50/- for every kilogram of the load which they carry on their heads. Thus, a bag of cement costs Rs. 3,000 in Vijaynagar. One kilogram of salt costs Rs. 80/- to 100/- while mustard oil costs Rs. 150/- per litre. Only two Maruti vans are there in Vijaynagar—one belongs to Indian Air force and another of the Assam Rifles. No public distribution system is there in Vijaynagar which means that the residents have to buy provisions from the Miao market at exorbitant prices. Every year from the month of July to October, there remains crisis for salt and mustard oil. For travelling by air, a passenger has been given subsidized rate of Rs. 676/- per trip from Mohanbari (Dibrugarh). There are flights from Mohanbari air port to Vijaynagar for four times in a month. There is no electricity supply in the frontier settlement of Vijaynagar. A hydro electricity project had been started in Gairigaon (Gorkha Busty at Vijaynagar) in early nineties but it has been discontinued due to lack of adequate fund from the government. All the building materials have to be imported from Miao Bajar of Changlang district of Arunachal Pradesh. No television set is there at Vijaynagar till today. They do not have therefore mobile sets also to contact their far off relatives and friends. If any resident wants to phone his relatives he has to do so from the Circle Office which has one INMARSAT satellite phone that has been frequently remained out of order. Earlier, to call for one minute, one had to pay Rs. 50/-. Only one school up to a class nine standard is there and for further study, one has to go out of Vijaynagar to Miao or Margherita/ Digboi of Assam. In this way, only the boys are going to Miao as well as Margherita/Digboi and therefore the girls are debarred from acquiring higher education in Vijaynagar. There is only one health centre with a doctor. Dr. Mopi Loyi is the doctor who has married a Lisu woman and settled there from 2006. He is serving the local people in the health centre where all the residents of persent 14 villages of Vijaynagar come for treatment. It is proposed to have been repaired a road made in 1972 but abandoned due to landslide from Vijaynagar to Miao. If it is done then instead of walking for six days for Vijaynagar one can reach Vijaynagar from Miao town within five to six hours. But the Forest department of Arunachal Pradesh is of the opinion that if the road is reopened then the Namdhapha Tiger Reserve Park will be disturbed. Yet the proponents of the road stated that a constant vigil by forest authorities can easily protect the Namdhapha Tiger Reserve Park. However, according to the Field Director of Namdhapha Tiger Reserve Park, the opening of the road cannot disturb the tiger reserve as he is confident enough to restore the ecology of the region but the only light vehicle can be allowed for transport purpose from Vijaynagar. This will help the Vijaynagar residents to have food security especially in the monsoon season of the year.

In this way, the whole border areas of Changlang district were explored and inhabited by the Gorkhas. In fact, still these areas are considered as the buffer zone of India to Myanmar having poor communication system and other infrastructural facilities. One feels the same regarding Changlang as might have been felt by the scholars like Verrier Elwin, Captain Vetch, Geoffery Tyson, L. W. Shakespeare, Pemberton, Mackenzie etc. while visiting the frontiers before writing their books like History of the Assam Rifles, The Forgotten Frontier, Philosophy of NEFA, The North East Frontier of India etc. in Changlang, Tirap and Lohit districts. Thus, the life in Changlang district is full of uncertainty and insecurity due to the isolated enclaves and battleground of NSCN and other terrorist outfits.

LITERATURE SURVEY ON GORKHAS OF ARUNACHAL PRADESH

So far, hardly any research study has been conducted (Bhattcharjee: 2005) on the Gorkhas of Arunachal Pradesh. However, in 2005, Dr. Khemraj Sharma studied the Gorkha tea plantation workers of Lohit district of Arunachal Pradesh. His book entitled **Sociology of Indian Tea Industry (2005)** is the first empirical study on the Gorkhas of Arunachal Pradesh. In this way, except the Census Reports of India on Gorkhas of the state, no scholar has so far dared to study the Gorkhas of Arunachal Pradesh. But unfortunately, all the Census

Reports of India highlighted that the Gorkhas are immigrants and thus unfortunately not a single line of appreciation has ever been quoted in the Census Reports till today about the contributions being made by the Gorkhas of Arunachal Pradesh to the state economy.

Scope of the Study

The present study will be an immense support to the future scholars who may be utterly interested to conduct the research studies on the Gorkhas of Arunachal Pradesh. Due to the strict compliance accorded for application as well as implementation to the Inner Line Permit System of Arunachal Pradesh in Changlang district by the government, not a single scholar has so far dared to visit the Changlang district of Arunachal Pradesh and study the Gorkhas who are mainly concentrated in the agrarian sector of Arunachal economy.

Objectives of the Study

The cardinal objective of the present study is to look into the agony of socio-economic living of Gorkhas at the Changlang district of Arunachal Pradesh. The enquiry into the history of Gorkha settlement (Rana: 2008) in forest fringe and unused as well as the barren land of Diyon river basin and Jhum (shifting) cultivation land of the tribals has been attempted in the present study. The study shall also highlight the fact that the Gorkhas of Changlang district of Arunachal Pradesh are still in the primitive stage of economic development.

Universe of the Study

The Miao and Nampong on the Diyon river basin is the universe of the study in the Changlang district of Arunachal Pradesh. The Miao and Nampong villages are the locations where my field observation had been done. The approach of the study is Anthropological ones as the Arunachal Pradesh is very fertile for Anthropological method of studying the Gorkhas in the tribal dominated society. The Miao of Changlang district is situated at the distance of 110 kilometers away from the Tinsukia town of Upper Assam. Here, more than fifty Gorkha households had been studied as a sampled village and the Nampong village of the Changlang district of Arunachal Pradesh as another sampled village which is situated at the distance of 112 kilometers away from the Tinsukia town of Upper Assam. The Miao was developed after the formation of Arunachal Pradesh as a state of North East India in 1987, while the history of Nampong starts from 1945—aftermath of the Second World War (1939-1945). Here, at Nampong, in order to fight with the Japanese force being backed up by the Burmese people, the British Government constructed a road known as Stilwell Road (1943-1945). Now, the name of the road is National Highway No. 153 that goes up to the Pangsau Pass of Myanmar (Burma). We found the same bridge being constructed at that time over the Nampong River. The name of the bridge was Borgolai Bridge. In fact, the Stilwell Road was constructed from Ledo (Assam) via Jairampur to Pangsau Pass of Arunachal Pradesh. It is found that the Nampong-Jairampur (a Check Post is there) area was the battleground where many British Allied Force including the soldiers of Gorkha Regiment and Assam Rifles died in the Second World War fighting with the Japanese force. To construct the Stilwell Road, many Gorkhas had been bought from Burma as Coolies (Sinha: 1986) as well as the porters by the British Government. The war symmetry made during the war period is still found there at Jairampur where I was able to calculate at least twenty graveyards of the Gorkha soldiers who died in the Second World War. After the Second World War, the Gorkha Coolies and porters were lured to settle down at the Nampong Gaon permanently by the British Government. Therefore, the data collected from Miao have been adequately supplemented by the data collated from the Nampong of Changlang district of Arunachal Pradesh in the present study.

Methodology of the Study

In Miao, I visited the villages like New Singpoo Gaon, Wailaf Gaon, Civil Power Line Gaon, Garo Line Gaon, L.C. Link Gaon, 10th Mile Gaon. Upper Colony Gaon, Police Colony Gaon, Miao Bajar Gaon, Kali Mandir Gaon, Brake Line Gaon, TVS Gaon, 6th Mile Gaon, Namchik Gaon, Kharsang Gaon and in Nampong, I visited the Kharsang Gaon, Nampong Gaon, Nampong II Gaon and Jairampur Gaon to supplement the data of the Miao villages.

The present study, due to lack of literature, on the Gorkhas of Arunachal Pradesh, is purely based on my personal observation and case studies from Changlang district of Arunachal Pradesh. Miao and Nampong where I conducted my field work for the research study are the two sub-divisional towns of Changlang district of Arunachal Pradesh.

II

The Gorkhas of Changlang District

There is no authentic source that indicates the exact numerical strength of the Gorkhas in Changlang district of Arunachal Pradesh. But it is estimated by the offices of the Sub-Divisional Commissioners of Miao and Nampong that now at least there are thirty thousand Gorkhas in Changlang district of Arunachal Pradesh. They are all found in various villages of the district. The villages are located mainly in hills and foothills of the district. The universe of the present study was Miao supplemented by the Nampong villages. The Miao is having more clustered villages Gorkha population while the Nampong villages are having scattered Gorkha households. In Nampong, there are 200 Gorkha households consisting of 1500 population. They are all the tenants of Tangsa tribes who have 27 sub-tribes with 3000 population in Nampong and Miao areas of the Changlang district. It is found that even the ex-government Gorkha employees of lower grade like peon, Chowkidar, primary school teachers, clerks etc. are also staying at the rented houses of Tangsa tribe in Nampong. It is also observed that even the Gorkha ex-soldiers of Assam Rifles in Jairampur are staying at the rented houses (Vara Ghars) of Tangsa tribes. Altogether, there are 600 Gorkhas in Jairampur area. The Jairampur, historically speaking, was the Zonal Headquarters of Assam Rifles. Now, 18th Battalion of Assam Rifles is there at Jairampur. 50 per cent of the Battalion soldiers are Gorkhas. In the olden days, people used to go to Pangsau Pass from Jairampur. In those days, at Pangsau Pass, a weekly Hat (market) used to take place on Thursday but now it is closed down except once in a year due to the security reason. In the weekly Hat day, lot of Gorkha food items like Gundruk, Kinema, Jhar-Rakshi, Rayako Sag, Sinki, Dale Khorsani (mainly the fermented foods of the Himalayas) (Tamang: 2009) used to be sold by the

Gorkhas. Here, almost all the Gorkhas are having Burmese (Myanmar) (Sinha: 1986) and Assamese background. They had to come to Nampong villages due to the cultural exploitation by the Burmese and of course, with the insistence of British Government as well as to some extent by the exploitation of the Assamese people in Assam. They had to forcefully adopt the Burmese culture including the Buddhist religion in Burma. According to Nampong Gorkhas, cultural exploitation of the Burmese people upon the Gorkhas was the immediate cause for the Gorkhas Return Migration (Sinha: 2007) to Nampong. Majority of the Gorkhas are Matwalis in Nampong. Altogether, 500 Puras (1 Pura=5 Acres of land) consisting of 25,000 acres of land are taken on lease by the Gorkhas in Nampong from the Tangsa tribes for agriculture, animal husbandry and floriculture. Again, about 200 Tangsa landowners are found at Nampong. These Gorkhas, as already mentioned in the study, have their settlement history in the region after the Second World War (1945).

Coming to the question of Miao where more than 12 thousand Gorkhas are there, the Miao is consisting of Miao, Singpoo Gaon, New Singpoo Gaon, Namphai I and Namphai II villages. In fact, the New Singpoo Gaon was my sampled village for the study. The Gorkhas had been settled in the New Singpoo Gaon from Namphai I and Namphai II villages of Miao ever since the last thirty years. At that time, all the Gorkhas were being invited by the Singpoos of the Singpoo Gaon to cultivate their land and also to pursue on animal husbandry as well as floriculture. Altogether, I found fifty Gorkha households in New Singpoo Gaon. The statistical break up of the Gorkha households of the New Singpoo Gaon is as follows:

Bahun	10 Households
Mangar	25 Households
Gurung	5 Households
Limbu	2 Households
Rai	3 Households
Chhetri	5 Households
Total	**50 Households**

Source: Field Work: 2011.

Interestingly, unlike Diyon, Dewan, Nampong, Kharsang, Namphai I and Namphai II villages of Changlang district, there is no Tamang (mostly they are called Lamas in Arunachal Pradesh as a whole) caste in New Singpoo Gaon. The Gorkha castes such as Tamang and Limbu as in Darjeeling-Sikkim, are not considered as Scheduled Tribes in Arunachal Pradesh. The caste like Manger, Gurung, Rai, Limbu and Chhetri of New Singpoo Gaon had their ancestors who belonged to the Assam Rifles and agrarian sectors of this region of Arunachal Pradesh and Assam.

There is Namdapha National Tiger Reserve Park that falls in the Changlang district of Arunachal Pradesh and the park is situated at the distance of 35 kilometers away from the Miao Bajar (Thapa: 2008) and also the park is located at the Myanmar border. At least 15 Gorkha households mainly belonging to the Tamang caste are found as the caretakers of the National Tiger Reserve Park at Namdapha. They are also found to have been pursuing on dry land cultivation by raising rough terraces on the steep Himalayas of Dewan region where the park is situated. The entire area is called Dewan region from where the people go to Vijaynagar by foot for six days. However, up to Dewan Bajar, there is a motorable but rough road from Miao Bajar.

At Miao, the fifty Gorkha households of New Singpoo Gaon have 500 cattle stocks. There is a grazing land for these cattle stocks of the Gorkhas located just below the Miao Bajar at the side of Boorie Dehing and Dehing (Nau Dehing or Diyon) rivers. Both the rivers are the tributaries of Siyang (Brahmaputra) river. The Boorie Dehing and Dehing rivers meet the mighty Brahmaputra at the Assam plains.

Pondering on the caste composition of Gorkha population of New Singpoo Gaon, it is observed that historically, these people were found to have been the most suited human resource stock for the British army and the agrarian sector economy during the British period and independent eras of the Indian Government. The Gorkhas have taken land on lease (rent) by paying Rs. 3500/- per Pura per year today both in Miao and Nampong villages. These Gorkhas who have been staying at the tribal houses have to pay Rs. 320/- per month irrespective of the size of the tribal houses. For staying at the huts constructed by the Gorkha themselves, each Gorkha household dweller has to pay Rs. 120/- per month irrespective of size of the hut. It shows that both the land (Pura) and house are absolutely under the possession of the tribal people. The above description shows that the Gorkhas have no stackholding in the Changlang district of Arunachal Pradesh except they have earned the status of Sukumbasis (temporary settlers) ever since the British days and therefore they have never been considered as Raithanees (permanent settlers) by the tribals in the villages of

Changlang district of Arunachal Pradesh of North Eastern Frontier of India.

POLITICS ON GORKHAS LIVING IN ARUNACHAL PRADESH

From the observation made in the Changlang district, it is found that uncertainty is the cardinal feature of Gorkha living in Arunachal Pradesh. The Gorkhas have no landownership right. They are all non-tribals in the land of tribals of Arunachal Pradesh. The Arunachal Pradesh along with Mizoram, Nagaland and Meghalaya is the tribal state (Rana: 2008) of North East India. Again, the Gorkhas have no voting right for Lok Sabha and Rajya Sabha Members of Indian Parliament. Of course, the Gorkhas have given voting right for Panchayat Members (three tier Panchayati Raj System in Arunachal Pradesh) and Members of Arunachal Legislative Assembly elections. No Gorkha has been given permanent Inner Line Permit. Every year, their Inner Line Permits have to be renewed from the Office of the Sub-Divisional Commissioners at Miao and Nampong of the Changlang district. In this way, their participation in the electoral process (Upadhaya: 2007) of living is almost nil in Arunachal Pradesh. No Gorkha can purchase land in rural areas of Arunachal Pradesh although a few Gorkhas have purchased land and constructed house in towns like Khonsa (Tirap district), Changlang (Changlang district) and Tezu (Lohit district) prior to 1987. In spite of this, very interestingly, why the tribals want to keep Gorkhas in their land—it is really a mystic and full of dilemma. It appears from the present scenario at Changlang district that settled cultivation is a big problem for the Arunachal tribes so as to pursue themselves on the agrarian economy because traditionally they were not accustomed to the settled cultivation. Considering the ground realities pertaining to the wet rice cultivation, the Gorkhas are absolutely the only option left out to the tribals of the Arunachal hills as well as the foothills of North Eastern Frontiers. In this way, the tribals are fully dependent upon the Gorkhas for state agrarian economy. This is due to the fact that historically the Gorkhas were the exponents of terrace wet rice cultivation in the Himalayas (Sharma: 2005). This had also been translated into bare reality in Arunachal Pradesh due to the British colonial policy in North Eastern Frontier of the then NEFA (Mackenzie: 2011).Here in this respect, no systematic study has been done on the contribution of Gorkha community on the agrarian economy and thereby the tribal society of Arunachal Pradesh. Historically, it is also found that the then NEFA was the destination for "Dukhi Gorkhas"—the poor Gorkhas (Hut: 2009) of Assam, Burma, Nepal and even Darjeeling-Sikkim and Bhutan due to the presence of virgin forest land, "Chars" and other unused or unclaimed land of the tribals. Then, most of the tribals of Arunachal Pradesh were nomadics of barbarous type roaming around the forests for hunting and gathering as well as catching the horns of wild elephants and doing Jhum cultivation in the frontier hills adjoining the Burma (Myanmar). Being the worshippers of agrarian economy including Cow-Dharma (worshippers of cows) approach of the Gorkhas, the British Government allowed the Gorkhas to clear the inaccessible forests and pursue on agriculture and animal husbandry (Chhetry: 2007). First, what the Gorkhas had to do was to prove themselves as good pastoralists and secondly they had to prove themselves to be the perfect cultivators later on by raising terraces on the foothill forests and also in the steep hills for dry land (Sukha Kheti) cultivation. The Gorkha settlers in Arunachal Pradesh have introduced terrace wet rice cultivation (Pani Kheti) in comparatively high altitude areas. In Changlang district, the Chakma refugees and Gorkha settlers are efficient rice growers. They show efficiency in crop production than the local tribes (Choudhury: 2009). The Gorkhas loved cows and thus they could very easily pursue on milk dairy business as their favourite profession everywhere in North East India. Miles together in North East India there were/are Gorkha Gai Goths (cow sheds) both in the past and even today more particularly in the Arunachal frontier region (Sharma: 2005). There is not a single Gorkha household in Miao and Nampong villages without having the cattle stocks at home and Byasis (low land located at the river basins and stream sides).

Another aspect of the politics on Gorkha living in Changlang and other frontier districts of Arunachal Pradesh is that since the British days, local tribes could not successfully pursue on agriculture and animal husbandry as desired by the colonial government to have good state revenue for the government. In fact, no tribe wanted to be the settled cultivators as they were then the stern believers of Jhum (shifting) cultivation. Secondly, in the olden days, they had slavery system which was completely banned by the British Government from 1838 onwards resulting which there was no other community like Ahom of Assam of the past to work as slaves on the land of the tribals in Arunachal Pradesh. So, after independence of the country, the tribals renewed their possession of forest fringe and foothills of Changlang and other unused land of the frontier districts of Arunachal Pradesh and leased out their Jhum and forest fringe as well as unused land to the Gorkhas. So, the agrarian perseverance, loyalty to the tribal landowners and commitment to agrarian economy of the state appear to have been the obvious reasons why the local tribals who were/are very indolent and less achievement oriented (Sinha: 2007) communities of hills had/have no other alternative except to lease out their land to the Gorkhas. In fact, the Gorkhas proved to be "Khati Khaney Jati"—laborious community (Sharma: 2010) in the world. Thus, the Dependence Syndrome of the tribals upon other communities of the country including the Gorkhas is the inherent politics on Gorkha living in Arunachal Pradesh in general and Changlang district in particular.

Still another special aspect on Gorkha living is that they are warlike people (Rana: 2011) who do not mind to kill enemy or to be killed himself at the hands of enemy while fighting with the enemy on the battleground with Khukuri (Liwang: 2011). It is a hearsay that most Gorkhas especially the Changlang Matwalis of the Gorkha community have been taught by the tribals to keep arms secretly at home. This may be true to a great extent as I found lot of open arms and ammunition shops in Changlang, Lohit and Tirap districts of Arunachal Pradesh. Their martial characters have enabled them to live in the most inaccessible as well as hostile environs of Changlang district. Most Gorkhas of Changlang district belong to the Matwali group who are hardly scared of wilderness living. They pay rent not only for land and house as well as cattle stocks to the tribal owners but also "Chanda" or locally called "Salami" (present) or sometimes food and other logistic supports to the terrorist outfits that are locally called Jungle Parties who belong to mainly the Nagas of NSCN groups and Naga sub-tribes of The Liberation Tigers of Arunachal Pradesh. In fact, all the tribal landowners called themselves as NAGAS. So, a kind of ethnic affinity has been restored well between the Naga landowners and NSCN groups that has helped the Gorkhas to be on the safe side from the NSCN attacks. Again, the tribal character of the Gorkhas has helped a lot to assimilate themselves into the tribal society of Arunachal Pradesh in general and Changlang district in particular. All the tribal landowners have constructed *Pucca* houses here while all the Gorkhas have constructed thatched roof huts. In this respect, every Gorkha says that he does not want to construct *Pucca* house here because of his uncertainty in terms of his staying at Arunachal Pradesh as hardly a tribal landowner leases out his land to him beyond thirty years at a stretch. The Gorkha house is called "Camp" having thatched roof, bamboo walls and pillars or posts polished with wet mud framed structure. As soon as the leased out land taken back from the Gorkhas, the tribal landowners again lease out their land to another new set of Gorkhas for next thirty years at a stretch. Sometimes, as soon as the leased out land is taken back from the Gorkhas, the tribal landowners either opt for Jhum cultivation or change the tenants for another thirty years. Although the Government of Arunachal Pradesh is interested for settled cultivation (Mishra: 1994) in the state including the hills of Arunachal Pradesh, the Jhum cultivation is still sustaining well due to the politics of tribalism of the Government of Arunachal Pradesh considering the interest of dominant local tribes of the state. Many tribal elites have pursued themselves on small grower tea plantations ever since 1999. But the percentage of such tribal tea planters is most negligible as the major percentage (99.9%) of the tribals is still found to be clinging on to the Jhum (shifting) cultivation. This may be the apparent reason why the Gorkhas as a whole have not been deported by the Government of Arunachal Pradesh as out 335 villages of Changlang district, there are Gorkhas in all the 335 villages. To the tribals, the Gorkhas are their best tenant-slaves who do not at all speak anything on their fundamental rights. Everything of the Gorkhas is theirs, even the beautiful daughters who are very often forcefully married to the tribal men. Every Gorkha whosoever I met at Miao and Nampong told me that he has to by hook and crook keep his tribal landowner (Malik) always happy so as to enable him to survive in the most hostile environment of Changlang district. The Gorkhas pay visit to the tribal landowners to receive the Tika (Rice mixed with vermilion powder) on their forehead at the time of Dasai (Dashara) festival as Tika is believed by the Gorkhas as a mark of blessing from elders under the Gorkha culture for their future, peace and prosperity.

Till 1987, Changlang district was under the administration of the Tirap Frontier Tract having Khonsa as its district headquarters. Thus, Changlang district under the Tirap Frontier Tract especially the hill areas was mostly under the Jhum cultivation leaving the foothills unused where almost all agrarian population belonged to the Gorkha community. The Government of Arunachal Pradesh felt it better to keep hill tribes in the hill areas only of the North Eastern Frontier bordering Myanmar. This is apparent from the fact that most Singpoos of the region have close association with the Myanmar Singpoos both during the British period and independent eras.

Other Reasons on Politics of Gorkha Living

Talking about the politics on Gorkha living in Arunachal Pradesh, a pertinent question that comes to our mind is that why instead of calling the Gorkhas as immigrants, outsiders, foreigners and non-tribals in the tribal land of Arunachal Pradesh, the tribals prefer the Gorkhas in their land. Following may be the obvious answers:

(a) Not only the Gorkhas are the exponents of terrace cultivation and also the dry land cultivation in hills, foothills and plain areas;
(b) But also, the Gorkhas practice animal husbandry and floriculture (Sharma:2003) because the so-called land leased out to the Gorkhas by the tribals are absolutely kept fertile by pouring cattle dung as natural composts for cultivation of high degree to produce the best crops;
(c) Expectation level of the Gorkhas is very low compared to the other castes and tribal communities of North East India;
(d) The Gorkhas are not well organized and therefore they have very weak social solidarity structure with reference to Arunachal Pradesh;
(e) All the so-called Gorkha elites of Arunachal Pradesh are encircled either around the urban belts of Arunachal Pradesh or Guwahati—the central niche of North East India due to the modern way of life or availability of the modern amenities.

Apparently, it is also observed that the Arunachal Gorkhas have triangular status. One type of Gorkhas have urban status leading the urban way of life. The second type of Gorkhas belong to ex-soldiers of Assam Rifles and finally majority of the Gorkhas of Arunachal Pradesh are simply tenants of the tribals. The first and second types of Gorkhas have been enjoying some kind of the socio-economic and political privileges in Arunachal Pradesh while majority of the Gorkhas (agrarian Gorkhas) do not at all have any kind of right or privilege as enjoyed by the urban Gorkhas who are treated as Raithanees in Arunachal Pradesh. Therefore, from this point of view, we can classify the Gorkhas of Arunachal Pradesh with a bipolar classification model that unfolds the Gorkhas as a whole into Raithanees and Sukumbasis. As far as the politics on living of the agrarian Gorkhas of Changlang district is concerned, they have the apparent options like:

(A) Stick to the Puras with Dukha or full of sorrows;
(B) Migrate to Assam or other parts of the country;
(C) Return Migration to Nepal Terai region or Siliguri (WB).

Very interestingly, as Micheal Hut in his article entitled "Where is Home for an Indian Writer" on *Indian Gorkhas*: *Issues and Perspectives* (2009) edited by Subba *et al*., observed that Dukha or sorrow legacy brought from Nepal by the Gorkhas hardly encouraged the Gorkhas of agrarian sectors of Arunachal Pradesh to go back to the Nepal Himalayas. This may be the reason why most of the Gorkhas of Changlang district are not sure about their living in Arunachal Pradesh but as they said that as soon as they become little bit richer, they will either purchase land in Assam or Siliguri (West Bengal) and construct house so that at their old age they can shift their family there permanently. Unlike the Arunachal Pradesh, they can purchase land in Assam or Siliguri (West Bengal) where since time immemorial the Gorkhas have prominent locus standing in both the socio-economic as well as the political dynamics of living.

Another issue is that why and how the Gorkhas are being well adjusted with the tribal society. It is due to the inter-clan differences that are still persisting as in the past among the tribal groups in Changlang district in particular and Arunachal Pradesh in general. What I found among the Gorkhas of Changlang district is that the Gorkhas are dwelling under the culture of utter silence. They do not at all want to speak anything openly about the tribals as they are scared of their ousting from the land of the tribal landowners. They rather suspect any newcomer to their villages. Hardly, they talk about the Gorkha-tribal relationship. They are, therefore, found to prefer to be completely introverts. But the Gorkhas of urban areas of Changlang district like Changlang and Khonsa of Tirap district are found to be little bit extrovert in regard to the Gorkha-tribal relationship because they are having government professions with higher educational standards. Many Police officers belong to the Gorkha community. Shri Tek Bahadur Chhetry, the Officer-in-charge of Miao Police Station told me that unfortunately the Gorkhas are simply the tenants of Nagas and Singpoos in Changlang district over the last 200 years.

They are all illiterate and thus they do not have highhandedness on any matter of their villages.

In spite of such a living at the Changlang district of Arunachal Pradesh, the Gorkhas as a whole have made lively living in the state due to the existence of 110 tribes and sub-tribes in the state of Arunachal Pradesh. Each tribe or sub-tribe is different from others in view of culture, dialect and tradition. Table 2.1 portrays the heterogeneous socio-cultural characters of the tribal communities of Arunachal Pradesh.

Table 2.1: Tribes and Sub-Tribes of Arunachal Pradesh

Sl. No.	*Name of the Tribe/Sub-tribe*	*Sl. No.*	*Name of the Tribe/Sub-tribe*
1.	Abor	2.	Adi
3.	Adi Gelang	4.	Adi Minyang
5.	Adi Padam	6.	Adi Pari
7.	Aka	8.	Apatani
9.	Ashing	10.	Bangi
11.	Banghi	12.	Bangro
13.	Bagun	14.	Bokar
15.	Bolak	16.	Bondo
17.	Bori	18.	Bat Monpa
19.	Dafla	20.	Darok Tangsa
21.	Deori	22.	Digru/Tarin Mismi
23.	Dirang Monpa	24.	Gelang
25.	Haisa Tangsa	26.	Halsi Tangsa
27.	Hill Miri	28.	Hotang Tangsa
29.	Idu/Chulikata Mismi	30.	Jambo
31.	Kaman/Miju Mismi	32.	Kaska
33.	Hatin Tangsa	34.	Kansing Tangsa
35.	Khalim Tangsa	36.	Khamba
37.	Khamiyang	38.	Khampti
39.	Khowa	40.	Khodang Bangoi
41.	Kamkor	42.	Kongbo
43.	Korang Tangsa	44.	Langkai Tangsa
45.	Libo	46.	Lichi Tangsa
47.	Liju Nokte	48.	Longchang Tangsa
49.	Langine Tangsa	50.	Langin Tangsa
51.	Langfi Tangsa	52.	Longsai Tangsa
53.	Loangsang Tangsa	54.	Loang Tangsa
55.	Meyar	56.	Miji
57.	Mikir	58.	Milang
59.	Milang Ebor	60.	Minyang
61.	Mising/Miri	62.	Mismi
63.	Moglun Tangsa	64.	Momba
65.	Monpa	66.	Morang Tangsa

(*Contd.*)

Table 2.1 (*Contd.*)

Sl. No.	*Name of the Tribe/Subtribe*	*Sl. No.*	*Name of the Tribe/Subtribe*
67.	Mosang Tangsa	68.	Muktum
69.	Namsang Tangsa	70.	Nimang Tangsa
71.	Nishang	72.	Nissi
73.	Nokte	74.	Nanang
75.	Padam	76.	Pailibo
77.	Padam Monya	78.	Pangi
79.	Pasi	80.	Ponkong
81.	Fang Tangsa	82.	Pothari Nokte
83.	Ramo	84.	Rangai Tangsa
85.	Saske Tangsa	86.	Rongrang Tangsa
87.	Sherdukpen	88.	Simong
89.	Simsa Tangsa	90.	Sinpoo
91.	Siram	92.	Sulung
93.	Sulung Wangni	94.	Tangin
95.	Tangin Boraghi	96.	Taisan Tangsa
97.	Tangs	98.	Tangeg
99.	Taram	100.	Tarang Monya
101.	Waikhampti	102.	Tikhak Tangsa
103.	Takha Nokte	104.	Namko
105.	Yanu Bangui	106.	Watong
107.	Yabin	108.	Yangkuk Tangsa
109.	Yangi Tangsa	110.	Jakin

Source: Census of India: 2001.

It is very transparent from Table 2.1 of the study that altogether there are 110 tribes and sub-tribes in Arunachal Pradesh and therefore they are obviously found to have 110 dialects. However, they have a common language known as Nefamiz. Each tribe has its own culture and tradition. The Buddhists are the major population of the state.

Linguistic Heterogeneity of Arunachal Tribes/Sub-tribes

The interesting point to note here for the survival of the Gorkhas in Arunachal Pradesh is due to the linguistic heterogeneity of the tribals. It is really transparent from Table 2.1 that there are 110 tribal dialects. This linguistic heterogeneity of the tribals has enabled the Gorkhas to comfortably adapt the local tribal environment. Due to this linguistic heterogeneity of the tribals with the occurrence of some kind of inter-tribal feuds and frictions, every tribe rather prefers the Gorkhas in their land as tenants (peasants). Of course, as already mentioned in this chapter, they have common language known as Nefamiz in North

East India. But looking at its popularity among the tribal population of the state of Arunachal Pradesh, hardly 10 per cent of the Arunachal tribes can speak the Nefamiz language. The communicators of this Nefamiz language are hailing merely from the elite circle of the tribal society. The common tribals, however, are not found to have been speaking the Nefamiz language in Arunachal Pradesh today.

Living Rights of the Gorkhas

The Gorkhas of the remotest villages of Changlang district feel quite comfortable in the sense that at least there they are able to manage two square meals which their predecessors who before coming to Burma and Assam could not at all manage the same in the Nepal Himalayas. Thus, living right is most primordial necessity rather than acquiring the identity right since they do not at all bother about the identity right because they are simply concerned with living right having two square meals per day in the Arunachal Pradesh in general and Changlang district in particular. The tribal development process of Arunachal Pradesh simply allows to acquire this living right to the Gorkhas with two square meals per day rather than acquiring the consciousness of ethnic identity in the district of Changlang. This may be the reason why the Gorkhas have assimilated themselves into the tribal way of life in Arunachal Pradesh in such a way that it is very difficult to distinguish the Gorkhas from the local tribes in their day-to-day life. Many Gorkha boys and girls have taken tribal titles to acquire the tribal benefits from the Government of Arunachal Pradesh. The Gorkha women like the tribal counterpart also wear the tribal "Lungi" made in the tribal households. This along with the facial similarity with the Arunachal tribals, the Gorkhas mostly Matwali group appeared to have been assimilated into the tribal way of life. I found that the Gorkhas speak the local tribal dialects fluently and most of the tribals also speak the Gorkha/Nepali language not only in Changlang district but also the other remaining fifteen districts of the state of Arunachal Pradesh (Sharma: 2005).

The inter-community marriages between the tribals and mostly Matwalis from the Gorkha community made the Arunachal agrarian society thoroughly integrated. At the Nampong and Miao villages, at least 20 per cent of marriages have taken place between the Gorkhas and tribals. However, it is also observed that the Tagadhari group of Gorkha community is found to be little bit conservative than the

Matwalis as they hardly marry the tribal women and *vice versa* as most Tagadharis have still kept the Hindu tradition of Purity-Pollution model in tact as in the past. The tribal societies are complex from the point of view of religious affiliation also. Hardly, the tribals found today to be the followers of their original form of Animism. I found that the Tangsas are mostly Christians while the Singpoos, the Buddhists. Interestingly, I also found that the Wanchus, Noktes and Tangsas are in favour of religious conversion into Christianity because they belong to the Naga sub-tribes and the Nagas are perfectly Christians. This is the religious scenario of Changlang district. Such divergent religious affiliations of Tangsa, Nokte and Wanchu tribes are also being followed by the Gorkhas in Changlang district and this has indirectly helped the Gorkhas to easily adopt the local tribal environment. Moreover, there is no unity among the Naga tribes due to their divergent religious affiliation to Buddhism and Christianity today and that is reason why the Gorkhas are living here quite comfortably. This caused for the tribals to prefer the Gorkhas particularly Matwalis in their land as Gorkha Matwalis are less conservative in regard to Purity-Pollution model of Hindu religion as they are having high level of cosmopolitan approach into their life in every nook and corner of Arunachal Pradesh as well as the other seven sister states of North East India.

Fear Psychosis among the Gorkhas

It is observed at Miao, Nampong, Bordumsa and Diyon areas of the Changlang district that the tribals want to keep the Gorkhas in their land due to the reason that unlike other ethnic communities such as Bihari, Marwari, Punjabi, Muslim etc. who mainly do pursue on business, the Gorkhas as poverty ridden human stock of the Himalayas can be kept under the fear psychosis of calling deported or escalated or ousted migrant community from Burma, Assam, Nepal and other parts of the country. They were/are all poorest of the poor even in their native villages of Nepal Himalayas. There is hardly any Gorkha from Terai areas of Nepal in both the Miao and Nampong villages. The tribals know that the Gorkhas are weak, meek and poor and therefore they can be easily tamed in their own fashions as the agrarian folk (peasants), as porters and as low grade casual employees in government departments of the state of Arunachal Pradesh. The agony of ousting from the Arunachal Pradesh is really the fear psychosis which the local tribals always want to inject into the minds of the Gorkha populace. This creates a kind of uncertainty of their living in Changlang district in particular and Arunachal Pradesh in general. However, the uncertainty enforces the Gorkhas to be always stubborn with perseverance, commitment to hard work or work as fast as they can do to earn more and more money within short span of time and thereby invest the money earned there either in other parts of the country or Nepal Terai belt. For evolving future alternative, they are now keeping close touch with Assam, Siliguri (West Bengal) if not the Nepal Terai belt. Not a single Gorkha of the Changlang district stated that he intends to revert to the Nepal Himalayas provided he is deported from the Changlang district of Arunachal Pradesh in future.

The "Basai Sarnu" System

The term "Basai Sarnu" in the Nepali/Gorkha language means the shifting the place of habitation as per the Gorkha legacy that they have inherited from the Nepal Himalayas; due to "Dukha" or sorrowful living in the agrarian sectors of Nepal Himalayas, Burma and Assam plains. Both at Nampong and Miao, I found that the Gorkhas are not allowed to stay beyond 30 years at a stretch in the land of a particular tribal landowner. Although their migration history in the region is beyond 200 years, still they take for granted the "Basai Sarnu" as an integral part of their lifecycle in Arunachal Pradesh of North East India. Such "Basai Sarnu" phenomenon is not however found to be on vogue among the Assomiya Gorkhas (Nath: 2009) of North East India today.

The terms like "Basai Sarnu"—shifting the place of habitation, "Kheti Garnu" cultivating the land, "Gai Goth Banaunu"—constructing cow sheds and "Gothala Basnu"—pursuing on cattle stock care-taker job might be the cultural traditions of Gorkhas that enable them to be in the remotest villages of the Changlang district of Arunachal Pradesh in particular and North East India in general. The "Gothala Basnee" profession might be the responsible factor for working in the lowest cadres of employment such as Chowkidar, Peon, Guard, Constable, Gate-keeper and Sepoy in police department and militia all-over the world. Due to the existence of sufficient forest resources in Arunachal Pradesh (82 per cent), the Gorkhas appear to be comfortable in "Basai Sarnu" from one location of Arunachal Pradesh forest to another location. Even at their native villages, after doing "Angsa Banda" (culture of distribution of parental property among the sons), they used to shift home from parental residence to another corner of allotted plot of land as given by their parents. The "Basai Sarnu"—the act of shifting the place of habitation involved lot of constraints and adventures which the Gorkhas were used to dare as part and parcel of their lifecycle. The Gorkha lifecycle process called as "Basai Sarnu" made this Gorkha community really Globalized (Sharma: 2009) since time immemorial. The "Basai Sarnu" cannot be purely comprehended as migration as the other communities of North East India understand it but very wrongly. It is a holistic process as the Gorkhas after shifting over to the new places of habitation, whole-heartedly made the respective places as home, hearth and also graveyards with their blood and sweats. They easily adopt the local culture and environment with utmost dedication and commitment, loyalty to the masters and even they display their life struggling with hard notes till their last breath.

This is the ground reality of the Gorkhas of Changlang district of Arunachal Pradesh where till the last thirty years back hardly any other ethnic community of the country used to dare to penetrate into as easily as the Gorkhas used to do. For the Gorkhas, dense forests, isolation and adventurous life, fighting with wild animals of the forests etc., are very enjoyable and pride making efforts of claiming themselves as martial race for which the world communities called them "Bahadurs". The term "Bahadur" is still found to be uttered eloquently by most of the Indians and others to the Gorkhas in the world. Here, in this context, it is found that unfortunately the Gorkhas feel proud of claiming themselves as "Bahadurs" by others as the people belong to a martial race. Sincerely speaking, historically, this pride making drama unfolded with "Bahadurness" was the responsible factor for the Gorkhas that caused them to be recruited as Sepoys in Assam Rifles or Gorkha Regiments to selflessly serve the British Colonial masters and after independence, the Indian masters. Even the Gorkhas were very happy to be called as 'mercenary force' during the British period. Thousands of Gorkha soldiers died in different wars both during the British period and independent eras of the country (Muktan: 2009).The British Government has still kept three Gorkha Regiments in U.K. All the present Gorkha Sepoys of the Gorkha Battalions are called "Commandos" of the Indian Army. At least, there are fifty thousand Gorkha soldiers today in India.

Most of the Gorkhas as ex-soldiers in the Changlang district of Arunachal Pradesh are settled down in the agrarian sectors of the state as agriculturists and also pursuing on animal husbandry (Gai-Vastu Goths) and horticulture by domesticating cows, buffaloes, pigs, goats and poultry farming; flower nursery raising for the flower garden etc. Whenever the Gorkhas go on shifting the place of habitation (Basai Sarnu), they take all their livestocks with themselves in the new habitations (villages). This is the regular feature of the Gorkhas since the last 200 years in the Changlang district in particular and Arunachal Pradesh in general. This has been mostly found in Arunachal Pradesh only unlike other states of Meghalaya, Mizoram and Nagaland of North East India where today Gorkhas can hardly go on "Basai Sarnu" as they are not allowed to do so there. Rather, the Gorkhas have to leave the places of habitation if deported to either Assam or Siliguri or Nepal Terai areas from Manipur, Meghalaya, Nagaland and other states of North East India. This is due to the problem of the Government of Arunachal Pradesh pertaining to the practice of Jhum cultivation of local tribes on the one hand and indolent and less achievement oriented nature of the Arunachal Pradesh tribes (Sinha: 2007) on the other. Otherwise, if the Government of Arunachal Pradesh was really in favour of the total extinction of the Gorkhas from the state of Arunachal Pradesh, then how today there are over one lakh Gorkhas in the state of Arunachal Pradesh. Moreover, with the passage of six decades of independence of the country, the Gorkha population has been fully increasing in Arunachal Pradesh. In fact, the Government of Arunachal Pradesh having no other alternative wants to have settled cultivation in Changlang district as in the other districts so as to realize good revenue from the agrarian sector. But its declared objectives incorporated in regard to the tribal development policy (Das: 1995) appears to be antithetical to its state agrarian development policy through the tribals who are still found to have strong conviction towards the Jhum cultivation. This is adequately proved by the fact that more than 700 acres of Changlang hill land are under Jhum cultivation of the indigenous tribes.

The Gorkhas as Reciprocal Citizens

Although the Gorkhas are reciprocal citizens of India in the light of the provisions of Indo-Nepal Peace and Friendship Treaty (1950), they are still treated as immigrants having Nepamul background (Sinha: 2007) especially in Arunachal Pradesh of North East India.

This may be the reason why once the forest fringe, "Chars" and unused land are made arable or habitable by the Gorkhas, the tribals do cast their jealous eyes and become successful to own the land with the patronage of the Government of Arunachal Pradesh that resulted into the Gorkha deportation from the land of Arunachal Pradesh. In this context, it is observed in Nampong village that at least 2000 Gorkhas have been deported so far since the last two decades. Even some of the ex-soldiers of the Gorkha community had been deported from Nampong as they were suspected to be the informers of army, police and intelligence departments of the government. The deportation of Gorkhas from Nampong is quite easy because the Gorkha households are very scattered by location as each Gorkha has taken land on lease of at least 20 to 25 Puras. So, another Gorkha household is located at the distance of 5 to 6 kilometers. In fact, Nampong like Miao is the last village of India besides Vijaynagar of the Changlang district. The Vijaynagar, as described above, is another village which is also called by the Gorkhas as Kalapani (Thapa: 2008) from the point of view of communication facilities. The Vijaynagar was explored by the Gorkha soldiers of 7th battalion of Assam Rifles. As informed by Shri Kedarnath Sharma, an ex-employee of SIB department of Government of Arunachal Pradesh of Nampong that in the olden days there were six villages but now there are fourteen villages where the Gorkha ex-soldiers are staying from early 1960s. Shri Sharma was posted at Vijaynagar of Arunachal Pradesh for five years from 1990 to 1995. Shri Sharma said that today there are 3500 Gorkhas and 1600 Yabin/Lusi tribe. In 1960, the Government of India through 7th battation of Assam Rifles consisting of Gorkha soldiers lured the Gorkha ex-soldiers to settle down there and pursued on agriculture and animal husbandry with free ration, medical facilities, providing free education to their children and free agricultural land as the Government Grant land for next few years i.e., up to 1970. Actually, the Vijaynagar was explored by Krishna Bahadur Rai, Bhim Prasad Sharma etc. of the 7th Assam Rifles (Thapa: 2008). It was claimed that prior to the British occupation of Upper Burma in 1826, Vijaynagar (the then unnamed place) was inhabited by the Burmese Singpoos and Yabin/Lusi tribe. Lot of Buddhist statues are still found there at Vijaynagar. After 1970, all the facilities provided to the ex-soldiers of 7th Assam Rifles had been stopped by the government. In this way, all the Gorkhas were made merely the agriculturalists and pastoralists. As mentioned above, Vijaynagar is still unconnected by the road communication. It takes 6 days walk to reach Vijaynagar from Miao Bajar or Dewan. Now all the Gorkhas of Vijaynagar are simply the tenants (peasants) of Yabin/Lusi tribe of the locality as per the Government policy of Arunachal Pradesh for the tribal development. The example indicates that the Gorkhas once upon a time during the British period were confirmed to be called with the term "mercenary force" and the same is still followed by the Government of Arunachal Pradesh. The colonization of Vijaynagar had been absolutely materialized through the contributions of the Gorkhas only. The process of consolidation of North Eastern Frontier was since the British days exclusively fulfilled by the Gorkhas as no other local tribe was in favour of British Government in this venture and even today most of the frontier tribes have a kind of nostalgia to be called themselves as Indians or to be on the Indian union. It is proved by the fact that the frontier Naga tribes are found to have been exclusively supporting the NSCN and ULFA terrorist outfits in their villages. They ask the Gorkhas not only to pay land tax and house rent as well as cattle stock tax to the tribal landowners but also the "Chanda" or cash as contribution to the NSCN terrorist activists (locally called Jungle Parties) who have their training camps at the Indo-Myanmar borders. This may be the obvious reason why most of the Gorkhas are trying to impart excellent education to their children outside the Arunachal Pradesh so that their children in turn can out rightly go out of the Changlang district for getting good job. It is simply because of this reason that even an educated Gorkha boy and girl does not get government job in Arunachal Pradesh particularly after 1987. Some Gorkhas have been employed as casual workers in the government offices but they have been hardly regularized in their services instead of working there as casual employees for the last two decades. For instance, at Miao, Smt. Leela Sharma has been working as a casual employee for the last 20 years in Public Works Department of the Government of Arunachal Pradesh but her service has not been regularized in spite of repeated persuasion done by Smt. Leela Sharma to the Superintending Engineers of the Public Works Department of Miao although she is being constantly given assurances by the office of Superintending Engineers of PWD, Miao for regularizing her service but in vain till today. Such examples are plenty in the Changlang district. This appears to be the apparent reason why the Gorkha children once educated hardly stay in Arunachal Pradesh rather they prefer to go out instantly and do not at all ever come back to the state. For example, Shri Jharen Sharma of Vijaynagar is now in USA as a computer engineer. He did not come back to Vijaynagar since his joining the job in USA in 1995. Similarly, hundreds of Gorkha educated boys and girls of Nampong and Miao as well as Diyon villages generally left for elsewhere the country and hardly come back there later on. Only the uneducated Gorkhas have been left out as Naga tenants (peasants) in the region.

The Gorkha Contributions

The first Gorkha teacher of Arunachal Pradesh was Shri Man Bahadur Sunar of Pasighat Lower Primary School of East Siyang district. Similarly, Mr. Hari Bhakta Sharma was the first teacher in Changlang district at Nampong Lower Primary School. Mr. Dil Kumar Gurung, Havildar of 8th Assam Rifles was the man who explored the Abor hills of Arunachal Pradesh to be bought under the British administration. Mr. Nandalal Manger, the Havildar of 11th Gorkha Regiment assisted Shri Stilwell to explore the possibility of constructing Ledo-Pangsau Road which was later on known as Stilwell Road (Deka:2005) that connected India to Myanmar (Burma). The Kharsang villages of Miao and Nampong were perfectly the creation of Gorkhas. Now, the tribal elites are establishing their small grower tea gardens at Miao and Nampong employing the Chakma and Bangladeshi workers from Bangladesh. But it is found that all the managers of these small grower tea gardens of tribals are Gorkhas by ethnicity because the Gorkhas due to their bravery have comfortably been able to tame the savage Coolies in the isolated enclaves of Changlang district of Arunachal Pradesh.

Interestingly, it is also observed from the study that Tagadharis mainly the Bahuns (Upadhayas-Jharra Tagadharis) and not the title by "Sharma" who are in fact considered as Jaisis (Not Upadhaya; non-pure Bahuns) in North East India, have been found to have been continuing their priesthood jobs and pastoral occupation and therefore hardly the Upadhaya Bahuns do agriculture to that extent as done by Matwalis of the Gorkha community in Changlang district. Even the tribals pay due respect to the Upadhaya Bahuns as priests and Pandits. They call Upadhaya Bahuns as Pandits-Porohits. It means that only the Jharra Tagadhari (pure) Bahuns i.e., Upadhayas can pursue on priesthood as in the past. Hardly Jaisis (Thimaha Tagadharis-non-pure Bahuns) are found to have been pursued on traditional profession

(Sharma: 1997) of preparing Janam Kundali (birth certificate) in Changlang district along with the pastoral occupation (Sapkota: 2007) in the region.

In Nampong, 25,000 acres of land with 5,000 cattle stocks are being mostly reared and therefore perfectly managed by the Chhetris (Thimaha Tagadharis) and Matwali castes of the Gorkha community. In Nampong, only 10 number of Tangsa tribal families, mainly the tribal elites (Mishra: 1994) have been pursued on small grower tea plantation on their earlier Jhum land. The green tea leaves so plucked in their small grower tea gardens of Nampong are sent to Jairampur Bought Leaf Factory. In fact, it is found that the industrialization as a process of social change has not yet stepped into the Changlang district of Arunachal Pradesh while altogether there are twenty two tea gardens in the neighbouring Lohit and Tirap districts of Changlang. Besides the tea plantation industry, saw and veneer mills are also flourishing in Lohit district (Sharma: 2005) of Arunachal Pradesh. But the Changlang district being the untouched district of Arunachal Pradesh till 1987, the industrialization as a process of social change has not yet reached there. In fact, the Changlang district is the buffer zone of India adjoining Myanmar having mostly the steep hill terrains, the industrialization has been avoided well by the Government of Arunachal Pradesh for security reasons. In the border between India and Myanmar, only the dense forests under the administration of Arunachal Pradesh Forest Development Corporation Ltd. are kept in tact ever since the British days. Below the Patkai hills of Changlang district of Arunachal Pradesh bordering Myanmar, the foothills are consisted of agricultural land of the tribals being well cultivated exclusively by the Gorkhas. In this way, the Gorkhas have become safety valves of the Indian Government in so far as keeping safe the eastern frontiers of India is concerned. It is also heard at Nampong that the Myanmar areas bordering India are also having lot of Gorkha villages. Thus, on both sides of India and Myanmar; the Gorkhas have served as buffer zone dwellers or as the most peripheral community (Sinha: 2007) of these two countries of South East Asia.

The Gorkhas as "KAM CHALO VARO, AFAL TERO THARO"

As the Gorkha proverb states "KAM CHALO VARO, AFAL TERO THARO" meaning thereby the Gorkhas are used at work extensively and thrown out to dust bin on the moment the selfish motives of the Government of Arunachal Pradesh and also the tribal people are fulfilled. The tribal people appreciate the Gorkhas till their vested interests are acquired. But on the moment their interests are fulfilled, they deport the Gorkhas to nowhereelse. This was not there in the olden days. Today, since the tribals are in the so-called process of transition (Das: 1987) by civilizing themselves (Sinha: 2007) as per the dictates of modernity, they are doing this against the Gorkhas. This is the inherent reason why the Gorkhas of a particular village as found today will not be found there in the same village after 30 years. There, we will find a new set of Gorkha dwellers. Presently, the question of security has become very urgent for the Gorkhas of Arunachal Pradesh than in the earlier eras as the then local tribes were merely savage nomadic tribes who were totally concentrated in the hill areas of Changlang district. The earlier term used for Arunachal Pradesh as "Enchanted Frontiers" during the British period can no longer be called as "enchanted" for the Gorkhas as they are being made exclusively the "**KAM CHALO VARO, AFAL TERO THARO**".

The Gorkhas in Chars, Forest Fringe and Unused Land of Tribals

The locations of Gorkha villages of Changlang district are mainly near the Diyon, Dehing or Nau Dehing, Boorie Dehing and other rivers like Nampong, Miao and small streams, Chars, forest fringe and Jhum land of the tribals. They have mainly settled in the lower altitudes to get sufficient water for irrigation on their wet land and grazing land (Chhetry: 2009) for cattle stocks while their tribal landowners are staying at the higher altitudes as they do not require much water for irrigation to wet land and grazing land for cattle stocks in their day to day life.

Tribal Vigilance on the Gorkhas

In both the Miao and Nampong villages, mostly the tribal landowners normally visit the Gorkha huts to investigate whether the Gorkhas are mixing up with outsiders or not. The tribal landowners ask the Gorkhas to avoid outsiders coming to their homes. If the Gorkhas do not complaisant the oral orders of their tribal landowners then they will be excommunicated from the land immediately.

With the inauguration of the Stilwell Road in 1943 (Deka: 2005), the Gorkhas as refugees mainly from Burma were bought and settled down at Nampong villages when the local Tangsa tribes were simply the nomadic tribes at the Indo-Myanmar borders. Fortunately, the Tangsas got special privileges from the Government of Arunachal Pradesh after 1987 only when they claimed the foothill land theirs and then forcefully converged all the then agrarian Gorkhas under their tenancy system as peasants. Interestingly, due to the establishment of Assam Rifles Zonal Headquarters at Jairampur (now there is 18th battalion), the Gorkhas do not have to pay "Chanda" or contribution in terms of cash to the NSCN and other terrorist outfits although the Tangsas of Nampong are found to be the covert supporters of NSCN and other terrorist outfits giving ethnic affinity to the Nagas as Tangsas also belong to the sub-tribes of Naga community. Sometimes as reported by the Nampong Gorkhas, the NSCN activists come to their homes and demand for logistics and the Gorkhas at this juncture have no other alternative except to cook food and feed the terrorist activists. But they are not supposed to pay any cash (Chanda) to the NSCN and other terrorist outfits of Arunachal Pradesh.

Among the Gorkhas, Tamang (locally, all Tamangs are called "Lamas" in Arunachal Pradesh), Gurung, Manger and Thami of the Nampong villages being traditionally Buddhists and to be very much nearer and dearer to the Buddhist Tangsas although most Tangsas are Christians, are found to be visiting the Nampong Buddhist Monastery where most Lamas (priests) belong to Tangsa tribe. Again, many Matwalis mainly Rais, Limbus and Sunuwars are Christians at Nampong. But at Miao and Diyon villages, the Gorkhas are mostly Hindus as Singpoos unlike Tangsas do not allow the Gorkhas to be the Buddhists and visit their monastery. Historically, Tangsas, Noktes and Wanchus as Naga sub-tribes do not have good association both on socio-economic and political spectrums with Singpoos of the Changlang district. Till the establishment of British sovereignty over the hills of Changlang district, the Singpoos were treated as the enemy of these Naga sub-tribes. Very frequently, the Singpoos including the Burmese Singpoos used to attack the Naga sub-tribes of the Changlang hills (Mackenzie: 2011). Thus, the Buddhist Tangsas are also very happy with the Gorkhas because of the close relationship of Tangsas with the Gorkhas on the religious front. Again, the Christian Tangsas are also happy with the Gorkhas who are being converted into Christian religion at Nampong. Till today, unlike the Tangsas, Noktes and Wanchus, the Singpoos are purely Buddhists (Hinayana Sect). They have drawn hatreds towards Christainity ever since the British days in Changlang district as the British people were purely Christians by religion. This along with the inter-community marriages has enabled the Gorkhas to adjust the volatile as well as hostile environment of Nampong villages.

The old Stilwell Road with the name of National Highway, No. 153, is under construction as per the Look East Policy of Government of India to connect India with Myanmar and other South Eastern Asian countries as per her latest bilateral diplomatic engagement with Myanmar, Thailand, Korea, Cambodia, Singapore and of course, the China (Singh: 2009). It is comprehended that the Stilwell Road (Deka: 2005) once completed will definitely help the Tangsas to transform themselves into modernity. Lot of small shops of Biharis, Marwaris and Gorkhas have mushrooming at Nampong. This will definitely help the Tangsas to transform themselves into the modern way of life. This in turn can also erase out their culture of suspicion towards outsiders including the Gorkhas. However, during the recent years, frequency of tribal vigilance on the Gorkhas as in the past has been decreasing considerably at Nampong. Lot of Television towers, cello phone towers and Radio transmission centres have come up both at Miao and Nampong of Changlang district. Now, the tribals are found to be coming to shopping complex at Tinsukia town of Upper Assam (six districts) and eastern districts (Upper Dibang Valley, Lower Dibang Valley, East Siyang, Lohit, Tirap and Changlang) of Arunachal Pradesh. In this way, now the Tangsas and Singpoos who used to be tilted towards Myanmar in the past are trying to integrate themselves with the national mainstream. This has enabled the policy of national integration to make a place among Tangsas and Singpoos of the Changlang district so as to establish relationship with other communities of the country including the Gorkhas. The habit of calling Gorkhas as "outsiders", "foreigners" or "immigrants" by the tribals as in the past is being slowly but very steadily erasing out at Nampong although it is found to be more in practice at Miao of the Changlang district. Further, it is also noted that the implementation of Inner Line Permit System is very strict in Changlang district than other districts of Arunachal Pradesh—the land of rising sun. This system of Inner Line Permit is found to be the responsible factor for the emergence of suspicion of the tribals towards outsiders including the Gorkhas. This Inner Line Permit System has been sustained well by the

Government of Arunachal Pradesh due to so-called sensitive Changlang district strategically bordering the Myanmar. But Changlang district is the district where the Burmese Gorkhas are also staying ever since 1945 and they had relationship with the Gorkhas of Arunachal Pradesh prior to their coming to the state since time immemorial (Singh:1986) as today also we found four lakh Gorkhas in Myanmar (Burma). In spite of utter negligence shown by the Government of Arunachal Pradesh towards Gorkhas, the Gorkhas have at turn become directly or indirectly very beneficial to the local tribals through their vocations (Sinha: 2007) both during the British period and independent eras of the country.

Permanent Settlement of the Gorkhas

After the formation of a full-fledged state of Arunachal Pradesh in 1987, only those Gorkhas who were then working in the government services of Arunachal Pradesh are given citizenship status in the state with the right to cast vote in Panchayat, Municipality and Member of Legislative Assembly elections and provide ration cards as well as the identity cards. But such Gorkhas are hardly estimated to be around 10,000 in Arunachal Pradesh today. They are mostly serving the Police Department of the Government of Arunachal Pradesh while there are over one lakh Gorkhas who are not treated as the first class citizens of the state of Arunachal Pradesh as the Gorkhas as a whole are considered to be the non-tribals in the tribal state of Arunachal Pradesh. Although, the ex-Gorkha soldiers of Assam Rifles have not been officially ousted from their settlement, they are also not allowed to purchase land in the state. In this respect, both the Government of Arunachal Pradesh and the Government of India are silent. However, the Government of India quite often makes statements in her Gazette notifications that the problems of Gorkhas of Arunachal Pradesh is the matter of the concerned state Government of Arunachal Pradesh. This is mainly found at Jairampur, Miao and Nampong of the Changlang district. In this way, the Gorkhas of Changlang district in particular and Arunachal Pradesh in general are treated as good as second class citizens of the country. The Coolie Kam (Job) along with the agricultural and pastoral professions as started during the British period is still on vogue among the Gorkhas of Arunachal Pradesh. It appears from the present scenario that to aspire for permanent settlement by the Gorkhas in Arunachal Pradesh is really a myth and distant dream (Sharma: 2005).

III

The Gorkhas in Arunachal Pradesh Socio-economic Setting

The Gorkhas have never become free from soldering the curse or blemishness of immigrants from Nepal, foreigners, immigrants as well as outsiders in spite of their sincere services rendered to the Indian soil of Arunachal Pradesh for the last 200 odd years. This becomes most apparent when we visit Arunachal Pradesh today and see the pitiable condition of the Gorkhas in the socio-economic setting of the state. Studying their socio-economic condition in the Changlang district of Arunachal Pradesh, it has been realistically comprehended that nothing is there with the Gorkhas before the eyes of Government of Arunachal Pradesh also to the local tribals. Although the Gorkhas are whimsically called as immigrants especially from Nepal, hardly 2 per cent of the Gorkhas of Miao and Nampong have been found to have direct connection with Nepal. In fact, they are also staying at Changlang district for the last fifty years. Sincerely speaking, till today, there is no government mechanism to ascertain adequately as to which Gorkhas are from Nepal; which Gorkhas are from Burma and which Gorkhas are from Assam in Arunachal Pradesh. Most of the Changlang Gorkhas among these 2 per cent of the first generational immigrants also do not have any connection with Nepal today. Of course, these 2 per cent Gorkhas of the first generational immigrants of Miao and Nampong belong to the Eastern Nepal background prior to their coming to the Changlang district of Arunachal Pradesh.

To be more specific in explanation, if we see the migration history of Arunachal Pradesh population, every caste and tribal community has respective socio-cultural background of their places of origin. For instance, Naga tribes of Changlang district have Nagaland and Myanmar background. Similarly, Khamtis of Lohit, Tirap and

Changlang districts have Myanmar (Sharma: 2005; Bose: 1987) background. So, it is probably the most unfortunate part of the whole history that described the Gorkhas as immigrants in Arunachal Pradesh while the tribals—so-called sons of the soil are considered to be the permanent residents of the land. Therefore, the whole history ever written by the British authors is biased in the sense that they did not mention anything in details about the Gorkhas of Arunachal Pradesh. Even the scholars like Elwin, Koopland, Hattman, Dundas, Mills, Mackenzie and others have failed to mention in their reports about the establishment history of the Arunachal Gorkhas on whom the British Government was rather totally dependent especially on the agrarian front as well as the British militia including the Gorkha Regiments and the Assam Rifles. Only L.W. Shakespeare in his book *History of the Assam Rifles* (1977) has mentioned the involvement of Gorkhas in political and economic consolidation of North Eastern Frontiers (present Tirap, Lohit and Changlang in particular and Arunachal Pradesh in general). The British colonial policy is found to be the primordial reason for having the present pitiable platitudes of Gorkhas in Changlang and Tirap districts of Arunachal Pradesh. If the Gorkhas as pastoralists and agriculturists did not have come to the Changlang as well as Tirap districts, then all the tribals would have been still found to be pursuing on animal hunting and Jhum cultivation (shifting cultivation) as well as the wild elephant catching in jungles.

In the foothills of Changlang district, the Gorkhas ever since 1826 started wet rice cultivation (Panikheti) by raising terraces and provided sweat rice to the tribals who then instantly became conscious of the value of their wet rice land which is called in Assamese language as "Pather" and on the basis of the tribal development policy of the Government of Arunachal Pradesh, they captured all the land of foothills of Changlang district as well as the foothills of Lohit and Tirap districts of North Eastern Frontiers into their grip and distributed the forest fringe and other land among the tribal themselves through their tribal councils by deporting the then Gorkhas who were cultivating the foothill land ever since 1826. This is in short the history of Gorkha deportation from the frontier region of Arunachal Pradesh ever since 1987.

The socio-economic life of Changlang Gorkhas is same today as it was there prior to the independence of the country. The same thatched roof huts along with Gai Goths (cow sheds) and Khutti around their huts are the areas or jurisdiction on which the Gorkhas are making fortune as their global destiny. They are totally unknown about anything beyond the Changlang and Tirap districts. To keep the Gorkhas in darkness, the tribals in the remotest villages, do not even allow the Gorkhas to purchase television sets and if any Gorkha is found carrying television from town may be confiscated by the tribals or terrorist outfits on the way before reaching his village and in this way, the Gorkhas are devoid of enjoying the television programmes at homes. No electricity facility is there in the Gorkha huts. This is apparent as we see that only there are "Chor Battoes"— small short cut foot paths and thus there is hardly any motorable road in the Gorkha villages. To go to the Gorkha Gaon like Makantong and Joynagar of Bordumsa of the Changlang district, one has to spend the whole day on walking. He cannot come back to Bordumsa Bajar in the evening of the same day. Talking with the Gorkhas of Changlang district, it is understood that no Gorkha is optimistic about their future in Changlang district or the Arunachal Pradesh as a whole. They have to be always mentally prepared for their deportation from the tribal land any time or from the Changlang district. However, a section of Gorkhas stated that they have been developing a kind of "assertiveness" (Nath: 2007) so as not to leave the agrarian land that they have made arable with their blood and sweat over the last two centuries even if they have to die there itself fighting with the tribals for the cause.

In order to make a significant place in Changlang district by creating pressure onto the tribals, many able bodied Gorkha boys and girls (Limbu, Manger, Rai, Tamang and Gurung) have joined NSCN and ULFA terrorist outfits so that the local tribals cannot easily deport the fellow Gorkha village brothers and sisters. In this context, many Gorkhas stated that the NSCN and ULFA terrorist outfits help them to rescue from the helpless situations mostly pertaining to the Gorkha deportation from Changlang and Tirap districts of North Eastern Frontiers.

I came to know from the Gorkhas of the Changlang district that the NSCN and ULFA terrorist activists speak Nepali/Gorkha language fluently. As an officer of the Central Government, I met some of the ultra activists in many village training programmes of the Central Board for Workers Education, Ministry of Labour and Employment at Lakhipather, Kakapather, Miao and Saikhowa areas where they talked to me in the Nepali/Gorkha language only with all well mannered jesters as they found me a qualified Gorkha Central Government Officer from Darjeeling. They did not disturbed me in conducting the CBWE training programmes rather they requested me to conduct the training programmes without inviting any sense of insecurity into my mind. In very many situations, I had to face the army operations also. However, I could save myself in the situations by showing my official identity card to the army officers on operations and also at the check posts of Dirak (Lohit district), Jairampur and Namchik (Changlang district) of Arunachal Pradesh. Unlike the other frontier districts like Lohit and Tirap, only two day Inner Line Permit (locally called Pass) is being issued to the outsiders in Changlang district for security reasons. Talking about the terrorist activists, it is found that both the local tribals and Gorkhas have soft corners in their heart to the terrorist activists because they have to live in the remotest villages of the country where hardly army and police force can make frequent access (visits) to rescue them from the attacks of terrorist outfits in the villages. The terrorism has been increased in Changlang and Tirap districts over the last two decades due to the birth of Arunachal Naga Liberation Tigers in these two districts of Arunachal Pradesh. Secondly, most of the Naga Noktes, Wanchus and Tangsa tribes of Changlang District have enabled big access to the Naga Liberation Tigers of Arunachal Pradesh due to their ethnic affinity to the terrorist outfits.

It is observed from the present study that the persisting form of tribal slavery system having Gorkhas as their slaves can only be found in Changlang and Tirap districts of Arunachal Pradesh. This kind of Gorkha slavery system is similar to the earlier form of slavery system that we have noted in India in the early part of 18th century. Here, of course, we found an overt form of slavery system of Gorkhas by the tribals while we found a covert form of Gorkha slavery system in other areas of North Eastern Frontiers of India.

The Nepali/Gorkha language as the only string for Gorkha solidarity (Upadhaya and Adhikari: 2007) in India is not allowed to teach in most of the schools and colleges of North East India. Except in some colleges of Assam, Gorkha as a subject being incorporated in their curriculum has not at all been allowed in the entire North Eastern region. In Changlang district, it is found that many Gorkhas do not want to speak in Nepali/Gorkha language or they intentionally want to avoid to speak anything in the Nepali/Gorkha language with the fellow Gorkhas especially the outsider Gorkhas as they think doing this, their tribal landowners will be disappointed and therefore annoyed with the Gorkhas as a whole. Most of the Gorkhas normally speak in Hindi language only in day to day socio-economic dynamics. However, at homes, they communicate in Nepali/Gorkha language. So, the Nepali/Gorkha language as an integral part of the Gorkha culture is also not being recognized by the tribals on the one hand and the Government of Arunachal Pradesh on the other. Rather I was really perplexed to hear from some tribals speaking the Nepali/Gorkha language for fond sake in places like Nampong, Miao, Kharsang and Bordumsa as well as Changlang of the Arunachal Pradesh.

Once in a year during the Singpoo cultural festival or it is also called Patkai cultural festival at Miao, the Myanmar borders remain open for a day or two when the Burmese (Myanmar) Singpoos and Gorkhas from Myanmar (locally Burma is more popular than Myanmar) do easily migrate to India and such Burmese (Myanmar) Gorkhas and Burmese Singpoos have been found to be easily accommodated or settle down in forest fringe, Chars and land of tribals as tenants (peasants) while hardly the Gorkhas from Myanmar (Burma) can come to Manipur, Mizoram and Nagaland easily today and settle down there as they are not allowed to do so ever since the last two decades. The Changlang tribals do normally allow the Burmese (Myanmar) Gorkhas to settle down in the Changlang forest fringe after clearing the jungles there but after the forest clearance being done by the Gorkhas, the land automatically come under the possession of the tribals. In fact, it is to be taken for granted that any new land being cleared at the forest fringe becomes the land of tribals in the light of the law of the land of Arunachal Pradesh.

Since the last two decades, it is observed that tribes like Singpoo, Nokte and Wanchu have started learning the Nepali/Gorkha language due to their marriages with the Gorkha women. Doing this, they have been able to exploit the Gorkhas more easily because whatever the Gorkhas talk, they comprehend very easily. Secondly, the Gorkhas with inborn qualities like sincerity, stubbornness, bravery and commitment to the tribal causes for economic development of Arunachal Pradesh have completely attracted the minds of not only the tribals of Changlang and Tirap districts but also the Government of Arunachal Pradesh especially after 1987.

In spite of possessing the above mentioned qualities by the Gorkhas, so far, no remarkable effort has been made by the local tribes to condemn the Gorkha deportation from the soil of Changlang and Tirap districts. This is indicated by the fact that for the last two decades, at least ten thousand Gorkhas have been deported from Changlang and Tirap districts of Arunachal Pradesh. From safety point of view, it is found that in earlier days, the Gorkhas had no problem except they had obligation to pay taxes regularly to the British Government. But now, the Gorkhas have obligations to pay money not only to the tribal landowners but also the Government of Arunachal Pradesh, tribal society and terrorist outfits. It is seriously viewed by the concerned people as how long the Gorkhas can soldier such multi-faceted obligations in North Eastern Frontiers of Changlang and Tirap districts of Arunachal Pradesh? This may be the reason why the present generation of Gorkha families are going out of Changlang and Tirap districts for ever and hardly come back to serve the Government of Arunachal Pradesh. Unlike in the past, the Gorkhas do not prefer to join the Police Department of Government of Arunachal Pradesh. It is heard from an ex-police officer that prior to 1987, most of the Arunachal Police force was consisting of Gorkhas only either as ordinary constables or as officers. In this respect, I found 20 boys from Miao and 15 boys from Nampong as soldiers in Assam Rifles have planned to settle at Guwahati (Assam) or Siliguri (West Bengal) after their retirement and not a single Gorkha boy or girl showed willingness or inclination to settle down in Arunachal Pradesh after his/her retirement from the service of Assam Rifles or Police Department of the date. Although presently, the Assam Rifles authorities have some kind of nostalgia to recruit the Gorkhas as in the past, the Gorkhas are still mostly preferred as they are called brave soldiers of the world. In fact, the Assam Rifles authorities cannot disown the abilities of the Gorkha soldiers of Assam Rifles especially in civilizing, taming and controlling the savage tribals on the one hand and terrorist outfits on the other with reference to the eastern most frontiers of Changlang and Tirap districts of Arunachal Pradesh.

Organising the Gorkhas in Changlang District: Case Studies

With the help of an Additional District Commissioner of Miao, one Mr. Khagendranath Sharma, priest by profession, formed a Gorkha Kalyan Samaj at Miao in 2007 with 80 households from the Gorkha community of Miao villages. But as soon as the Additional District Commissioner was transferred from Miao, Shri Khagendranath

Sharma, as the General Secretary of the Gorkha Kalyan Samaj, had been threatened by the local Singpoos to such an extent that finally in 2009, Shri Khagendranath Sharma had no other alternative except to abandon the Gorkha Kalyan Samaj. At that juncture, as he stated that he could not get the support of his own Gorkha community also. Every other Gorkhas of the area complained him that they were at peace there without being organized among themselves. They did not want to invite troubles by forming the Gorkha social organization. This indicates the fact that Gorkhas normally fight for others' consolidation (Sinha: 2007) rather than the consolidation of their own community. It is heard at Miao that the Gorkha Police officers are found to be very active in beating the Gorkhas even unto death at smaller pretensions than the tribal police officers of Arunachal Pradesh. This may be the reason why every time, the Government of Arunachal Pradesh keep Gorkhas either at Police Station or at the office of Additional District Commissioner compulsorily to tame the Gorkhas of the area in such a way that they should not have been organized well in any way. Shri Sharma of the Gorkha Kalyan Samaj of Miao was being out rightly threatened to be deported from Miao by a Gorkha Police Officer of the Miao Police Station.

Shri Kedarnath Sharma of Nampong told me similar story. As soon as Shri Kedarnath Sharma tried to organize the Gorkhas of Nampong, he was transferred to Vijaynagar (Kalapani) of Arunachal Pradesh for five years in 1995. Interestingly, it is found that some educated/conscious Bahuns of Changlang district tried to organize the Gorkhas but in vain as they did not get the support of majority of Gorkhas who belong to the Matwali castes of the Gorkha community. Mostly, the Matwalis do not support Bahuns because the Matwalis called Bahuns as most cunning as well as exploiting caste (Bhatto Jat) whose predecessors exploited the Matwalis in the Nepal Himalayas while they themselves called "Latto Jats" or innocent castes. Matwalis still are of the opinion that the Bahuns of Gorkha community exploited their Matwali predecessors both in Nepal and India with the patronage of Government of Nepal and also the Indian Government. This is one of the weakest points of Gorkha diversity everywhere in India without generating concrete unity among themselves in clear sense of the term.

Secondly, hardly there are few Bahuns (about 5%) in Changlang district. They are very poor (Daridra-Dukhi-Garib Guruba) compared to other Gorkhas who belong to the Matwali group of the Gorkha society. So, the Bahuns do not have any locus standi in Changlang society and thus they are highly uncounted and therefore probably most unaccountable.

Thirdly, the Bahuns are suspected to be the well-wishers of Government of India having purely the Indo-Aryan background while the Matwalis, as Mongoloids of Tibeto-Barman race background being very much akin to the tribal physiology as well as way of life in the Changlang district and the entire North East India, do not have much loyalty to the government.

Fourthly, Bahuns of the Gorkha community are more conservative than Matwalis in so far as their religious commitment to Hinduism is concerned.

From the above observations that are being made by myself in Changlang district, it is very transparent that there is a remotest chance to have Gorkha solidarity in Changlang in particular and Arunachal Pradesh in general in future years.

Strings for Gorkha Existence

In spite of having unorganized structure of the Gorkhas in Changlang district, Dasai-Tihar festivals are the cultural strings to perceive the Gorkha existence and solidarity. Not a single tribe of the Arunachal Pradesh has so far interrupted the Gorkhas from observing their cultural festivals. Rather, the tribals have also found to be actively participating themselves in observing some of the Gorkha festivals like Dasai and Tihar and share "Shell Roti"—the Gorkha cuisine, although they spell the Gorkha cultural cuisine called Shell Roti as "Sheloti". During the recent eras, due to the influx of Biharis and Marwaris in Changlang district, Deepawali festival is also equally celebrated by the Gorkhas. Many tribal boys have made Gorkha women as their adopted sisters and as the adopted sisters of the tribal boys, the Gorkha women give "Bhai Tika" to the tribal brothers on their forehead during Tihar festival of the Gorkhas. Another area of Gorkha-tribal integration is in respect of sharing the Gorkha "Jhar"—the mountain beer and Rakshi (wine) made of the fermented millet and rice by the Gorkha Matwalis with the tribals. The Jhar-Rakshi has good nutritious value for the Himalayan people (Tamang: 2009). Every tribe knows that the Jhar-Rakshi prepared by the Gorkhas is found to be very tasty, beneficial and enjoyable. Whenever the tribals pay visit to the Gorkha huts, they ask Jhar-Rakshi for drinking and enjoying on the moment. It is very commonly said that the Gorkhas are very much merry-making martial race of the world and that may be reason why the Gorkhas are used to be called as "Johny Gorkhas" by the British officers in India as well as the World. The open-heartedness of Gorkhas might have been another reason why they have been accommodated well by all the tribals of Arunachal Pradesh although officially, the Gorkhas are most unaccountable or peripheral community (Sinha: 2007) in Arunachal Pradesh from the point of view of socio-economic as well as political dynamics. The Gorkhas laugh when other people laugh and shade tears from their eyes on the sorrows faced by others; may be there is no benefit for Gorkhas to laugh when others laugh and cry with tear when others cry. Hardly, any report is found which has been prepared that has appraised well by the Government of Arunachal Pradesh regarding the contributions made by the Gorkhas to the Arunachal economy. Instead of this, still the Gorkhas support the Government of Arunachal Pradesh blindly in most of the situation. The reason behind their laugh and cry are yet unknown to themselves. This is because of the fact that the Gorkhas are very sentimental race in the world being commanded by the emotional upsurge in different odd situations of tribals. No logic as well as rationality is being administered by the Gorkha themselves in such respective situations of their acts and activities. They do that which their masters instruct to do so in all walks of their life. This may be the appropriate reason why Dr. Khemraj Sharma (2011) called the Gorkhas as Moharas (shields) for other communities of the world.

Culturally, most of the Gorkhas of Miao and Nampong organized to celebrate marriage ceremonies of their sons and daughters either at Mergherita or Digboi or Tinsukia or Guwahati of Assam in order to be free from the obligations put forwarded by the system of providing Inner Line Permits to the bride and bridegroom parties in check posts of Changlang district. Secondly, the terrorist outfits also disturb the Gorkhas in such occasion if the marriages are held there in the villages. Rather they arrange separate feasts for the local tribals later on after the completion of marriage ceremonies in Assam region. Interestingly, it is also observed that hardly the tribals invite the Gorkhas of the region while observing their cultural festivals both at Miao and Nampong villages. However, it is also found that many Tamang, Gurung, Manger and Thami being traditionally Buddhists are formally invited to attend the tribal Buddhist monasteries but they are informally invited by the tribals in their cultural festivals although many Gorkha Buddhists normally attend the same. However, as part of the government programme, the Gorkhas of Miao and Nampong villages attend and participate the Patkai cultural festival held every year in the month of January-February at Jagun (Assam) ever since the British period. The Gorkha cultural food items, equipments, vessels and cultural songs and dances along with the tribals are displayed at the Patkai cultural festival. This Patkai cultural festival has its own history from the British days. The British administrators, in order to assimilate the hill tribes of Changlang, Tirap and Lohit districts with the Assamese society, used to organize the Patkai cultural festival especially after 1838 in Jagun—the earlier habitation of Singpoo tribe of Changlang district (Mackenzie: 2011). The Singpoos had to left Jagun of Assam as soon as their slavery system was abolished in 1838 by the British Government when hundreds of Singpoos belonging to Assam plains had to liberalize their slaves borrowed from the Ahom community of Assam. This may be the reason why after the Singpoos left Jagun in 1838, the entire areas of Jagun remained under the dense forest and after 1950 earthquake, about 500 Gorkha families being affected by the earthquake had been shifted from Saikhawa to Jagun (Assam). Very recently, due to the immigration of Hill Miris as well as Singpoo—Tangsa (Nagas) from Arunachal Pradesh to Jagun, the Government of Assam tried to restructure the Jagun area calling as a Scheduled Tribal Area. But as there are 95 per cent of Gorkha population in Jagun (Assam) today, an agitation took place in 2009 when at least 5 Gorkhas had been died on police firing and presently the Government of Assam has kept the matter at abeyance, may be for the time being. This indicates a glaring instance of vindictive attitude of the Government of Assam towards the Gorkhas as a whole as the Gorkhas are staying there beyond 80 years or more by developing the region in all aspects of life. Talk about the cultural development, talk about the economic development and again talk about the strategical safety of the region, Jagun is really a place that can be purely called as a buffer zone of Assam/Arunachal Pradesh to Myanmar. This attitude of the Government of Assam has been of late borrowed by the Government of Arunachal Pradesh also in so far as the deportation of the Gorkhas from Tirap and Changlang districts is concerned. All Assam Students Union (AASU) and United Liberation Front of Assam (ULFA) activists wanted to deport those Gorkhas who had immigrated to Assam after 1970. This issue had cropped up well during the Assam

Movement (1979-1982) by AASU when thousands of Gorkhas of far-flung areas of Assam were deported forever from their centurion old living in Assam. I came across such deported Gorkhas of Assam to the tune of 200 in number at Kadamtala, Salbari, Salugara, Badogra etc. of Siliguri town of West Bengal. The Gorkha deportation took place following the Assam example in Meghalaya in 1987 (Subba: 2007) and also in Manipur later on during the 1990s. The same thing had been happened in Arunachal Pradesh especially at Itanagar and Khonsa where the Gorkhas were asked to leave the homes of tribals and go to Nepal. However, at that juncture, the Government of Arunachal Pradesh had to seriously review the situation considering the importance of state agrarian economy of North Eastern Frontier (Changlang and Tirap districts) being pursued well by the Gorkhas. In that situation, Shri Mani Kumar Subba, the then standing Member of Indian Parliament from Tezpur (Assam) pursued the matter to the Government of Arunachal Pradesh and Assam. This may be the reason why the Gorkhas of North Eastern Frontiers of Arunachal Pradesh were somehow saved from frequent as well whimsical deportation. The deportation of Gorkhas from North East India is a regular feature. It is but observed that the Gorkhas as a whole in North East India have been carried the image of Essentialism from their places of origin in agrarian economy which cannot be undone by the terrorist outfits and those tribal elites who try to brainwash the local common tribals of Arunachal Pradesh. As elsewhere mentioned in the study that the Gorkhas are wanted for work and work only for others as "Kam Pyaro Ki Mam Pyaro"—as per the proverb of the Gorkha community. The proverb indicates that everybody loves Gorkhas for work done by the Gorkhas with sincerity, devotion and commitment and this really is a strong string for their existence in Arunachal Pradesh as well as the entire region of North East India. Every tribal community of Arunachal Pradesh wants to avail the services of the brave Gorkhas in hills, foothills and plain zones.

Prof. Sinha (2009) has very categorically stated that hardly the Gorkhas hesitate to do any kind of difficult jobs. It is found that they are ready to fight with leopards, tigers and bears at Changlang forests while carrying out the job of forest clearance for settled cultivation and tree cutting as carpenter who are in Gorkha society called "Arawal". In Miao, three Gorkhas died fighting with the tigers coming down from the Namdhapaha National Tiger Reserve Park in 2008. Shri Dhan Bahadur Rai of Kharsang village of Miao had killed 2 bears with his Khukuri (Gorkha weapon) in 2000 A.D. when he was clearing the forest fringe near the foothills of Changlang district. The majority of workers (200 workers) at Kharsang Oil Refinery (Miao) of Changlang district and also at the Kharsang Colliery of the same district are Gorkhas since the last one century. Majority of Chowkidars at Namdhapaha National Tiger Reservc Park are the Gorkhas. Most of the security personnel at the government offices are Gorkhas both at Miao and Nampong of Changlang district. No other people hailing from other communities of the country dare to go to such places of Changlang district of Arunachal Pradesh and work in such adverse situation. Shri Man Bahadur Sunar (Attendant) of Nampong Inspection Bungalow is working for the last thirty years as a casual worker. He is from Vairawah of Nepal. He stated that although he wants to stay at Nampong permanently after his retirement but he is not allowcd to do so by Tangsas of the locality. So, he stated that he will purchase a small plot of land at Siliguri (West Bengal) and settle down with his family members after his retirement. Whatever he is saving from the income he earned there, he will invest the same in Siliguri for his retired life. Interestingly, what he said to me is that he feels himself simply as a "Gothala" or caretaker in the Inspection Bungalow for the last thirty difficult years. What he has furnished the reason of such platitude is due to the poverty ridden Nepal. All the Gorkhas of Nepal called him "Pravasi Gorkha" or foreigner Gorkha whenever he visits Nepal and they do no want to issue him the "Nagarikta Praman Patra" or citizenship certificate of Nepal. The same explanation is being given by most of the Gorkhas of Changlang district in regard to issuing Nagarikta Praman Patra calling them as surplus Pravasis of Nepal. They simply come to Nepal on "Return Migration". This has enforced many Gorkha Matwalis to marry the tribal girls and settle down forever in the remotest villages of Changlang district. They are made immigrants in their own land of Nepal. To marry the tribal women is only the viable alternative for the Gorkhas to articulate their survival in Arunachal Pradesh

Very interestingly, as soon as a Gorkha marries a tribal woman, he is entitled to avail most of the facilities of the state except citizenship certificate. But culturally, he is totally tilted towards the tribal way of life. But his children are given the same facilities as enjoyed by the children of the tribal society because the tribal society has given equal importance to matrimonial system in Arunachal Pradesh along with Meghalaya, Nagaland and Mizoram. This is another string for their survival in Changlang district. Many Gorkha Christians of Nampong have married Tangsa women who are mostly Christians and they are therefore staying there forever. They stated that at least there, they do not have to bother about two square meals unlike in Nepal Himalayas as in the past. The "Anikal Lagnu"—spreading famine as used to be taken place in Nepal Himalayas very frequently, is not known here in Arunachal Pradesh. This is what exactly told by their predecessors who came from the Nepal Himalayas. Presently, many educated tribal girls want to marry the Gorkha boys considering their sound economic status due to their positive attitude to lead a settled life. This has been supported the fact that most tribals still reflect nomadic culture. Unlike the Myanmar border tribals lingering with the legacy of nomadic attitude, the tribals of the Changlang district have no more been attuned to the instinct to dwell themselves there with nomadic legacy of the past due to their transition to modernity. But most of the tribes of the Changlang district of Arunachal Pradesh, of course, love for hunting and gathering as well as wild elephant catching in forests while hardly any Gorkha pursues himself on hunting and gathering as their cultural legacy. In reserve forests, hunting is prohibited by the Government of Arunachal Pradesh. Even the tree cutting business in reserve forests has been abolished from 1987 by the Arunachal Pradesh Forest Development Corporation Ltd. In spite of this, quite often, the tribals try to pursue on forest tree cutting ventures due to their whimsical claim to settle down permanently as per the tribal development policy of Government of Arunachal Pradesh in Changlang district which has still the prevalence of Jhum (shifting) cultivation being done by Singpoo, Tangsa, Nokte and Wanchu tribes. In fact, what I found here is that the Gorkhas taught the tribals the ways and means of permanent settlement. Raising terraces in foothills are exclusively done by the Gorkhas. Now, this is followed to some extent by the local tribes also. But interestingly, it is also found that still the tribes are not much successful in this venture for settled cultivation due to the reason that tribals do cultivation in a particular plot of land till the plot of land remain fertile and as soon as the fertility of particular plot of land is decreased they lease out the plot of land to the Gorkhas or keep the land barren for years together. In fact, I did not find any tribal who is domesticating cattle stock which provides the natural compost from the cattle dung while every Gorkha has cattle stock in "Goth"—the cattle sheds. The cattle stock keeping at homes has enabled the Gorkhas to have good crops that ultimately fetch good revenue for the government through the tribal landowners. Therefore, it can be generalized from the above discussion that conversion of barren land, "Chars" and forest fringe into rich agrarian niche is being exclusively done by the Gorkhas and Gorkhas only who have to be therefore kept there in the tribal land at least for thirty years at a stretch. Otherwise, all the tribes of Changlang and Tirap districts will be nowhere. Neither they can revert to nomadic life as it is banned by the Government of Arunachal Pradesh nor hunting and gathering in the forests as in the past prior to 1987.

Quality of Life of the Gorkhas

Coming to the question of quality of life of Gorkhas, comparing the tribals, it is observed that although the Gorkhas have thatched roof huts, they keep their huts clean being polished with cow dung and reddish mud on the floor and bamboo framed mud walls. This is not found in case of the tribal houses as the tribals hardly clean their house as the Gorkhas do. Every Gorkha house owner has reared floriculture at homes (Sharma: 2005). The Gorkhas are fond of flowers both for worshipping their god and goddesses at home and temple as well as observing Pujas (socio-religious ceremonies) and festivals at home while the tribals do not have such interest to have flowers and thereby developing floriculture by raising the flower gardens (*Ibid.*) at homes and agrarian land.

The Gorkhas vs. Gorkhas in Changlang District

The Gorkhas do not have organic solidarity. This is proved by the fact that once Shri Ratna Bahadur Rai (Miao) while going to Chenai to undergo medical treatment of his mother was looted by another unknown Gorkha fellow in November, 2010 at Guwahati with the medicine being put on the tea cup that caused him unconscious. Many Gorkha women are trafficking from Changlang district by the Gorkha themselves. Trafficking Gorkha women (Chhetri: 2009) is a common incidence in North East India. In fact, to look at the Gorkha girls, they appear to be very beautiful having Mongoloid face which is very much in demand in the brothels of Mumbai, Kolkata, Delhi and other metros of the country with worth Rs. 70,000 to one lakh as price for a single Gorkha woman to be supplied to the brothel. This may be the reason why the Gorkha women are not safe in North East India. In all cases of women trafficking, Gorkhas are fully involved. Otherwise, how a Gorkha girl of Nampong of Changlang district had been traced out at the Mumbai brothel in 2010? Shri Dhan Bahadur Chhetri of Nampong told me that his beautiful daughter had been eloped by a Gorkha boy and sold at Kolkata brothel (Sonagachi) or red light area in 2009. Plenty of such instances are there from all-over the North Eastern Frontiers. Fair complexion, sexy outlook, outspoken habit and open-heartedness of the Gorkha women are responsible factors for Gorkha women trafficking from the Changlang district of Arunachal Pradesh. In this respect, the Tagadhari women are found to be rather quite conscious as they hardly talk or mix up with men-folk of the villages of Miao and Nampong. If a newcomer visits a Tagadhari house, only the male members of the house become quite vocal while the woman members of the house remain inside the house only. While travelling from Tinsukia (Assam) Railway Station to New Jalpaiguri (West Bengal) Railway station, I came across many Gorkhas who do not at all openly mix up with other unknown Gorkhas. Many Gorkhas told me regarding their queer experiences as to how they were cheated by the unknown Gorkha fellows on their journey at various places of the country.

IV

The Gorkhas in Inherent Dilemma

The observations made in the earlier chapters of the study indicate that the Gorkhas are completely accustomed, adopted and adjusted to the Arunachal environment that is consisted of the Pahar-Parbat (hills), Khola Nala (streams and drains), Jungle or forest and unknown barren land as well as Chars of Arunachal Pradesh. Ever since the days of "Burma Ko Dhawa"—war with Burma (1824-1826), the Gorkhas appear to have been faced Dhawa everyday or doing struggle everyday for their survival. When he is to be ousted from the Changlang district is not known to him, when he has to loose his leased in operational landholding and other property is not sure and when he is to loose the two square meals for himself and his family, he is not all ascertained. The uncertainty, uncertainty and uncertainty is the way of living of the Gorkhas in Arunachal Pradesh in general and the Changlang district in particular. This has made the Gorkhas since the last two centuries, the conflict afflicted human resource stock (Nath: 2007) of the Arunachal Pradesh as well as North East India. Of course, unlike Assam where we found the afflicted Gorkhas in overt form, the afflictedness of the Gorkhas is in covert form as hardly we found the conflict afflicted Gorkhas in action in Arunachal Pradesh of North East India.

Living and Dying in Changlang

It is observed from the study that the Gorkhas are trying to adjust the local environs and if not die fighting with Khukuris against the enemy whoever the enemy may be whether men or wild animals of the locality. Over the last 200 odd years or so, the Gorkhas of Changlang district have been tolerating the attacks of the tribals but it appears from the way they are living that they are ready to die in Changlang district only rather than leaving the battleground of Changlang district of Arunachal Pradesh for elsewhere. They have no other viable alternative elsewhere to go on "Basai Sarnu" (Hut: 2009) to Arunachal Pradesh or even in other parts of the country as a whole except to face difficult situations there itself. Since they are manual agrarian workers and peasants, they know that they will not be accepted in any other part of the country. Comparing other states of North East India, Arunachal Pradesh is having very thin population structure as Arunachal Pradesh has just eleven lakh populations with 82 per cent of land under the forest cover and as most tribals are staying in hill areas, the Gorkhas have been living quite comfortably in the foothills of all North Eastern Frontier of India. Economically, hill areas of Changlang district are not so lucrative to the Government of Arunachal Pradesh having acute dry land. So, the government encourages, of course, unofficially for the immigration of Gorkhas in the foothills which are mainly the central niches of the Arunachal agrarian economy due to sufficient rivers that are flowing down on the foothills from the hills of Changlang. The river water as well as the river basins are left to no use for the tribals. This is the main reason why the Gorkhas have with all stubbornness converted the foothills into the rich agrarian sector of Arunachal economy.

All the Gorkhas of Miao and Nampong have their "Byasis"—the land near the river or stream sites at the lower altitudes where they can comfortably keep their cattle stocks in Goths (cow sheds). The Gorkha culture of keeping "Byasis" has enabled the Gorkhas to live both in high land and low land in all seasons in Aul/Lekh (high altitude and low altitude niches) are equally come under the preference structure of the Gorkhas in so far as their living is concerned. This may be the accurate reason why both in Nampong and Miao, the Gorkhas are staying in high as well as low altitudes while the tribals are mostly staying in the middle altitudes where there is water scarcity and lack of greeneries. Both high land and low land (Lekh and Aul) are habitable to the Gorkhas with their assertiveness.

If situation demands, a Gorkha does not hesitate to chop up the head of enemy on the ground using his Khukuri. Although the civilized Gorkhas may call this act as an act of foolishness but at the Changlang situation, Khukuri is only the answer as it is the only weapon to be used for personal safety by the Gorkhas that helps them to survive in the hostile situation of Changlang district. Here in this situation, what a Gorkha can do if his enemy comes in front of him to kill him on the spot? So, to survive himself is always the first human right of the Gorkha fellow. Even women folks have also been found carrying the Khukuris. Although the so-called civilized Gorkhas may call it as an apparent foolishness but for the Gorkhas who are staying in such a volatile situation insisted them to use Khukuri as only the wise alternative for their survival. Since the Changlang Gorkhas have been kept at periphery bordering the Myanmar (Sinha: 2007), the Khukuri is only the weapon for their security not only to kill the wild animals but also the savage tribal enemy whosoever he may be. As the Changlang villages are as good as the villages as we found in the earlier stage of human civilization, here the logic, ration and consciousness of human kind have no place to comprehend giving compliance and compliment in clear sense of the term. Many Gorkhas of the areas so described in the study, stated that such and such Gorkhas might not have been killed by the wild animals or enemy provided they could have kept Khukuris with themselves on the stipulated hostile situations of Changlang district.

Mr. R. P. Bhattacharjee (2005) in his article entitled "Security and Development in Arunachal Pradesh" has stated that Changlang and Tirap districts have become the battleground for Naga insurgents of Khaplang and Issac-Muviah groups where simple and innocent villagers are being brainwashed and terrorized. Here, in this context, the so-called traditional tribal bodies like Kebang, Mele, Nogongthing, Jungpblue, Buliang, Wancho-Wangas, Kava, Keba, Tso-Tsorgin etc. had been found in the past to settle the crimes have also lost their grip over the tribals giving solutions to the occurrence of frequent crimes in the villages due to the presence of Naga insurgents who stated that the so-called tribal bodies are rather the well-wishers of the government. Besides Naga insurgents, very recently other insurgent groups like Liberation Tigers of Arunachal Pradesh, United Liberation Tigers of Arunachal Pradesh and Revolutionary Army of Arunachal Pradesh have also sprung up in Changlang and Tirap districts of Arunachal Pradesh. The Government of Arunachal Pradesh has failed to finish up the ultra outfits in Changlang and Tirap districts. Thus, it is proved by the ground realities that security rather than development is the real malaise of Changlang and Tirap districts where the Gorkhas are merely living with Khukuris in the battlefield. When a Gorkha is going to be killed nobody knows before hand. Restoring peace is the main agenda for the Government of Arunachal Pradesh through different government packages initiated recently for the tribal development in the state. It is found that 80 per cent of the budget of the government of Arunachal Pradesh is spent on salaries (*Ibid.*). Thus, a package on tea cultivation is on vogue since 1999. But it is again found that due to the security reason, whatever the tribal elites who had pursued the project in the initial stage on tea cultivation have leased out to the Marwaris of Tinsukia, Digboi and Margherita of Assam. In fact, it is seen that most of the outside entrepreneurs do not want to invest their money on projects of variety in Changlang and Tirap districts due to the security lapses. All these have led the Changlang and Tirap districts to unsolved dilemma or unresolved phenomenon.

If this is the overall scenario of Changlang and Tirap districts, then just imagine the socio-economic conditions of Gorkhas there. It is really very worrysome situation to live in Changlang and Tirap district villages. This has led the Gorkhas to be very vulnerable in so far as leading their descent life in Changlang district is concerned. Hand to mouth situation is also very frequently found in some of the remotest villages of Changlang district. The highhandedness of underground outfits made the Arunachal Police force helpless. I found that common people do not believe on the Police force there rather they are ready to cooperate the underground terrorist activists who in many difficult situations support common people in the Changlang villages. This may be the reason why the Changlang villages appear to be desolates, post-war fields and the affected people there are under the so-called rehabilitation programmes of the government in Camps. In every rehabilitation camp, I found hundreds of Gorkhas besides Chakma and Bengali refugees from Bangladesh. The above observation indicates that dwelling in dilemma and dilemma only is the normal process of Gorkha living in Changlang district. Hardly any Gorkha thinks for better life in Changlang district tomorrow. This may be again the apparent reason why a Gorkha has to stand up and sit down till his tribal landowner asks him to do so in his day to day life. He cannot simply talk with high rhythm (voice) with tribal landowner neither he can easily resist a tribal fellow in case he is beaten up by him and sometimes a tribal fellow may even finish him up to death.

Tradition of the Gorkhas as a Mercenary Human Resource Stock

Once upon a time during the British period, the Gorkhas were used to be called as mercenary force. The same legacy is still to be on vogue among the Gorkhas of the Changlang district. "Hire and Fire" the Gorkhas by the tribals have made them a mercenary force in Changlang district of Arunachal Pradesh. As non-tribals in the land of tribals of Changlang district, the Gorkhas are no more called today as reciprocal Gorkha citizens of the country as per the provisions of Indo-Nepal Peace and Friendship Treaty (1950). The Government of India is also keeping deaf ears to the problems of Gorkhas of Arunachal Pradesh stating it as the border state adjoining Myanmar, China and Bhutan.

Since the Gorkhas are found to be mum in Changlang villages, no government i.e., neither the Government of Arunachal Pradesh nor the Government of India thinks anything concrete about the pitiable platitudes of the Gorkhas. To keep the North Eastern Frontier safe, the Gorkhas are the best option left to the government since the Gorkhas hardly mind to donate their blood, sweats and life to the cause of Government of India or the Government of Arunachal Pradesh.

Keeping the Gorkhas unaccountable to the Arunachal Pradesh economy, society and politics, what the Government of Arunachal Pradesh is presently doing is that let the Gorkhas be there in the same geographical niche where they are staying with the same status since the last 200 years or so. In fact, the Government of Arunachal Pradesh knows it very well that the existence of Gorkhas in Arunachal Pradesh in general and Changlang as well as Tirap districts in particular is hardly realized rather the Government of Arunachal Pradesh has kept her ears deaf, eyes blind and attitude indifferent as of the British government had towards the Gorkhas. The Gorkhas have also kept themselves mum about their right to identity and for the realization of the Gorkha identity, they hardly complain the Government of Arunachal Pradesh. So, what the Government of Arunachal Pradesh does normally think is that the Gorkhas are very happy there as hardly the Gorkhas have created any havoc in Changlang district so far since the formation of Changlang as a separate district from Tirap in 1987. This may be the immediate cause why still the Gorkhas of Changlang and Tirap districts are considered to be the mercenary hands to the Government of Arunachal Pradesh and the local tribals. This is based on the simple logic that if a child does not cry, his mother hardly provides her breast milk to the child. The same is the situation of Gorkhas in the Arunachal Pradesh in general and Changlang as well as the Tirap districts in particular in the question of realizing right to ethnic identity of the Gorkhas in the state. There is no Gorkha organization of prominence to make the Gorkhas conscious of their rights pertaining to the realization and thereby restoration of their ethnic identity at the North Eastern Frontier of India.

The Gorkhas in Frontier Wilderness

So far, hardly any study has been conducted on the Gorkhas of North Eastern Frontiers wilderness of India. Prof. A.C. Sinha (2007) has stated in his article entitled "Indian North East Frontier and Nepali Immigrants" that "There is a hill, send up a Gorkha" may be quite appropriate in the context of seven sister states of North East Council. The direct contact between the Gorkhas and North East Frontier, as mentioned everywhere in the study, appears to have been occurred in 1817 when 1000 Hindustanis and Gorkhas took part in Shylet operation as part of the Cuttuck Legion (later on known as Assam Light Infantry). He further stated that after 1824, the Gorkhas started coming to the North Eastern Frontier. The story of the Gorkha involvement in the consolidation of the region under the British Empire is ably presented through the pages of Col. L.W. Shakespeare's "History of the Assam Rifles" (1977). In Assam Rifles, more than 50 per cent of riflemen were hailing from the Gorkha community. The Khukuri replaced the short sword on the flag and hats of Assam Rifles after 1865 in recognition of the sincere services rendered with Khukuris in the North Eastern Frontiers jungles. Later on, Khukuri was accepted as the emblem of the Assam Rifles as the custodians of the security of the region. Prof. Sinha (*Ibid.*) has further stated that the Gorkha Training Centres were established in district headquarters and as a district headquarters, a training centre had also been established at Khonsa of the Tirap district in 1852. Through Khonsa, the present Tirap and Changlang districts were controlled by the British Government. The Gorkhas were also stationed in hill areas of Khonsa and Sadiya frontier tracts. From Khonsa, at least five thousand Gorkha families had been settled at the place like Miao, Diyon, Jairampur, Lohitpur, Hailuang, Walong, Anini, Parsuramkund, Digaru of Changlang, Lohit and Upper/Lower Dibang Valley districts respectively. There are also a few Gorkhas in Lisok and Wintong areas of Changlang district. It is an established fact that all the tribal leaders are totally dependent on the Gorkha votes in Changlang, Tirap,

Upper/Lower Dibang Valley districts of the Arunachal Pradesh. All the Chief Ministers of the state of Arunachal Pradesh got the ample support from the Gorkhas in winning their elections.

The Gorkha Ex-soldiers

The Gorkha ex-soldiers were encouraged to settle down in the foothills, forest fringe and other strategic points of the North Eastern Frontiers of Changlang and Tirap districts. Prof. Sinha (2007) is correct as he has stated that "the peasant background and discipline of their strict military training, acquired an image as loyal citizens with pro-establishment attitudes towards the government. With their hard work, perseverance and investment of their pensions in agriculture, they have been able to turn out their newly acquired settlements as thriving centres of prosperous peasantry. Their apparent and visible prosperity among the relatively indolent and less achievement-oriented indigenous communities attracts jealousies".

Other Gorkhas in Changlang

A number of settlements like Sadiya (Assam), Khonsa (Tirap), Jairampur, Namphic Check Post, Nampong and Miao (Changlang) are located at the areas where there is a considerable movement of armed forces to contain secessionist and extremist activists in Changlang and Tirap districts of North East Frontier. This may be the reason why as I have noted in Changlang district that many Gorkhas were deported by the tribals blaming them as informers of Indian army and police force. It is told by the local people that these days, the job of informers is plenty for the youths and quite a good percentage of young boys and girls are doing this job both in Miao and Nampong. However, in such situation, mostly the Gorkhas have been found suffering a lot. This is due to the fact that Gorkhas have soft corner to Indian army and police force and thus they are suffering at the hands of terrorist activists mainly from the NSCN groups in Changlang district.

"The immigration of Gorkhas into North Eastern Frontier may be described as an administrative nuisance rather than a political menace" is correct as stated by Prof. Sinha (2007) as I found that the Gorkhas are being used as "Kam Chalo Varo, Afal Tero Tharo"— the Gorkha proverb states that once the vessel is used by you at the optimum level, you throw it out to the dustbin—is correct in case of Gorkhas of Changlang as well as Tirap districts of Arunachal Pradesh. It is interestingly observed that unlike Nagaland, Mizoram, Meghalaya and Manipur, no administrative report of the Government of Arunachal Pradesh has described openly the deportation of Gorkhas from the Arunachal Pradesh. Not a single British officer could unlike other communities of North East Frontier of India had made any contradictory remark on the problems created by the Gorkha settlers in Arunachal Pradesh (the then NEFA). The Gorkha "Khutis" (herdsmen's temporary sheds) consisting of herds of cows, buffaloes along with cultivation at the "Chars" had been tremendously encouraged by the British Government in Changlang and Tirap districts of Arunachal Pradesh. These Gorkhas have made the Changlang land fertile with the challenges afforded by the distinct isolated location into opportunities for overall economic development of Arunachal Pradesh, "with their qualities like cheerful, perseverance and sturdy hands, their ubiquitous Khukuri and readiness to do anything to make a lively living. With this temperament he easily combines a number of roles in himself as a dairyman, carpenter and even errand boy. When he comes to the North Eastern Frontier Tract of Changlang and Tirap, he invariably locates himself away from the tribal village on an inhabited possibly barren land and forest fringe areas. Often the local tribals make him guilty of felling trees, grazing land and even clandestine settlements on the reserve forests (*Ibid.*)" of Changlang and Tirap districts of Arunachal Pradesh.

The frugal habits, perseverance and industrious habit of the Gorkhas make them a difficult living for himself to begin comfortably. He is having all types of agricultural chores. His cosmopolitan social outlook, relative freedom from restrictions of Purity and Pollution in terms of food and drink and prevalence of polygeny enables him easily to acquire a female partner. An Administrator with about four decades of experience in North Eastern Frontier region came to the conclusion as "The Gorkhas are phenomenally fertile people and it is not unusual to find among their families where there are four to five wives and twenty to thirty children. It has been found that larger the family of the Gorkha the more prosperous it is (*Ibid.*)". I have also made the same observation in Changlang district where each Gorkha has at least 5 to 10 children if he has a single wife and 15 to 20 children if he has two wives. Mr. Lok Bahadur Chhetri of Nampong has two wives living in the same house having 12 children from his two wives. This has enabled him to keep 25 cows and 5 buffaloes which are looked after by his children only in the grazing field near the river Nampong. On the way to Nampong from Jairampur, I found hundreds of Gorkha children looking after the cows and buffaloes in the forests. The same observation I could make in Diyon, Miao (Changlang district), Lohitpur (Tezu) of Lohit district, Namphai-I, Namphai-II and Kharsang villages of Changlang district.

Cultural Traditions of the Gorkhas

Both the groups of Gorkha community (Tagadharis and Matwalis) are proud of their respective history, culture, religion, language and traditions. The Tagadharis feel that they are pure Hindus and the Matwalis also feel that they belong to martial race of the world. For the Tagadharis, India is not a new place to live on as their predecessors once upon a time in Muslim Rule in India had hailed from India only and the Matwalis are also proud of their respective traditions since Mahabharata days when they (probably all Matwalis) had participated and had to fight the Mahabharata war. By heart and soul, they considered the local tribals of Arunachal Pradesh as uncivilized, illiterate nomadic tribes having laziness in absolute sense of the term in all pursuits of Arunachal economy. This aspect has been nicely accorded by the Government of India as she knows it very well that the Gorkhas are very much pro-India on the one hand and very laborious community on the other since time immemorial while the local tribals as completely indolent and against the Indian Union. Their traditions and culture are being drawn mainly from Myanmar and Thailand—they therefore feel that they are very much foreigners to the Union of Government of India. This leads the government to keep soft corners to the Gorkhas of Changlang in particular and Arunachal Pradesh in general although officially the government can not apparently condemn the tribals of the state in favour of the Gorkhas. In fact, the Gorkhas have served the country by civilizing the tribal societies of Changlang and Tirap districts where hardly till few years back, the tribals could at all construct home and toilets. The Gorkhas always keep their home clean and construct toilets and urinals. To clean huts with cow dung is another area of Gorkha culture. However, today, these habits have also been slowly adopted by the local tribals. So, not only from the economic development point of view of Changlang and Tirap districts, the Gorkhas have also taught the tribals to clean houses so as to lead a healthy life.

Most of lower primary and primary school teachers in Changlang district are either Gorkhas or Biharis who inspire the tribal boys and girls to attend schools regularly. But as many teachers stated that most of the tribal boys and girls by heart and soul are fond of nomadic life by pursuing themselves on hunting, gathering and elephant catching in the forests as well as fishing at the rivers. They are also keen to have elephant horn business. It is also found that most of the tribal youths have very destructive attitudes to the government mechanisms. The conversion of hostile foothills of Changlang and Tirap along with the foothills of other districts of Arunachal Pradesh into cultivation made the Gorkhas unofficially recognized human resource potentials to the Government of Arunachal Pradesh. The Gorkhas do extend cooperation to the government mechanisms at the level of implementation of government projects in the state. It is also observed that the Tagadharis having rich Vanarasi, Patna, Vrindavan and Kashi religious as well as the educational legacy enforces most of the people of Arunachal Pradesh and even the tribals to pay due respect to all the Gorkha Pandits and priests. The Gorkhas are fond of Hindi film shows and due to the encouragement of Government of India in implementing the Rajbhasa Promotion Policy in North East India, the Gorkhas in fact have been able to teach Hindi to the tribal children. Moreover, due to the existence of 110 tribal dialects with 110 tribals of the Arunachal Pradesh, Hindi along with English languages are the medium of instruction in the schools, colleges and Arunachal University, Itanagar. So, talking about the Gorkha contribution to Hindi language as per the Rajbhasa Promotion Policy of Government of India, the Government of Arunachal Pradesh has also kept in tact the obligation for the implementation of Rajbhasa through the Gorkhas and Biharis in the state schools, colleges and university. Teaching Hindi in schools has helped the tribal young generation to properly feel the pulse of the Gorkha contribution to the tribal land of Arunachal Pradesh. And that is why some voices are being raised today against the real and putative problems of the Gorkha immigrants in the North Eastern Frontiers of India mainly in Changlang and Tirap districts. The Gorkhas in other districts of Arunachal Pradesh are little bit better than the Gorkhas of Changlang and Tirap districts. For instance, the Gorkhas are more secured in Lohit district as they are allowed to purchase land, construct Pucca houses ever since the British days. I found this at Allobari and Lohitpur of Tezu and Lohit district where the Gorkhas are having much better socio-economic status along with the right to cast votes for the Members of Indian Parliament. In this way, the Gorkhas' role on social consolidation of the tribals is also quite apparent since they have made many tribals their Mits (friends) and also married many tribal women. During the recent two decades, the percentage of Gorkha-Tangsa Mit relationship has been increased to two hundred times at Nampong. However, the Singpoos being little bit conservative in approach to the Gorkhas, this Mit system has not been coined well till today with significant percentage at Miao of the Changlang district.

Nepali vs. Gorkha Identity Question

It is observed that hardly the common tribals know the word "Gorkha". They call all the Gorkhas as Gorkhas in Arunachal Pradesh which has created lot of confusions among the Gorkhas as they are perfectly conceptualized to be the immigrants from Nepal only. But, in fact, ever since the last three decades, hardly the Gorkhas of Nepal have preference structure to come to Arunachal Pradesh. Most of the Pahari Gorkhas of Nepal Himalayas normally has been found to be comfortable to stay in the Terai belt of Nepal and Assam hills and plains. I talked to the educated Singpoos and Tangsas of Miao and Nampong about the name by which they address the Gorkhas of the region. Most of them informed me that the common name is Nepali rather than the Gorkha. By "Gorkha", they merely understand the Gorkha soldiers of Indian Gorkha Regiments. Like Darjeeling-Sikkim, hardly I found any Gorkha asking for clan background of another Gorkha. Mostly they ask the caste background of unknown Gorkhas whenever they meet in public places and as Gorkha guests who come to their houses. All the Gorkhas of Changlang and Tirap districts simply ask the caste background of another Gorkha. Forget about the clan background as it has no meaning in North East India. Simply they distinguish between the tribals and Gorkhas there. This is due to pseudo-Hindu racial stock composition of the majority of Gorkhas who are Matwalis in Changlang and Tirap districts. Historically, most of the Matwalis unlike Tagadharis are having pseudo- Hindu background. Many of them, in the past were Animists. Hardly 20 per cent of Gorkha Hindus speak pure Indo-Aryan Nepali/ Gorkha language as observed by Prof. Subba (2007) is found to be totally contradictory by connotation in case of the Gorkhas of Changlang and Tirap districts of Arunachal Pradesh where hundred per cent Gorkhas speak the Nepali/Gorkha language only as their medium of communication in day to day life. Even if they speak Hindi as medium of communication in public places, at home they all speak in Nepali/Gorkha language only.

Marginalized Status of the Gorkhas

Sharma's study on "Marginalization of Gorkhas in India: A Community in Quest of Indian Identity" (2011) indicates that all the sections of Gorkhas whether educated, uneducated, rich or poor, high castes/low castes, scheduled castes/tribes, Other Backward Classes or any other categories are being marginalized in different fashions in their socio-economic as well as political aspects of life by the mainstream societies of the country. One of malaises of the Gorkha community in India is that they openly agree for their marginalized status accredited by other communities of the country. Unfortunately, as Sharma (*Ibid.*) observed that in very many cases, the Gorkhas marginalize Gorkhas only for short-sighted vested interests. This becomes good stimulus for other communities like Bengali in West Bengal and also the tribals in North Eastern Frontiers of India to marginalize the common Gorkhas later on at random.

Tribals Versus Non-Tribals

It is observed from Miao and Nampong of Changlang district that due to the common Hindu traditions, the Gorkhas—Biharis as well as Marwaris have formed an informal group through the informal social linkage. Many Biharis are found visiting the Gorkha households with Chat Puja Prasad as "Thekuwa" and the Gorkhas also found visiting the Bihari households with Gorkha "Shell Roti" to be shared by the Bihari neighbours during the Tihar (Deepawali) festival. The Marwaris and Biharis invite Gorkha Pandits and priest Bahuns to do religious Pujas at their homes. Necessity makes no demarcation as well as differences in their relationship. The informal non-tribal group formation at Miao and Nampong has helped the Gorkhas to be safe from the treacherous acts and attacks of the tribals and terrorist activists. Now, the tribals do not dare to ill-treat the Gorkhas, Biharis and Marwaris in the old fashions as they are paying good income to the tribal land and house owners. Many Gorkhas, Biharis and Marwaris have hired the tribal houses for the shops of variety. The tribals also purchase goods and articles at the shops that have created a kind of concrete social networking which quite often enhances to reduce animosity between the tribals and non-tribals. Shri D.B. Gurung, a shopkeeper says that he has established good rapport with Tangsas of Nampong in such a way that he is going to open another grocery shop there itself very shortly. Shri D.K. Sunar and Shri R.K. Sharma (teachers) of Nampong High School stated that they have been respected by the Tangsas of Nampong like anything. Both of them have married Tangsa women. I found both the Tangsa women (wives) of Shri Sunar and Shri Sharma although belonging to Tangsa tribe of the locality, speak Gorkha/Nepali language in such a way that nobody can really call them Tangsa tribal women. Even their etiquette and jester as displayed to me really resemble with the Gorkha counterpart. They were so happy to see me there in place like Nampong where hardly any scholar has dared to visit till today. They said that Tangsas are also human beings. If it is so, they further said that why the people of India do not ventured to come to Nampong which is also an integral part of the country. The Tangsas of Nampong stated that they are happy with the Nampong Gorkhas who live and die with the tribals, become benefactor, friend, guide and philosopher to each other at times of their need. Not a single Gorkha has been so far being exploited out of way by the Tangsas and vice versa; rather the Gorkhas have sacrificed a lot for the cause of the Tangsas. For instance, many Gorkhas have joined the Christian Church of the Tangsas and also married many Tangsa women. This case study shows that Gorkhas are being fully adjusted with and assimilated into the Tangsa way of life at Nampong. Similar cases are also found at Miao of Changlang district in significant percentage. The Tangsas said that they are unnecessarily called savage, uncivilized and illiterate tribes and even they are also being blamed for the supporters of terrorist activists in Changlang district. Shri Atem Mele of Miao told me that his two sons are serving the Assam Rifles. Mr. Mele also said that if he was really anti-government in his approach, then why he has sent both sons to serve the Assam Rifles of the government that too both of them are posted at the Myanmar borders of the country. Again, some of the Singpoos also informed me that they are the descendents of Besa Gam, the famous Singpoo tribal chief who was thoroughly pro-establishment (Government) during the British period. In fact, it was Mr. Besa Gam who supplied the tea seeds and seedlings to Mr. Robert Bruce in 1830 (Sharma: 2009; Mackenzie: 2011) and the tea seeds and seedlings supplied by Besa Gram were later on planted at Chabua tea estate of Dibrugargh district (Assam) as the first tea estate of British Empire in India.

The Identity Syndrome

The concept of Gorkha identity is found to be more pronounced among the educated urban based Gorkhas in Changlang and Tirap districts. The common Gorkhas of villages do not however have any sense of having Gorkha identity crisis in Changlang and Tirap districts. What I found is that except a few Tagadharis and little bit educated Matwalis, the common Gorkhas do not at all talk anything about their identity crisis in Changlang district of Arunachal Pradesh. To the common Gorkha villagers, the concept of ethnic identity is very vague because they are very much concerned with domestic and agrarian chores and do not at all have any moment at their disposal to think about the issues pertaining to ethnic identity crisis. They feel comfortable provided they have living right with two square meals per day for their families. They said that why they should be communal with the local tribes since they have to live and die with these tribes only. "Taroko Deota Ra Nagik Ko Bhut Ma Nagik Ko Bhut Nai Kam Lagcha" meaning thereby the nearest ghosts or evil spirits come to rescue a person in his bad days than the distant gods or goddesses who can hardly do it to the Gorkhas. This entails hundred per cent realities in Changlang and Tirap districts where hardly except the tribals, nobody can come and rescue them from outside on the moment when the terrorists activists ransack the villages. The common tribals come to save the Gorkhas, counteracting the terrorist activists because the tribals also speak the Nagamese language with the terrorist activists and convince the terrorist activists to go back to jungle as 'Jungle Party' from the villages. In the situation, many tribals also die as it happened in recent past in the Changlang district of Arunachal Pradesh.

The identity syndrome for the Changlang Gorkhas appears to be a false hypothesis for their existence as they do not have long term commitment to the locations of their staying today. This is so as they live with utter uncertainty and die with utter uncertainty. They do not have Mai-Bap (father/mother) in the Arunachal Pradesh. If it is so, where is the significance of having identity crisis that might have been felt sincerely by the Gorkhas in Changlang and Tirap districts of North Eastern frontier of India? In fact, to the Gorkhas of Changlang, to manage "Dui Bela Ko Bhansa or Khana"—two square meals per day—is their bare expectation as well as their expected living right realized in the sate of Arunachal Pradesh. So, to manage two square meals per day is the prime objective here besides to save something from their income so as to be invested in Assam or Siliguri or Nepal Terai belt and impart education as far as possible so that their children can go out of Arunachal Pradesh to get jobs of their choice.

From the above discussion, we evolve out an academically generalized conclusion that the Changlang Gorkhas might be having identityless status to the perception of Gorkha academicians and so-called Gorkha elites of the country but not to the common Gorkhas of Changlang district. This may be the reason why some conscious Gorkhas called Changlang Gorkha villagers as "Gorkha Tribals" as they have least sense of ethnic identity realization and restoration and undertake struggle for acquiring the Gorkha identity in Changlang district. What I personally feel after my intensive interactions with the Changlang Gorkhas is that injecting identity consciousness forcefully in the minds of the Changlang Gorkhas would rather further create more complexities and commotion into their existing agony at the local situation. At least, they can make safe living with whatever identity they have so far restored of their 200 years of odd existence by generating enough confidence among the tribals of the Changlang district. Therefore, no meaningful injection on the restoration of Gorkha identity can be administered among the Gorkhas to avoid conflict afflicted situation between the tribals and Gorkhas in Changlang district. No new agony can be afflicted upon the Gorkha community at Miao and Nampong along with Diyon and Changlang. The best option left to them is to encourage mobility of their children from the Arunachal Pradesh to either Assam or other parts of the country because no more they want to left "Munglan" or India for Nepal Himalayas. It is also observed that most of the Gorkha children are interested to go to Assam or Siliguri (West Bengal) as their destination besides the Indian metropolis as their first preference or option in order to avoid the agony that their forefathers had to undergo in the history of 200 odd years of living in North Eastern Frontiers of India.

The Immigrants Once and forever

The Gorkhas are made immigrants once and forever by all communities of the country and by all the government agencies. In spite of living in the North Eastern Frontiers of India for the last 200 odd years or so, everybody including the intellectuals, professors and bureaucrats of the country do not have left the habit of stating the Gorkhas as immigrants from Nepal. Why they do not at all call the tribals of Arunachal Pradesh also the immigrants from Myanmar, Korea, Thailand, Tibet etc.? It is what I believe is due to the non-written specific history of the tribal immigration to the Arunachal Pradesh while the Gorkhas have specific written history of their immigration to North Eastern Frontiers of India including the Arunachal Pradesh. The fact to be realized by all concerned is that may be the Gorkhas had immigrated to the Arunachal Pradesh or other states of North East India little bit later than the tribals who immigrated to Arunachal Pradesh from Burma, Thailand, Korea and Tibet. So, to be unbiased in generating specific explanation, it can be said that like the Gorkhas, all the tribals are also the immigrants to the soil of Arunachal Pradesh from Myanmar, Thailand, Korea, Tibet and other South East Asian countries. This statement can well be supplemented by the fact that all the tribals of Arunachal Pradesh drew their traditions and culture from the country called Myanmar (Burma), Thailand, Korea, Tibet and China. In fact, they too appear to be the earlier immigrants to the land of Arunachal Pradesh which was mostly the integral part of Myanmar and Tibet prior to 15th century. This is further supplemented by the fact that even the then Ahom kings of Assam did not have clear cut concept about the exact borderline (boundary) between the Upper Assam (Mackenzie: 2011) and Myanmar and also China. This might be the reason why very often, the Myanmar (Burma) Singpoos used to invade the North Eastern Frontiers even after the consolidation of North Eastern Frontiers by the British Government in 1842. Still today, many Burmese (Myanmar) Singpoos come to the North Eastern Frontiers of India especially at the Changlang, Lohit and Tirap districts with malaise attitudes to India as they have relatives here in these districts and settle down while the Burmese Gorkhas have left their relatives at Myanmar (Burma) and this might be reason why in very many situations, they also get the Outer Line Permit (Pass) to go to Myanmar (Burma) to meet their relatives. This is supported by the fact that there are over four lakh Gorkhas in Myanmar (Burma) today, mainly they have been pursued themselves on agriculture and pastoral professions. Hardly, here at Miao and Nampong, the Gorkhas have been found to go to Nepal Himalayas to meet their relatives. Now with the introduction of Look East Policy of Government of India in the North Eastern Frontiers (Singh: 2009), the National Highways are under construction to connect India with Myanmar through Arunachal Pradesh, Manipur and Mizoram as well as Nagaland. The inter-relationship between the Gorkhas of Arunachal Pradesh and Myanmar (Burma) is expected to increase further and the question of calling the Gorkhas as immigrants will become more and more redundant in realization and actualization for the tribals of Arunachal Pradesh in particular and the people of North East India in general. Therefore, till today, the Gorkhas of North East India have been centred on the subjectivity by explanation rather than having objectivity in generalizing that will erase out instantly in the light of Look East Policy of Government of India. This is the reason why the terrorist outfits do not want to have the Indo-Myanmar (Burma) connectivity through the National Highways as quite often I found that they are creating havocs in the National Highways like Stilwell Road at Nampong in Changlang, Anini in Upper Dibang Valley and other places respectively of the North Eastern Frontiers of India adjoining the Myanmar (Burma). The terrorist activists try to brainwash the local tribals stating that their culture will be finished, their tradition belied and therefore their very existence in Arunachal Pradesh will be at stake once the national highways are completed. But very interestingly, it is found that not a single Gorkha talks anything negatively regarding the implications of the construction of Stilwell Road. Many Tangsas at Nampong stated that they will be nowhere (Deka: 2005) as soon as the Stilwell Road (153 National Highway) is completed. Here at Nampong, Shri Kedarnath Sharma, an ex-employee of SIB department of the Government of Arunachal Pradesh stated that through the Stilwell Road, people of Nampong may avail better opportunities that will come to their doorsteps. Here, the people may get multifarious opportunities. Further, he stated that Nampong will be exposed to the nation having movement of the people from across the different countries of South East Asia. To Shri Sharma, opening of old Stilwell Road may help to flourish Nampong with adequate infrastructural facilities like telecommunication and other communication media. Hardly there are newspaper field reporters at Nampong today. No newspaper reporter wants to go Nampong from Tinsukia or Digboi for news collection to be published in Arunachal Pradesh Newspapers because the newspaper reporters are intentionally harassed and assaulted by the local Tangsa anti-social elements. Only in 2010 November, a Tangsa boy, as a reporter of 'Arunachal Times' was beaten to death. A young boy belonging to Tangsa community at Nampong told me that as to what is the use of studying college since he does not expect to get government job today in the Liberalization, Privatization and Globalization era. This is due to the absence of developmental packages of Government of Arunachal Pradesh as well as Government of India (Bhattacharjee: 2005) in Arunachal Pradesh. The non-availability of government jobs is a common problem in Arunachal Pradesh as elsewhere the country. I could collect lot of information from the Nampong government offices about this problem of the region. With the discontinuation of forest based business, many young boys have become unemployed and that may be the reason why many of them join the terrorist outfits (*Ibid.*). The government officials at Nampong feel that they are punished by posting at Nampong because Nampong is the remotest location of Changlang district besides Vijaynagar which is also called KALAPANI by the local Gorkhas of Changlang district and the government servants clearly informed me that they simply do paper works including the preparation of reports at Nampong offices only (Sinha: 2009) justifying their inability to do the job perfectly as per the instruction of the Government of Arunachal Pradesh. Here even if any government official goes on for genuine developmental work for the region, he will definitely be harassed by the local unemployed youth organizations of the tribals which ask for 10 per cent commission from the project amount and sometimes the terrorist outfits (Jungal Parties) also demand handsome share from the project fund to meet their expenditure at the jungle training camps as well as training centres in the Indo-Myanmar (Burma) borders. So, the government projects are very frequently made nuisance and unaccomplished there. This might be the obvious reason why the Changlang district still appears to be the most undeveloped district in Arunachal Pradesh. So, the employment opportunities in the government offices is almost nil at Nampong. By and large, the same situation is there at Miao, Diyon and Changlang.

Although the bus services are there from Nampong, Miao, Diyon and Changlang, there is no morning bus services from Tinsukia town

(Upper Assam) to the above mentioned places or towns of Changlang district. Only the morning bus services are there from these towns of Changlang to Tinsukia and the same buses come back to Miao, Nampong, Changlang, Diyon etc. in the evening. It indicates that Changlang district is in the initial stage of economic development because of its isolation till 1987 from the mainland of Arunachal Pradesh or the country as a whole. In fact, the Changlang district although incorporated in the political map of Arunachal Pradesh it was meant for army and police stations along with the Gorkha villages to merely restore the boundary intact with Myanmar. This is the reason why all the hill tribes of the past possessed the forest fringe for settled cultivation to be comfortably done by the Gorkhas. The ten kilometer land beyond Nampong adjoining the Myanmar (Burma) is no-man's land today being simply protected by the Indian Army and Assam Rifles. The present Tangsas of Nampong villages used to stay in this ten kilometer area in the past but now they all have been shifted to the Nampong villages due to the instruction of Government of Arunachal Pradesh.

V

Rescuing the Arunachal Gorkhas

The term "Rescue" involves security for the development of Arunachal Pradesh along with the safety and security of people thereof. In the present section of the study, we will dwell on the authenticity of providing security to the people of Arunachal Pradesh frontier regions in general and Gorkhas of the state in particular. As mentioned in the earlier chapters of the study that among other districts of Arunachal Pradesh, Changlang and Tirap districts are most unsafe districts due to the presence of terrorist outfits headed by the NSCN groups belonging to the Naga insurgents. Even the Government of Arunachal Pradesh has accepted this fact during the recent years. So, leave aside the question of full security, rather simply it is expected to have rescue of the people especially villagers from the attacks of terrorist activists in the district of Changlang. In fact, rescuing is being substituted for security of the people especially the Gorkhas followed by other non-tribal population of the district. By "Rescuing" in this study, we mean to save the people from the attacks of the terrorist activists in Changlang and Tirap villages. Rescuing involves preparation for safety at the time of pre- and post-terrorist operations.

Pre- and Post-Terrorist Operations

It is observed that except at Jairampur, Miao and Nampong Bajars, there is hardly any army and police camp to rescue the Gorkhas from the attacks of terrorist activists. In 2009, one of the pockets of Kharsang village near Miao was attacked by the NSCN group when five Gorkha villagers died. The rescue team of army force arrived there after 12 hours of the incident. This indicates the casual preparation of army to counter the terrorist activists in Changlang district. If it is so, who comes there to rescue the Gorkhas; it is very much comprehended that the Gorkha themselves have to rescue with their Khukuris. But the Gorkhas with Khukuris can hardly serve the purpose much before the sophisticated weapons that the terrorist activists have procured from Myanmar (Burma) and China for the operations.

Now coming to the question of post operation and rescue thereof of the people, the Gorkhas as well as others are getting cooperation of some of the Christian missionaries which come forward to rehabilitate the Gorkhas in some locations. This is seen mostly at Miao villages where lot of Christian missionaries are working these days. The Christian Singpoos, Noktes, Wanchus and Khamptis are found rushing to the devastated Gorkha villages by the terrorist outfits. Sometimes, the tribal councils come forward to merely rehabilitate the deserted Gorkhas of the villages. They supply food, medicine and other temporary camp relief materials to the rehabilitation camp dwellers. Again, sometimes the Gram Panchayats also come forward in this respect. Interestingly, it is observed that the Gorkhas do easily forget the agonies incurred on them due to the terrorist operations at their villages. They said that this is quite usual as there is no other alternative place for them to shift to rehabilitate so as to repair the lost done by the terrorist outfits both in terms of manpower and property (cattle stocks and food) that they have managed to earn and invested in the land of their tribal landowners. It is also found that most of the victims of terrorist operations are females and children. Finally, the Government, Police and Army come to rescue the Gorkhas but then everything turns out to be normal in the Gorkha villages. The same life process is being resumed by the Gorkhas with the same cheerful jesters at the isolated villages. Looking them cheerful, energetic and well instituted, the government reports in positive way stating that the Gorkhas of the villages are rehabilitated well. The situation continues for some months or the years. To avoid the same situation in near future, the Gorkhas are forced to pay something to the terrorist outfits rather than inviting further troubles to themselves in near future.

Compared to Miao, Nampong is free from terrorist attacks due to the establishment of Assam Rifles Zonal Headquarters at Jairampur of Changlang district. It is found that mostly the Army and Assam Rifles are kept at important places because it appears from the local situation that hardly government is satiated with police services in these areas. At Jairampur, besides Police Check Post of the

Government of Arunachal Pradesh, it is seen that the Assam Rifles has also taken over the charge of the Check Post near the camp of Assam Rifles that starts the Changlang district of Arunachal Pradesh beyond Jagun of Assam bordering the Pangsau Pass of Myanmar while I did not find any army as well as Assam Rifles camp in Miao region. This might be the reason why Miao Gorkhas are under the problem of frequent attacks of the terrorist activists than the Nampong Gorkhas. Everytime, a terrorist outfit says that it has not attacked the villagers rather the outfit says that some other groups might have attacked the villages. It is due to the reason that it is very difficult to distinguish a terrorist outfit from another because all the insurgents of the terrorist outfits look like same physiologically or otherwise unless the terrorist activists become vocal about their group that they belong at the situation. Mostly, the Nagas are insurgents not only in the NSCN groups but also in the terrorist outfit called the Arunachal Pradesh Naga Liberation Army. This is the reason behind the failure of police and army that could not distinguish an insurgent group from another. However, it is found that ninety-nine per cent of terrorist activists claim themselves as Naga activists of NSCN groups.

Politics of Rescuing the Gorkhas

On the one hand, the Gorkhas are sturdy hands for the tribals and tribal encouragement to the terrorist outfits for operations in the Gorkha villages on the other. This is really a big dilemma for the Changlang Gorkha villagers. In fact, this is the matter of great confusion. Why the tribals have followed such a dual policy in Changlang district? This is the issue for thorough introspection by all concerned. However, it is found that separately the Gorkhas are not the subject of terrorist highhandedness but apparently it is the failure of the Government of Arunachal Pradesh to tame or finish up the terrorist outfits in the state. The police department is in very many situations not free from making casual approach to the terrorist outfits in Changlang and Tirap districts. Secondly, blood is thicker than water. The Changlang tribals being Naga sub-tribes appear to have soft corners to the NSCN and other Ultra outfits. Thirdly, the Gorkhas do not have strong organization to fight against the terrorist outfits in Changlang and Tirap districts. Fourthly, the Gorkhas belong to most neglected community in North East India. Finally, the Gorkhas do not acquire supports from Government of Arunachal Pradesh in rescuing themselves in these districts. One of the weakest points of the Gorkhas in Changlang is that they do not show assertiveness to the tribals because to show assertiveness means to invite conflicts which again finally lead them to deportation from the Changlang or Tirap districts of Arunachal Pradesh.

Every time, after the terrorist operation, the Gorkhas make compromises with the situation expecting better tomorrow. Thus, compromising attitude of the Gorkhas has been damaging the very image of the Gorkhas in Changlang and Tirap districts. In fact, both the terrorist activists and local tribals have close linkage as well as affinity to each other in the districts. It is due to the ignorance of the local tribal people of the state. The tribals do not know the negative implications of supporting the terrorist activists who always remain in the mood of realizing their vested interests from the people of the region. Neither the terrorist groups allow to restore inter- community harmony in clear sense of the term in the region nor allow peace in the land. Therefore, to bring or restore safety and security for the development of Changlang and Tirap districts of Arunachal Pradesh really calls for a new approach to be followed by the Government of Arunachal Pradesh in near future.

Politics of Ultra Surrenders

Like the United Liberation Front of Assam (ULFA), the National Socialist Council of Nagaland (NSCN) outfits and others offer themselves for their surrender to the government. Due to the liberal policy of government, the ultras in few numbers come to the mainstreams but most numbers of them do not really surrender and come to the mainstreams. They try to cheat the government mechanisms in very many situations or in different ways. Rather, the so-called surrendered ultras (SULFA- Surrendered Ulfas in Assam- for example) become the informers of the terrorist outfits later on with some ransom from the terrorist activists in action. As in Assam, the same is also found in case of Arunachal Pradesh ultra outfits. Instead of decreasing the number of terrorist outfits, more and more outfits are emerging in Changlang and Tirap districts. This may be the apparent reason why China through Myanmar (Burma) is restoring stronghold in the Indo-Myanmar and Indo-China borders.

Thus, the ultras have established a close link with Myanmar (Burma) as they have training camps at the Myanmar bordering India.

Therefore, the question of surrender to the national mainstream is mostly a whimsical and half-hearted effort of the terrorist activists. Rehabilitating terrorist activists in the national mainstream involves huge amount of government money. Lot of designated ultra camps are there in Arunachal Pradesh and at ULFA dens in Lakhipathar, Kakopathar and other areas of Upper Assam. Those ultras who want to surrender to the government are comfortably staying in designated camps where neither the Indian army nor police force of the state government can go to counter the so-called surrendered terrorist activists. It is also heard that if ten ultras surrender another 20 ultras are collected from the villages and they are given rigorous training at the training centres with the sophisticated weapons that are very easily procured from Myanmar (Burma) and China. Considering the present situation at the Changlang and Tirap districts of Arunachal Pradesh, there is a remotest chance of complete surrender of the terrorist activists in near future to the national mainstream.

The Compromising Situation

Under the situation as described above, most of the Gorkhas living in rural areas stated that they have no other alternative except to surrender to the terrorist outfits. They want, in fact, to be in the good book of the terrorist outfits so that they are not disturbed to smoothly pursue on agriculture and pastoral activities in the region. This may be the background why the terrorist outfits mostly do not disturb the Gorkhas in Changlang and Tirap districts unless and until their interests are jeopardized by the Gorkhas of the region.

It is also found that the terrorist activists come to the villages to even celebrate Gorkha Dasai and Tihar festivals. The terrorists say that they may be terrorists in the eye of the government but they are friends to the villagers both in the hills and foothills of Changlang district. It can be nicely comprehended from the above discussion that terrorists here rather appeared to be quite close to the helpless Gorkhas of Changlang and Tirap districts. If really the ultras as a whole would be the enemy to the Gorkhas, then by now, there would have been not a single Gorkha in both the districts of the North Eastern Frontiers of Arunachal Pradesh. It is further observed that many educated terrorist activists suggest the Gorkhas to impart good education to their children and send them outside for good jobs. If any family member falls sick, the ultras help to provide even the medical treatment hiring the doctors from nearby towns. If there is any unemployed Gorkha youth roaming round the village having no work at his hand, the terrorists ask the tribals of the locality to lease out their forest fringe to the Gorkha guy so that the unemployed Gorkha guy can cultivate the land as well as pursue himself on animal husbandry. In fact, the terrorists appear to be the friends to friends to every community and enemies to those who go against their interests. All these eventualities led the Gorkhas to be pro-terrorist outfits by force although they are by heart and soul pro-government. Although the Gorkhas are pro-government in approach, but it is found that the government is totally indifferent to the Gorkhas as it is seen that the Government of Arunachal Pradesh has been failed to rescue the Gorkhas from the terrorist attacks in the North Eastern Frontier regions. So, they have best option to support the terrorist outfits here in Changlang and Tirap districts of Arunachal Pradesh.

The "Ghar- Lauri"—visiting the Gorkha and tribal houses through the process of ransacking by the terrorist outfits is quite common feature or method of recruitment of young boys and girls in terrorist organizations. It is found that the terrorist organizations are having their own structure and function as it is heard from Changlang people that those who are working as the soldiers of ultra outfits get pension after their retirement from the organization. They have the same system as of the Indian military force in so far as recruitment, functioning in the organization and retirement from the organizations is concerned. After the youths being collected from the "Ghar- Lauri" process, they take them to the training camps. Imparting two years of rigorous training in the training centres, they are sent for different places for operations. In Nampong, I found ten Gorkha boys and two girls from Tangsa community were taken forcefully to the training camps of Arunachal Pradesh Liberation Tigers. Again, in Diyon, 25 young Gorkha boys were taken by force through "Ghar-Lauri" by the Arunachal Pradesh Liberation Tigers in 2010. In this context, the role of government appears to be a futile endeavour. While pursuing the "Ghar-Lauri", it is seen that not a single villager dares to retaliate the terrorist activists. This is in fact, the regular feature in the Changlang and Tirap districts especially in rural areas. Whatever the police and army camps are there in these two districts, they are mainly centred on the towns of the Changlang and Tirap districts. This may be the reason why the terrorist activists as stated by the villagers, hardly miss the chance to ransack the village, nabb the youths or kidnap the youths and even rape the beautiful women of the villages. However, many youths of the towns of Changlang and Tirap districts are also being kidnapped by terrorist activists when the terrorist activists get opportunity to catch the town youths outside the towns or Bajars in the villages.

Of course, the Government of Arunachal Pradesh, in 2002, passed The Arunachal Pradesh Control of Organized Crime Act (Act No.5 of 2002) with 30 sections (Bhattacharjee:2005), "the state is constantly facing the problem of crimes due to the origin of Liberation Tigers of Arunachal Pradesh, United Liberation Tigers of Arunachal Pradesh and Revolutionary Army of Arunachal Pradesh since 1993 onwards. Very interestingly, instead of having the Act, so far not much have been done at the level of its implementation in Changlang and Tirap districts as NSCN Khaplang and Isaac-Muivah groups have become totally successful in their mission in the districts. In this context, Bhattacharjee (2005) observed that "NSCN (IM) made its presence felt since early 2000 A.D. Some sections of the people thought it was a good send. Let them fight it out, was what they say. This was the reaction of people against a powerless administration and the police force of the state that failed to make single conviction despite the increasing number of deaths, disappearances and blatant cases of extortion and intimidation". In this context, what the Gorkhas of Changlang district stated is that instead of adhering compliance to the Inner Line Permits to the Gorkhas, the civil administration should modernize the police and army to combat the NSCN (Khaplang and Isaac-Muviah) groups. Most of the Police personnel stated that how they can fight with NSCN groups who have possessed most sophisticated weapons being purchased from Myanmar (Burma) and China. They have to save their lives for their families while the NSCN groups have one point programme i.e., either "Do or Die". During the year, 2001, at least 68 were murdered, 47 burglary, 269 dacoity, theft 432, robbery 100, kidnapping 58, riot 20, culpable homicide crimes under Indian Penal Code was 2367 (*Ibid*). Among the 68 murdered cases in Changlang district, 51 were Gorkhas from Diyon, Miao and Nampong villages. During 2010, at least 30 Gorkhas died in Changlang district (Website: 2010) mainly they were the Gorkha villagers of Miao, Diyon and Namchik. The case study of Changlang, in this respect, indicates that every year, the number of murder cases are increasing by leaps and bounds. It is therefore apprehended that the Government of Arunachal Pradesh would be really doubtful to solve the problem of terrorism in near future. In 2010, at least 50 cows of the Gorkhas were butchered by the NSCN activists in Namphai I and Namphai II villages of Miao sub-division. Where is the safety and rescue of the Gorkhas in so far as their economy or manpower resource is concerned in Changlang district? This may be the reason why today 90 per cent of Gorkhas are mentally preferred to go either to Terai belts of Nepal or Siliguri (West Bengal) in their old age. Being a scholar from Darjeeling, I found many Gorkhas of Kadamtala, Salbari, Bagdogra, Salugara etc. of Siliguri from the Changlang district in particular and Arunachal Pradesh in general. The whole lot of present question of rescuing the Gorkhas and thereby awarding them overall safety is rather an apparent myth or hippie philosophy in the Arunachal Pradesh. However, the other ethnic communities by and large are not so much worst sufferers than the Gorkhas because the other ethnic communities mainly Biharis and Marwaris are purely living in small Bajars of Miao, Nampong, Diyon, Kharsang etc. where the insurgents hardly dare to attack the people as there are Police camps near the Bajars of Nampong, Miao, Diyon and Kharsang of the Changlang district.

In fact, I had a haunch that whether the Gorkhas are safe or not in Changlang district. Finally, I came to the conclusion that killing the Gorkhas falls on the selectivity or pick and choice of the insurgent groups. It is found that those Gorkhas fall on the hit list of terrorist outfits who always do intentionally instigate the common people of the villages against the terrorist outfits or work as informers to the government and police as well as army camp officers. The Police and army camps try to acquire as much as informers for them from the local villagers as they can. So, there is a rational logic to the commoners who doubt new faces appearing in their villages. The insurgent outfits also have their informers in the villages. As soon as a person is caught as culprit of being the informer to the government agencies or police or army, he is either butchered at forest or made victim under the bullets of the terrorist guns. This is exactly happening in the two districts of Arunachal Pradesh. Otherwise, the cumulative operation by the terrorist activists has hardly come to the notice of the people in the villages. Of course, if a conflict takes place between the army and terrorist activists in the villages, then sometimes the innocent villagers also come under the bullets of army and terrorist activists. The main fight is between the terrorist outfits and civil administration as well as army in Changlang and Tirap districts. Thus, in this respect, selectivity rather than cumulative terrorism is there in the two districts of the state of Arunachal Pradesh. Therefore, the question of safety and rescue operations are not so much to be worried by the people in general and Gorkhas in particular in Changlang and Tirap districts of the state.

Finally, it is up to the commitment of the government to restore peace and tranquility in the Changlang district. The matter of public safety is exclusively the sole challenge to the government during the recent years. This is due to the most laksadical approach of the Government of Arunachal Pradesh to the issue of public safety, security and rescuing the Gorkhas, Biharis and Marwaris and other non-tribal communities for the economic development of Changlang and Tirap districts of Arunachal Pradesh. If the government is really determined to extinguish terrorism from the soil of Arunachal Pradesh, there is nothing to perceive it as impossible. A Gorkha Subedar of Gorkha Regiment (5th Regiment) told me at Miao (Changlang) that if the government allows to operate the training centres or training camps of the terrorist outfits by the Gorkha Regiments in Changlang or Tirap districts, then it is according to him, a matter of just 24 hours to finish up all the terrorist camps. But the government has followed the Appeasement Policy to the terrorist outfits considering the rescuing problem of minority or non-tribal communities including the Gorkhas of Arunachal Pradesh.

Withering Away the Gorkhas

I asked whoever the tribal I met at Changlang district about their attitudes regarding withering away the Gorkhas from the Arunachal Pradesh foothills. They all stated that if the Gorkhas are absconded or evicted from the Arunachal Pradesh hills and foothills then which community will pursue on the agriculture and animal husbandry as well as horticulture in the region. No other communities are really interested to pursue on agriculture, horticulture and pastoral activities in the state. I also asked why the tribals do not want to replace the Gorkhas in agricultural and pastoral activities, they responded that the tribals are meant for landowners only and not the cultivators as per their tradition and culture (Mackenzie: 2011). Since the culture of Jhum (shifting) cultivation has been discontinued due to the pressure put on by the Government of Arunachal Pradesh, now they want simply to be the landowners. Again, the culture of hunting and gathering has also been considerably discontinued along with the discontinuation of slavery system of the past; they have hardly any urge for agriculture and pastoral professions in Changlang and Tirap districts of North East Frontiers which were their nomadic empire during the pre-British period and sovereign tribal principalities during the British eras. They found no other community in North East India to replace the Gorkhas in the agrarian sectors of Arunachal economy especially in the Changlang and Tirap districts along with other districts of Arunachal Pradesh.

The above observation made it very clear that the Gorkhas are kept in Changlang and Tirap districts for agrarian economy on the one hand and safety of strategically sensitive zones of the state adjoining Myanmar on the other. Thus, we can say that now the Gorkhas are being loved not for their cheerfulness, bravery etc. etc. but to fulfil the selfish motives of the local tribals on the one hand and the implementation of government policy on the other to have settled agrarian economy in the districts. This may be the apparent reason why Sharma (2005) while observing the socio-economic conditions of Gorkha tea plantation workers at Gunnanagar of Chowkham in Lohit district of Arunachal Pradesh found that the Gorkhas are kept at the industries also due to the fact that they are "Khati Khane Jati"—the laborious community of the Arunachal Pradesh. Rather, their perseverance, positive attitudes, stubbornness to commitments and sincerity in carrying out the responsibility as well as loyalty rendered to their masters are their real traditional qualities so as to survive themselves in such hostile environments of the districts like Changlang and Tirap of Arunachal Pradesh today. Similar picture is also found in other North Eastern states of India. The Nagas of Nagaland and Mizos of Mizoram have also no difference on their opinion regarding these qualities of Gorkhas. In spite of Gorkha escalation movement led by All Assam Student Union (AASU) under the Assam Gana Parishad Movement (1979-1982), more than six lakh Gorkhas are there in the state of Assam today surviving in various sectors of Assamese economy.

The above observations made it confirmed that withering away the Gorkhas from Arunachal Pradesh being launched by various insurgent outfits in turn will be a big loss or be a suicidal game to themselves although the Gorkhas have been accustomed to go on "Basai Sarnu"—shifting the habitation usually at the most cases. Therefore, deportation of the Gorkhas from Changlang and Tirap districts appear to be a hippie philosophy for the terrorist outfits and a few tribal elites of Arunachal Pradesh.

Retrospection of Settlement History of the Gorkhas

Retrospection of the settlement history of Gorkhas in Changlang district is apparent from Shri Harka Bahadur Rai, as an ex-soldier of the British Gorkha Regiment (8th battalion) who was the first Gorkha to settle down at Nampong and Shri Netra Bahadur an Ex-Subedar, of the 8th Assam Rifles was the first Gorkha who settled at Diyon of Changlang after the Second World War while at Miao, the Gorkhas had been settled after 1826 when the British Government entirely taken over Upper Assam that included all hills and foothills of North Eastern Frontiers of Arunachal Pradesh. The Gorkhas had been kept at Nampong and Miao, on Diyon or Nau Dehing as well as Boorie Dehing river sides. Diyon had villages of Gorkhas since 1838. The Singpoos of Changlang district had sovereignty over foothills and hills of Changlang district where they bought the Gorkhas from Khonsa and a few Gorkhas from Nepal as grazers and subsequently cultivators. It was Captain Neufvillee who settled the Gorkhas in Singpoo dominated area of Miao, Diyon etc. of present Changlang district in 1826. The above observation on the basis of my findings from the field i.e., Changlang district, makes transparent that without hesitation we can say that the Gorkhas are there in Changlang district from 1826 in few numbers as bought by Captain Neufuillee and in 1837, by Captain Hannay who bought more Gorkha in numbers. Third flow of Gorkhas in Changlang district had taken place from 1841 onward by Major White, Captain Vetch, Dundas and finally after 1948 from Assam, Burma and Nepal by the Government of Arunachal Pradesh.

Now, the Gorkha immigration is not so significant in Changlang district as in the past due to the emergence of terrorist outfits and antithetical attitudes of tribals in Arunachal Pradesh for newcomer Gorkhas especially by the educated tribal elites who spread over these wrong messages to the common tribals of Arunachal Pradesh. It is also found in agrarian sector of Changlang, due to the transition of tribals to monetized economy, the tribals are interested to lease out their land on "Bhagi"—share on fifty-fifty basis (share-cropping system) on the products on their leased out land that normally the Gorkhas produced every year, while the Gorkhas are interested for leased on land on rent with specific amount to be paid to the tribal landowners. This has caused for less number of Gorkha immigration to Changlang district since the last one decade compared to the past two centuries. Giving land on "Bhagi" is more beneficial to the tribal landowners while taking the land on rent is more beneficial to the Gorkhas counterpart. This process has been affecting the whole agrarian relations between the tribals and Gorkhas of Changlang district today. This sometimes creates a kind of duality of existence for Gorkhas in the region especially in the North Eastern Frontiers of India mainly Changlang and Tirap districts of Arunachal Pradesh.

In fact, the Singpoos and Tangsas of Changlang district failed to have agriculture as they were accustomed to hunting and elephant catching in jungles thereby leading an indolent and lavish way of living. This along with the discontinuation of slavery system of Singpoos and Tangsas, both the British Government and the then tribals invited, lured and indentured the Gorkhas to settle down in the grant land of the government, Jhum land of the tribals and forest fringe and "Char" in both the hills initially due to the similar physical environment of Changlang as of Nepal and Burma Himalayas and foothills of Changlang district later on. Sociologically speaking, the Gorkhas always called or remembered "Burma Ko Dhawa" meant both the Burmese invasion by the British Gorkha Regiment and influx of Gorkha Grazers and agriculturists in Burma. Thus, by "Dhawa", it is understood to be the effort to occupy the land of Burma as well as the land of Arunachal hills and foothills. The development syndrome of tribals was responsible factor for Gorkha immigration into the land of Arunachal Pradesh (Patkai hills) and Burma. On the Burmese side also, mostly the Singpoos could not however utilized the potentialities of land and that was the main reason why the British Government was forced to invite the Gorkhas to settle down there so as to accrue good revenue from the Gorkha grazers and agriculturists. Unlike Manipur side when the Gorkhas settled and also entered Burma in 1871, in Changlang (Patkai hills), the Gorkhas started to settle down on and around 1826 only due to the occupation of Upper Burma by the British Government after the Treaty of Yandabo with the Burmese Government. So, there is no point to call the Gorkhas as immigrants in Changlang and Tirap districts in particular and Arunachal Pradesh as a whole. Later on, as I used to hear in my childhood days that lot of Gorkhas from Kalimpong (Darjeeling district of West Bengal) used to go on migration to settle in NEFA.

Going to NEFA and settle down there, of course, involved complete adventure and pursuing on such adventure was another characteristic feature and nature as well as the culture of the Gorkhas since time immemorial as the Gorkhas were fond of pursuing on going to "Munglan" and become "Lahuree". Doing this, lot of Gorkhas died in Munglan including the Arunachal Pradesh. All these observations I could make in Changlang district however require further thorough empirical enquiry in future days by the scholars because till today, the Government of Arunachal Pradesh has not shown keen interest to allow the scholars from the country on pursuing research studies in the state (Bhattacharjee: 2005). Although , realistically, it is observed that the Gorkhas are indispensable resource for both the tribals and Government of Arunachal Pradesh, they belong to the most peripheral (Sukumbasis) community of the tribal societies which called their people as the sons of the soil (Raithanees) or calling themselves as the core communities (Sinha: 2007) of Arunachal Pradesh. In the context of settlement history of Singpoos and Tangsas of Changlang district, I asked them to tell their pre- British history and in this respect, most of them failed to answer me properly while I asked the same question to the Gorkhas who rather instantly said that their predecessors had hailed from Nepal and Burma and settled down in the "Attapee Jungles"—the dense forests of Changlang from early 1826. Lot of "Chautaros" (rest sheds) made of stones during their early settlement are found in Diyon, Miao, Nampong, Kharsang along with Siva and Vishnu Mandirs (temples) in Changlang district. Still "Byasis"—river side land have been possessed by the Gorkhas with "Khuttis"—cattle sheds. These Gorkha Khuttis are found in almost all the 335 villages of Changlang district. Both "Chars" and "Khuttis" of the Gorkhas are in fact the components of agrarian economy of foothills of the district. Without Khuttis and Chars, hardly the Gorkhas survive anywhere in Arunachal Pradesh and other North Eastern states of India. A Government Officer of Additional District Commissioner office (Miao) stated that what is the harm if the Gorkhas are making the land arable and paying good revenue to the government from the Khuttis (one cow= Rs. 50 per year) and tax (Rs.3500 per year per Pura) from the tribal landowners for their land being leased out to the Gorkhas. So, it appears from the discussion that instead of withering away the Gorkhas from Changlang district, it is very much wise for the tribals to give security and show kindheartedness to the Gorkhas. What the tribals can do with such vast barren land, forest fringe and "Chars" since no other communities are really interested to settle down in such sites as mentioned above in the Changlang district. Rather outside communities still scared to go there except the Gorkhas. Even if some Biharis and Marwaris are there in Miao, near Miao gate and Bajars of Nampong and Diyon, they hardly want to go to the remotest villages consisting of the Gorkhas, Chakmas, Deoris and Bangladeshi Bengalis.

It is also found that entertaining peace talks followed by thorough surrender by the terrorist activists is simply the temporary techniques of terrorist outfits in North Eastern Frontiers of India in general and Arunachal Pradesh in particular ever since the last two decades. The governments of seven sister states of North East India have completely failed to evolve out any permanent solution to the problem of terrorism in North East India. This I felt a kind of perpetual consternation to be left to the minds of outsiders whenever I used to do journey to places like Miao, Nampong, Diyon, Changlang, Khonsa etc. Every passenger especially outsider appeared to be under fear psychosis of terrorist activists on the way to their destination. Although the Government of Arunachal Pradesh and local tribals have soft corners to the terrorist outfits, the Government of India cannot just tolerate the open violence there officially as the region is also the integral part of India or "Akhand Bharat" in the light of Look East Policy of India (Singh: 2009). Therefore, the government cannot merely award credentials to the fissiparous tendencies of the people who are pro-terrorist outfits in the region but in fact the government also wants holistic development of the region. Every morning, we come across the news regarding the bomb blasts in the region. For example, on 30.11.2011, a bomb exploded at Imphal (Manipur) where the Prime Minister along with Smt. Sonia Gandhi (Chairperson of UPA Government) was supposed to visit on 3.12.2011. It shows that the terrorist activists do not want the hegemony of Central Government in the region. This may be due to the plan of the hideout terrorists who are in the habit of pursuing on to terrorize and brainwash the local innocent villagers. The same has been noticed in Changlang and Tirap districts of Arunachal Pradesh.

Talking the Assamese language makes the terrorists escaped from the check posts like Namchik, Dirak and Jairampur of Lohit and Changlang districts respectively. Although the Inner Line Permit system is still on vogue, the checking mechanisms of the Government of Arunachal Pradesh are quite casual in approach and action even though I found that the Assam Rifles is very strict in this matter at their respective check posts. But they have to abide by the instruction of the Government of Arunachal Pradesh through MLS and MPs who comprehand the local tribals as their vote banks. Rather, today what the choice that the officers of the check posts of the government have followed appears to be the middle range approach providing softness to the trespassers who pass through the check posts of Changlang, Tirap and Lohit districts. Only the Gorkhas are thoroughly harassed in the check posts. Surprisingly, what I have noted is that the Gorkhas, so harassed, may be due to having their no *locus standi* in Arunachal Pradesh. Otherwise, other communities also should have been thoroughly interrogated as well as harassed at the check posts. In fact, it is like Gorkha proverb as "Jo Hocho Uasi Ko Mukh Ma Gocho" meaning thereby one who is weakest is to be further pinched bitterly more especially in case of the Gorkhas in the Arunachal Pradesh check posts. I had a bitter experience at Namchik and Jairampur check posts of Changlang district where even I being an educated Gorkha officer of the Central Government of India had been profusely hackled, harassed and thoroughly interrogated while I was going to Miao and Nampong instead of showing my official identity card to the check post officials. These examples have supplemented the fact that how the Gorkhas are experiencing such step-motherly treatment particularly in frontier districts like Lohit, Tirap and Changlang of Arunachal Pradesh of North East India.

To conclude this chapter on rescuing the Gorkhas, it can be finally said that nobody except the Gorkha themselves can rescue them in the most volatile as well as hostile situations that are taking place in Arunachal Pradesh in general and Changlang district in particular.

VI

Strings for Gorkha Survival

The study on Gorkhas of Arunachal Pradesh is for the first time being dared to be conducted by this scholar in the most dangerous district of Changlang of Arunachal Pradesh. It is the most dangerous in the sense that if any terrorist outfit is informed that an outside scholar is conducting research then the scholar will be very instantly gunned down. Again, it is a dangerous district in the sense that no outside scholar can go there for research work as the Government of Arunachal Pradesh has also accepted the fact that Changlang and Tirap districts adjoining Myanmar are very disturbed districts and therefore the Government has banned for any research study there in these two districts till today. This is from the point of view of the conversion of Changlang district as the battleground by the NSCN (Khaplang-Issac-Muviah) groups. Besides NSCN, there are Arunachal Naga Liberation Front, Arunachal Pradesh Liberation Tigers, Arunachal Pradesh United Liberation Front etc. as the terrorist outfits which are creating havocs in frontier districts of Arunachal Pradesh during the recent eras. The local people called them "The Jungle Parties" who very often come to the residences of villagers carrying food and ask them to cook food in their houses and serve them the same. The terrorist activists sleep in their houses on the floor outside the house and early in the next morning they go to the jungle silently. However, as reported by the villagers, they are scared of the army only not the police force of the state. They do not disturb the family members at night nor ask any money from the villagers when they come to sleep overnight. Some Gorkhas told that the NSCN leaders ask the Gorkhas to earn as much as they can and invest the money anywhere else; their force will not extort anything from the Gorkha houses. Whenever the gangs of terrorist activists come to the Gorkha house, they bring one Gorkha fellow terrorist to communicate in the Gorkha/Nepali language so that the Gorkha villagers are enabled to know what the outfit activists want from their home. It is heard that the "Jungle Party" hardly disturbs the Gorkhas unless a Gorkha goes against the terrorist outfits.

Combating the Hostile Situation

Over the years since the last two decades, the Gorkhas are struggling hard due to terrorism in Changlang district with their boldness. But very interestingly, it is noted that the number of Gorkha population is increasing in Arunachal Pradesh. For example, in 1961, only ten thousand Gorkhas were there in Arunachal Pradesh while in 1991, their number increased to eighty five thousands (Dutta: 1981) and as per the Census of India, 2001, their number reached to ninety four thousands. Now, there are over one lakh and five thousand Gorkhas in Arunachal Pradesh and about thirty thousand Gorkhas are staying in Changlang district alone. Another twenty thousand Gorkhas are reported to have been found in Tirap district of North Eastern Frontiers of India.

This indicates that the Gorkhas have been nicely combating the volatile situation of Changlang district with their inborn qualities. It is adequately proved by the fact that hardly any tribes talks against the Gorkhas, although the tribals speak quite often that the Gorkhas are immigrants from Nepal. They do not have clear cut idea about the fact that the Gorkhas are also there in Assam, Darjeeling-Sikkim, Bhutan and other parts of the country. In fact, all the Gorkhas are being categorized into one group i.e., immigrants. This is quite natural because even the government has not been able to distinguish Nepamul Gorkhas—Nepal based Nepalis and the Gorkhas of Indian origin (Sinha: 2007) may be due to the allegiance of some of the Arunachal Gorkhas to Nepal especially the Terai belts as their ultimate destination.

Secondly, combating the volatile situation of Changlang, the Gorkhas have been followed the process of conciliatory approach with tribals of the locations under the study. The place like Miao, Nampong and Diyon of Changlang district are as such that isolation makes the Gorkhas to be accommodative to the tribal environment.

Thirdly, all the Gorkhas are in truest sense of the term either grazers or agriculturists in Changlang district. So, what they can do as the only option left to them is to win the hearts of tribals through their hard work although the tribals are, as per the Gorkha proverb "Ama Diyara Bau Na Hune Jats" meaning thereby the tribal communities and their people cannot become true fathers even if you give your own mother to the tribal men.

Fourthly, all the Gorkhas pursue on compromising attitude to the tribals and tribal way of life. Of course, making compromises with the tribals have made the Gorkhas as tenant-slaves or tenant servants of tribals in the Changlang district. Their safety is being ensured by the tribals only in the land. This, they have followed to avoid their oustings from the Changlang district.

The Gorkha Ekrupta

The question of Gorkha unity (Ekrupta) among the fellow Gorkhas is apparently a myth in Changlang district as the Matwali majority of the district among the Gorkhas are looked to be perfectly under the process of Tribalization through cultural integration with the tribals. Even some Limbus, Mangers and Rais have joined NSCN and other terrorist outfits. The cultural exchanges are in respect of marriage with the tribal men and women, Mit making system with the tribals, celebrating the tribal festivals, religious conversion to Buddhism and Christianity, drinking alcohols etc. The Gorkha Tagadharis (Bahuns and Chhetris) are however still clinging to their past Hindu fundamentalism. Absolute liberalization (by Matwalis) versus Absolute Hindu fundamentalism (by Tagadharis) is the inherent social trajectory that is operating in the Gorkha society of Changlang district. This process has therefore bipolarized the whole Gorkha society into two groups. It has absolutely hindered to restore the Gorkha Ekrupta or Unity in Diversity at the Arunachal situation. Here, the tribals are very happy to see the bipolar social structure of the Gorkha society. This may be the obvious reason why not a single Gorkha social organization has been evolved till today in Changlang district in particular and Arunachal Pradesh in general. So, there is a remotest chance to have Ekrupta in the Gorkha society of the Arunachal Pradesh in future.

Consciousness of the Kind

Of course, the question of separate Gorkha identity which always pinches the minds of all Gorkhas may be it is in their sub-conscious level of living in the most hostile situation of Changlang district. It is true that the Gorkhas as a separate category of ethnic group have not been able to make felt among the tribals in the sub-human situation of Changlang district. Even the Gorkhas have to fail to make tribals realized the Gorkha identity as there is not a single Gorkha organization to kindle the light of ethnic identity in the state. Not a single Gorkha is there as the Member of Legislative Assembly of the state to ventilate the grievances of Gorkhas in the Legislative Assembly of Arunachal Pradesh.

Poorest of Poors

The Gorkhas of Changlang villages comparing the Gorkhas of urban areas of Arunachal Pradesh are poorest of poor. They are as good as peasants. They have nothing to think better tomorrow considering the malaise attitudes of Government of Arunachal Pradesh to the Gorkhas of the state. Of course, no tribe of Arunachal Pradesh wants that the Gorkhas to have any say in the body politics of the state. This is the basic attitude of the tribals towards the Gorkhas as they think that the Gorkhas as "foreigners", "immigrants" or "outsiders" in the tribal land of Arunachal Pradesh forever.

Erasing the Title "Bahadur"

To be called "Bahadur" means possessing bravery as the only skill possessed by a Gorkha makes himself happy in most of the places of the country. It has now in fact become a curse on the part of Gorkhas as a whole and this makes the Gorkhas blatantly humiliated whenever realizing ethnicity issue everywhere including the Arunachal Pradesh. Now, is therefore the high time to be rather "Cowardice" like other ethnic communities of the country such as Bengali community of West Bengal rather than to be so-called braves for others causes. This is due to the fact that bravery shown in the pages of Gorkha history of the last 200 years in Changlang district could not really reap any tangible result in favour of the Gorkha themselves. What is the use of showing bravery for others' cause? Whoever the Gorkhas show bravery for others' causes, they are applauded like anything for the time being but again they are apparently escalated after some time by the same people whom the Gorkhas show their bravery at a particular point of time. But on the moment the Gorkhas try to realize their ethnic identity in the India, they are escalated by other people. Similar picture is also found in case of the Gorkhas of Arunachal Pradesh where on the moment the Gorkhas make unused land, Jhum land, Chars and forest fringe habitable or worthy to live on, the tribals put their jealous eyes and call all the Gorkhas as foreigners or immigrants, non-tribals rather than they simply labelled the Gorkhas as landless peasants, coolies, porters, grazers, casual employees in government offices etc. In fact, for the Gorkha themselves, they are cowards, self centred and absolutely stick to respective self-survival of the fittest. This indicates the Gorkha society is purely an individualistic society rather than a cumulative ones.

From Self Assertiveness to Cumulative Assertiveness

It is found that the Gorkhas at the individual level always display assertiveness for survival but the accumulative assertiveness is always lacking among the Gorkhas of Arunachal Pradesh. Unless and until the cumulative assertiveness can be displayed by the Gorkhas before the Arunachal tribals, there is a remotest chance of making their place in the Arunachal society. It is invariably proved by the fact that once in Miao; a Gorkha boy was assaulted by a Singpoo relating to the purchase of second hand bike by the Gorkha boy from a Bihari fellow. The Singpoo wanted to purchase the bike at lower price from the Bihari than the price that the Gorkha boy was ready to pay to the Bihari. In the incidence, the Gorkha boy had been beaten in such a way that the he had been hospitalized at Tinsukia for about two months. Here in this situation, nobody came forward to save the Gorkha boy. This is due to the lack of cumulative assertiveness of the Gorkhas of Miao—the dens of Singpoo tribe. What I feel about the background reason for lack of cumulative assertiveness among the Gorkhas is that the Gorkhas had been cursed by a "Sati"—the lady who was going to be buried along with the dead body of her husband in his funeral pyre and therefore the community may be called as "Sati Le Sarap Diaeko Jati"—a community being cursed by a Sati so as not to have Unity among themselves in the world. This is apparent even at the present Nepal where Madhesias (plain Hindi and other Indian language speaking people) have dominated the body politics of Nepal as there is the President—the highest constitutional head of

Nepal from the Madhesia (Hindi speaking) community of the Terai belt of the country.

"Basai Sarne" Syndrome of the Gorkhas

The "Basai Sarne" or shifting the place of habitation of the Gorkha cultural tradition is responsible factor for the existing pitiable socio-economic conditions of Arunachal Gorkhas. Hardly, the Gorkhas mind to change the landowners through the Basai Sarne process. They do not mind to shift their habitations from one village to another village in search of tenancy. They appear to be rather the ping pong balls that are being thrown from one corner to another corner of the table by the players. Here, in Arunachal Pradesh, the tribals are the players and the Gorkhas as the ping pong balls. Hardly, the Gorkhas mind to frequently shift their habitations at the insistence of the tribals. This is supplemented by the fact that hardly the Gorkhas are allowed to stay in the land of a particular tribal landowner beyond thirty years at a stretch. The question is that how long the Gorkhas can bear this curse to go on "Basai Sarne" endeavour in Arunachal Pradesh—nobody knows it exactly today.

A Speculation of the Tribal Highhandedness

It is speculated that a day will definitely come when the Gorkhas would be nowhere in the Changlang district where they will be vanished not only socio-economically but also culturally. The Nepali/Gorkha language as the component of cultural entity is being slowly forgotten by the Gorkhas. Speaking Nepali/Gorkha, I found that lot of Gorkhas mix the tribal dialects. I could not comprehend fully the Nepali/Gorkha language spoken by the Nampong Gorkhas especially the grazers and agriculturists who are centred around Nampong, Kharsang and 7th Mile villages while the Gorkhas of Jairampur mostly the ex-soldiers of Assam Rifles and Gorkha Regiments could speak the Nepali/Gorkha language very fluently without admixing the tribal dialects. In fact, if we see the history of the Gorkha community, linguistic homogeneity was the sole string to restore the ethnic solidarity. It is therefore apprehended by this scholar that the Gorkhas will not be there on the day when all the Gorkhas will speak the tribal dialects of Arunachal Pradesh. It is said that if you want to spoil an ethnic community then first you make them language-less entity or not known to speak their own language. The tribal highhandedness may defeat the Gorkhas if the Gorkhas totally fail to speak Nepali/ Gorkha language in Changlang district of Arunachal Pradesh in general and Changlang and Tirap districts in particular.

Inherent Reality and Existence

In Changlang district, cosmopolitan attitude of Gorkhas is responsible factor for their weakness in their living. To prefer the tribal women for marriage today seem to be the inherent reality of the Gorkhas to merely survive in the volatile environment of Changlang district. They do not know how their very ethnic existence is on the extinction. In fact, they are going to be a vanishing community in Changlang and Tirap districts of Arunachal Pradesh due to the reason for they have the structured preferencc to marry tribal women. The religious conversion into Buddhism and Christianity is another responsible factor for Gorkha extinction in Changlang district. It is in Miao and Nampong that although Diyon Gorkhas are little bit conscious of the Hindu religion; the Gorkhas are fully tilted to Christianity and Buddhism. It is also observed that the Gorkha Buddhists and Christians are hardly disturbed by the terrorist activists who are mostly the Naga Christians or Buddhist tribals of Arunachal Pradesh.

Politics of Duality

In normal times, the Gorkhas are ill-treated as immigrants either by the local tribal anti-socials or terrorist outfits but at the time of state elections, the Gorkhas are lured and brainwashed by the politicians of Arunachal Pradesh so as to get maximum Gorkha votes. This is the regular practice of politicians in Changlang district. But once the elections are over, the Gorkhas are brought back to the same platform where they were prior to holding the elections in the region. This is a kind of dirty tribal politics in regard to the Gorkhas. Crores of rupees are spent to the Gorkhas and tribals by political parties. Some candidates of political parties normally purchase bicycles, bikes, televisions etc. and distribute the same to the villagers. For months together prior to holding the elections, pre-election feasts are arranged for the villagers. The situation appears to be very festive in the region. For instance, Mr. Rajen of Chowkham (Sharma: 2005) of Lohit district of Arunachal Pradesh even distributed four wheelers to some of the influential leaders of Namsai sub-division of Lohit district in the last parliamentary election that was held in 2008. In fact, the politics of duality made the Gorkhas further messed with the tribal domination network in Changlang district in particular and Arunachal Pradesh in general. Apparently, the politics of duality is an easy weapon to hit upon the Gorkha community of the state along with other North Eastern states of India. The Indian Government has also the same approach to North Eastern Gorkhas during the last six decades of independence. Not a single remarkable effort for betterment of Gorkhas has been done by the Government of Assam or other North Eastern states rather in most of the cases, it is found that the government is having indifferent attitude to the Gorkhas. In most of the cases, government calls the Gorkhas as immigrants just to get supports from the tribals of Arunachal Pradesh. In very many situations, political parties evolve conspiracy through the local tribal anti-socials and also common tribal people to create nuisance against the Gorkhas of the region. Their land, cattle stocks, human resources and what not are confiscated or looted easily by the tribals in most odd situations. Even sometimes, the political parties pretend to cry with crocodile tears in relation to the mishaps or misfortunes taken place with the Gorkhas for the time being just to make pretension so as to collect Gorkha votes in the elections. In rest of the time, they do not have left the habit of designating the Gorkhas as immigrants in the Arunachal Pradesh land. This is most unfortunate process of the whole blemishness of characterizing the Gorkhas as "foreigners", "immigrants", "outsiders", "non-tribals" etc. in Arunachal Pradesh.

Culture is Wonderful

In spite of having total exploitation of Gorkhas in Arunachal Pradesh, cultural traits of the Gorkhas (Subba: 2009) have helped the Gorkhas to be accommodated in the state in general and Changlang district in particular. Flying with cold wind or breeze, churning with moments, singing with nature and accommodating other cultural traits of the tribals have been leading the Gorkhas to uncertain destiny. The cultural trait of synchronization with the local tribal cultures has really helped them to be busy with cattle stocks, "Kheti" and household chores. The culture is the lifeline of Gorkhas to live with Dukha (Hut: 2009) and take respiration in the clean natural habitat of Arunachal Pradesh. The Gorkhas say that at least here, air is pure, water is filtered and till now, having overall simplicity of the tribals of the region, have inspired the Gorkhas to lead comfortable life although in very many situations, they are hackled, harassed and exploited in different fashions from different corners of the state of Arunachal Pradesh. The culture as lifeline of the Gorkhas has been found to be the available means to live comfortably in the most hostile as well as volatile environment of Arunachal Pradesh.

The Homeless Gorkhas

Most Gorkhas of Changlang district stated that Nepal is even worst today as the Gorkhas of Nepal call all the Indian Gorkhas as "Pravasi Gorkhas"—foreigner Gorkhas. The Gorkhas of Nepal do not want to provide "Nagarikta Praman Patra"—citizenship certificate to the Pravasi Gorkhas from the offices of Chief District Officer (CDO) in Nepal. To go to Assam and West Bengal is therefore more safe for them once they earn something in Arunachal Pradesh. Whenever the Gorkha, Bihari, Marwari and others earn something substantive in amount in Changlang district, they go to their respective places of origin to invest the same. The homelessness made the Gorkhas everywhere servants (slaves) of the mainstream communities in the world. This is the main antecedent why most of the Gorkhas do not hesitate themselves to be merged with the global communities (Sharma: 2009). "Chora Ko Jat Ki Ran Ma Ki Ban Ma"—the Gorkha proverb states that a son of the Gorkha should either die in the war fighting with the enemy or at jungles fighting with the wild animals, is really a wonderful cultural note ever coined by the predecessors of the Gorkhas. It is seen in the Changlang district especially in towns that once the Gorkhas make inaccessible habitat theirs, they sale out their home and hearth and shift to another isolated enclaves for the same. The same story is found with the Gorkhas in Arunachal hills and foothills. "Bigreko Mancheko Bhatkiyako Ghar, Bhatkiya Pachi Ke Ko Dar" meaning thereby when a Gorkha becomes a bad man, he is not scared of spoiling his own home. This is exactly the situation of most Gorkhas in the Changlang district where they are damn sure in regard to their ousting from the land of tribal landowners tomorrow or the day after tomorrow. So, this may be the reason why the Gorkhas are not at all scared of "Basai Sarnu". They are sure that they will not be allowed to stay in a particular plot of a tribal landowner beyond thirty years at a stretch. On the basis of this observation, we can say that the Gorkhas are completely made homeless in Changlang district or other districts of Arunachal Pradesh.

Once Unorganised, Unorganized for Ever

The Gorkhas of Arunachal Pradesh were unorganized in 1826 and still today they are fully unorganized. Concept of organizing the Gorkhas under a common umbrella or banner appears to be a distant dream for themselves. If any educated or conscious Gorkha wants to organize the Gorkha community in the region, he will be first hackled, harassed and doing this if he is not tilted to the tribal interests, then he will be beaten to death. For instance, in 2007, Shri Khagendranath Sharma of Miao formed a Gorkha Kalyan Samaj at Miao, initially he was fully supported by fellow Gorkhas of the area and also the Singpoos of Miao but later on in 2009, he was asked to abandon the organization and in this context, even Mr. Sharma was warned to be ousted from the present site at New Singpoo Gaon, Miao. That pressurized Mr. Sharma to abandon the Gorkha Kalyan Samaj forever.

The Tagadharis ever since the freedom movement in the country appeared to be the extroverts whenever any Gorkha is exploited by others (Sharma: 2009). The Tagadharis complain and oppose for the exploitation done by others upon the Gorkhas. But it is seen mostly the Matwalis of Changlang district unless a Matwali is educated and conscious, hardly complain or oppose against the exploitation done by tribals. Rather, the Matwalis (drinking alcoholic castes of the Gorkha community) call the Tagadharis (wearing sacred threads castes of the Gorkha community) as Batho Jats (cunning castes) while the Matwalis call themselves as Latto Jats (innocent castes) both in Darjeeling- Sikkim (Sharma:1987) and North East India (Sinha:2009). In fact, the urge for being conscious comes through the minds of the Tagadharis due to their Hindu religious background of India and this may be also the reason why the Tagadharis want to do something remarkable for themselves and the entire Gorkha community. Mostly, the Tagadharis want to do this because they are cowards as well as they are educated while the Matwalis feel themselves brave. This bravery is responsible factor for inviting troubles in their day to day life. For example, very recently, because of this over-bravery, Shri Madan Tamang, the Gorkhali leader of All India Gorkha League was assassinated in Darjeeling town that too in the broad day light. This may be the reason why Matwalis are called "KAACHO JATS" meaning thereby the raw (wild) castes of the Gorkha community. Historically, the "rawness" of the Gorkha Matwalis made them to be enrolled into the Assam Rifles and Gorkha Regiments by the British and Indian Governments. "Hukum Ko Jawab Chaina"—the Gorkha proverb states that there should not have been any counter argument against an order ordained by the Master (whether in army or in civil life) made the Gorkhas, slaves who mainly belong to the dominant Matwali group of Gorkha community in North East India as immigrants from Nepal in general and the Arunachal Pradesh in particular. As in the past, today also, the Gorkhas have to present Hornbill feather to the Naga landowners at the time of Hornbill Festival in Changlang and Tirap districts of Arunachal Pradesh as the mark of respect to be ordained to the landowners. This indicates that keeping Naga tribal landowners always happy is binding on the part of the Gorkhas in Changlang and Tirap districts of Arunachal Pradesh as per the tribal tradition.

The Malaise Game

In the present study, I have experimented myself with the effort to write on the Gorkhas of Changlang district of Arunachal Pradesh and explicate many malaises as the components of easy game being played with Gorkhas by the Arunachal tribes as well as the tribal outfits in Changlang district. The whole malaise game is also being well played by the tribals with the patronage of the Government of Arunachal Pradesh with the Gorkhas. This is the most important mission of writing the present book for the academic world. The malaises need rectification from the above, i.e., the government level through her state policy for agrarian development of eastern most wilderness frontiers of India.

In the name of the tribal development policy, no such malaise game should be continued in Arunachal Pradesh paralyzing the Nation First Approach of whole fabrics of the Government of India. The malaise game has been damaging the National Integration Thesis in relation to Arunachal Pradesh in particular and North East India in general. Let the government come out with the solution to identify the Gorkhas of Nepal origin and the Gorkhas of Indian origin. In fact, what I believe is that the government simply cannot do it whimsically as it involves the Indians in Nepal in the light of Indo-Nepal Peace and Friendship Treaty of 1950. Even for an educated Indian Gorkha like me, the treaty is the sole responsible factor for creating dilemma and problem of distinguishing the Gorkhas of Indian origin from the Gorkhas of Nepal origin (Sinha: 2009). However, here I would like to contradict Prof. Sinha (*Ibid.*) on the ground that Indians in Nepal are much better in their locus standi than the Gorkhas in India. This is proved by the fact that a Bihari by ethnicity is the President of Nepal today along with more than thirty five Madhesia Members of Nepali Parliament. So, until and unless the Indo-Nepal Treaty of 1950 is abrogated or amended, the Gorkhas in India in general and Arunachal Pradesh in particular are not safe as it was harped by Shri Subash Ghisingh, the leader of Gorkha National Liberation Front in Darjeeling in 1987. This malaise game will be over on the moment the treaty is abrogated or amended (Subba: 2009) for the Indian Gorkhas. The sense of escalation I could feel well while working in North East India although nobody from the region could overtly escalate me in their environment but sufficiently I had the opportunities to sense to be covertly neglected, escalated and what not in the region. If the person like me is being ill-treated in such fashions, then just imagine the platitude of common Gorkhas in the land of tribals—Arunachal Pradesh in particular and North East India in general. Hardly, I found the North Eastern people who do appear to have been sufficient testimony to the mischievous intension that they have kept in their mind to the Gorkhas of the region. "Ama Diyara Bau Na Hune Jat"—the Gorkha proverb states that a tribal cannot be a true father even if you give him your own mother on marriage—appears to be hundred per cent truth especially in Changlang district of Arunachal Pradesh. What the tribals have to do now is to instantly leave the habit of being indolent, calling fear psychosis of losing tribal identity in Arunachal Pradesh if outsiders come there since they have their respective state government, government mechanisms and popular base in their body politics. I do not think of being scared of losing tribal identity by the Arunachal Pradesh tribes if the mainstream communities want to abode on the soil of Arunachal Pradesh to develop the state forever. The last word forever is that the Gorkhas do not damage the tribal identity rather help to prosper the same in the soil of Arunachal Pradesh.

Concluding Remark

The Gorkhas of Changlang wilderness of Arunachal Pradesh would be considerably safe if they become by heart assertive with new techniques of adjustment, assimilation and adaptation in the Arunachal environment. They must be more optimistic upon the situation to convert challenges into opportunities for the overall socio-economic development in the region. Instead of investing money earned in Arunachal Pradesh elsewhere the country or Nepal Terai belts, the Gorkhas should give more and more prominence to the education of their children so that they will be having high mobility preference structure across the globe today as Globalization and the Gorkha culture of "Basai Sarne" in the Arunachal wilderness are not antithetical to each other but complimentary to each other. Further to contain the mollified intention emerged among the tribals who blame that the Gorkhas invest money earned in Arunachal Pradesh at their respective places, the Gorkhas should now have to invest whatever the money they earned there in the state only so that the tribals will be pacified considerably.

VII

An Account of Gorkhas in the Sadiya Frontier Widerness

Quite a good many empirical studies have been conducted on the Gorkhas of Assam of North East India. Analyzing the studies on the Gorkhas of Assam, it is however found that mainly the Gorkhas of North East Frontier—the frontier on and around Arunachal Pradesh have been left out due to the inaccessibility of the region on the one hand and imposition of the Inner Line Permit system by the Government of India on the other. In the present section of empirical study, an attempt has been made to study the Gorkhas of the frontier region called Sadiya Frontier which was in the British Raj under the North East Frontier Agency (NEFA) of British Government and also during the independent era till 1954 (Gautam: 2009) of the Government of India.

Discussing the origin of Gorkhas in Assam, Jaisi (1990) stated that the relationship of Assam and Gorkhas through Coochbehar of present West Bengal was restored since early 6th century A.D. He has stated that Maleswar Neog, the Chairman of the Assam Sahitya Sabha (1974) informed that king Harsavardan of Kamakhya had married a Nepali princess in 153 A.D. Further, the Nepali princess Ratnakanti was married to Biswa Sing of Coochbehar (*Ibid.*). This indicates that the Gorkhas had been living in Assam since 153 A.D. The Sankerdev (the great Vaisnavite Guru of Assam) who is claimed to be a Gorkha by ethnicity stated that all Gwalas (milk suppliers) of North East India were Gorkhas. The Coochbehar kingdom was related to Assam and this may be the obvious reason why the Gorkhas came to Assam from Coochbehar of present West Bengal. In this context, Dr. D.R. Regmi in his book entitled "Modern Nepal", Vol. I (1975) stated that "further, we have suggested that several ruling families were mixed up in blood with royal dynasties (Coochbehar) which originated from the Mongoloid Kiratas or semi-Aryan Khasas. Such royal families might be those who ruled the eastern Terai (Darjeeling district) and Koch-Bihar of West Bengal. The Doinwars or Danuwars of Mohatari who ethnically allied to the Koches or modern Koch-Bihar are in particular seen in context with different ruling houses in the Chaubisi group (of Nepal). By Chaubisi, it was understood to be the various small principalities of Nepal". It is learnt from the Gorkha Conquest of Dr. Kumar Pradhan (1991), the great Indian Gorkha historian of Darjeeling, that South eastern part of Nepal had been the abode of the Kiratas (Rai and Limbu) although all the Matwalis of the Gorkha community now claimed themselves to be the descendents of Kiratis of Nepal and India prior to 6th century. Before the Aryans arrived there, the Kiratis and Khas groups used to be living in the area. It was through the Kiratis and Khas of eastern Nepal, we got the gods and goddess like Siva, Parvati, Ganga, Yakshya etc. In ancient time, the name of Tripura was Kirat. It is claimed that Koch, Mech (Bodo), Naga and Nepali Tharu of Napal Terai area, Rai and Limbu are the descendents of this Kiratas. The Mahabharat War which has taken place between Kauravas and Pandavas was also consisting of the Himalayan Kiratis. It is found that Arjuna had done war at Pragjyotispur which was the dominion of Kiratas. This has been elaborately discussed in "Kirantiajurnia"—the sacred book on Kiratas of Assam. In Puranas, it is stated that Kiratas used to live between eastern Nepal to mighty Brahamaputra. This was possible for the Gorkha Kiratas as they were easily accommodated and integrated (Sharma: 2012) with other castes and tribes of North-eastern India. In this context, Kanaklal Baruah in his article entitled "My Reminiscences" (edited by Maheswar Neog: 1973) on The Studies in the Early History of Assam has stated that "evidently in those days, the process of assimilating new immigrants into the indigenous society had been quite quick. This process has been going on in Assam since time immemorial and it is still working well in Assam. It is this process that the Assamese Hindu society has been built up that explains the complete fusion of the Gadiya, Utkal, Dravidi, Kamrupi, Maithili, Kanajia, Marwari and Gorkha Brahmins in the Assamese Brahmin society of the present day". It is claimed that Brahmins and Kasyaps (probably Gorkha Chhetris) might have come from Upper Bihar, Mithila and Kanyakubja which were once the integral parts of Nepal. It indicates that the Gorkhas were there in those days in the areas. The Assamese kings of Kamrupa had special regards to the Brahmins and Kshatriyas of Mithila, Kanyakubja and Upper Bihar. The Kamrupa kings brought Brahmins and Khatriyas (Chhetris) in Assam. Dr. Hutton in his study on the Origin of Races and Religion in India entitled "Studies in Early History of Assam" has eloquently stated that "Brahmins and Kayasthas of Assam are all imported from Northern India, mostly from North Bihar (Mithila) but the Assamese Kolita Brahmins are indigenous to Assam. The Mithila in early human civilization was part and parcel of Nepal. This has been the historical clue that indicates the Gorkhas were very much present there in India. The Nepal had areas in Mithila. This is proved by the stray notes on Buchanan's account of Purnea. Here Buchanan wrote that "By the Pandit, I am assured that Triabhukti in Sanskrit and Tirbhut in the vulgar dialect, are perfectly synonymous with Mithila and are in more common use, but Tirabhut is now applied by the English to denote the distinct adjacent of Purnea on the west, I shall in order to avoid confusion, always use the word Mithila to denote the old division of India which comprehends a great part of three districts under the company's government and a portion of the dominion of Gorkha (Nepal). We know that the racial, linguistic and cultural affinities between Mithila and Kamrupa (Assam) at one time were very close. In fact, during the zenith of the rule of the kings of Pushavarman's dynasty between the sixth and eight centuries perhaps the whole of Mithila was within the Kamrupa Kingdom". Ever since the Pauranik Age, the Kamrupa (Assam) had deep relationship with Nepal. Many parts of Nepal were included with Kamrupa. In "Yogini Tantra", we find the following description:

> "From the Mountain of Kancana in Nepal up to the confluence of the Brahmaputra, from the Karatoya to Dikkarasini, the northern limit in the mount Kanya, in the west of Karatoya in the east Diksu (Sikkim), O daughter of the mountains, in the south the confluence of Lakse with Brahmaputra, this is the territory which all treaties call by the name Kamrupa".

King Biswa Singh of Coochbehar married the daughter of king Ratna Malla of Nepal. A new generation from the Nepali queen flourished in Coochbehar. A son of Biswa Singh who was named as Nar Narayan and also called as Malladeb brought many Gorkhas as sepoys, carpenters, Pandits, Purohits, stone workers etc. in Coochbehar of present West Bengal.

The Gorkha Dasai-Tihar festivals are the indicators to prove that Gorkhas had a deep conviction as well as commitment to India. King Bali was the son of Lord Brahma. In Descriptive Account of Assam, Robinson in W.W.Hunter's book entitled "A Statistical Account of Assam, 1876" has mentioned that the "inhabitants asserts that Ban Raja (Bali Raja) was a demigod, sixth in direct descent from Brahma. He added that his dominions were situated on the banks of Narmada river that he journeyed into Kamrupa, Chaidar and other parts of Assam and was the first person who introduced the worship of Mahadeo or Siva into this part of India". The Bali Raja had his territory from southern Nepal to the banks of Narmada river. In Assam, it was the Bali Raja who introduced the system of Mahadeo or Siva worship. The Mahadeo, it is claimed in Puranas used to live in Nepal Himalayas. The Gorkhas were early worshippers of Siva and Bali Raja was also the worshipper of Lord Siva. The Bali Raja had therefore a close relationship with the Gorkhas. Near Tezpur (Sonitpur) of Assam, Lord Krishna had defeated Ban Raja. It is stated by Kautilya that an Easterner named Bana and his ancestors Bali and Virochana ruled Tezpur (Sonitpur) in Assam valley. During the reign of Bana and Bali Raja, the Nepalis of Nepal had established close relationship with Kamrupa (Assam). Rule of Tantrism and Tantris of Assamese society and Dhami-Jhankris as well as Vaidangs of the Gorkha community is still found on vogue in North-east India. This is adequately proved by the observation that has been done well by H.P. Sastri in his study entitled "Kamrupa and Vajrayana" that it is however quite possible that actually Nagarjuna dynasty flourished not long before. Alberuni's visit so that his fame as a alchemist easily reached. Alberuni came to India in about 1030 A.D. It is well-known that Sidha Nagarjuna was a famous Kaviraja or physician and certain medical pills, still in use in Assam valley, are associated with his name, being prepared according to his prescription. They are still famous in the Assam valley as Nagarjunar Bari (Nagarjuna's pills). A book containing his 100 prescriptions, known as "Yoga Staka" has been discovered in Nepal and Tibet, though he may or may not have been a native to Kamrupa.

Huien Sang of China while visiting Kamrupa of Assam stated that the then Kamrupa of Vasker Barman of Assam was consisting of Upper Bengal, East Bihar, parts of Bhutan and Nepal (Morang).

Vasker Varman was the descendent of Nepali Malla king (*Ibid.*). It is written in Kausika or Kauski that the fact probably is that at least the northern reaches of the Kosi of Nepal consisted of the western boundary of Kamrupa till the time of the later Maurya or the early Gupta dynasties. Within this boundary, it was included not only the northern portion of the district of Purnea but also the whole of Morang, south of Nepal. Within the Morang itself, it was the famous place known as Varaha Tirtha, the supposed birthplace of Narakasura, near the junction of the Koka-Kota with the Kosi. The earlier Kamrupa kings must have possessed this tract which contained the birthplace of their progenitors. The Kamrupa kings must have always longed to regain possession of this tract which contained the Varaha Tirtha (sacred place). When the Gupta power declined, the Kamrupa kings, taking the advantage, gradually extended their kingdom towards the north-west as far as Kosi and that is how Mahabhutavarman could grant lands near this river in sixth century. Towards the end of that century, however, their aggression brought about a conflict between Mahasena Gupta of the later Gupta dynasty and Susthiravarman, king of Kamrupa. In the end, the later was defeated and Kamrupa dynasty was perhaps pushed back to the Karatoya. In the early part of seventh century, Bhaskarvarman, together with Shri Harsha, conquered Gauda and Karnasuvarna. The Kamrupa boundary was then again extended to the Kosi and here Bhaskaravarman could renew the grant of his ancestor Mahabhutavarman.

According to Puranas, king Narkasur of Nepal (Barah district of present Nepal) had been the adopted son of the king Janak of Janakpur (Nepal). He killed Ghatsur king of Kamrupa. If the king Narkasur was from Nepal, then Nepal was for later Kamrupa kings, as the ancestral as well as sacred place. The Kamakhya temple of present Guwahati was constructed by this Narkasur king. The Narkasur also brought many Brahmins from Nepal. This may be the obvious reason why the Gorkhas visit Kamakhya temple in a large scale. There are still many Gorkha Pandits in Kamakhya temple. In the name of Kamakhya Devi, Gorkha Tagadhari women observed Swasthani Ko Brata (Puja) throughout the one month in Magh (Jan-Feb) every year. The Kamakhya temple attracted the Gorkhas to come to Assam and settle down there forever. Similar is the case of Vasistha temple.The Bhattarai Bahuns of the Gorkha community are associated to be the descendents of Rishi Vasistha (Purohit of Lord Rama). It also indicates that the Gorkhas were there in Assam from the days of Lord Rama.

At the time of Naranaryan's regime, Kamrupa had boundary up to the river Kosi of Nepal. Thus, many Gorkhas had been there at Kamrupa. According to Kamrupa and Vajrayana, as it was informed by Rana Suvarna Samsher Jung Bahadur, A.M., that according to tradition, still current in Nepal, Machindranatha and Minanatha were two different persons, though at the time or other, both were in Kamrupa. It is further said that there were a long continued drought in Nepal which led to famine. The king of being instructed in a dream by god, came to meet Machindranatha who was then in Kamrupa and took him to Nepal. The drought then had been ended. Machindranatha is still looked upon in Nepal as a saint by both the Hindus and Buddhists. Again, the same thing has been noted by some Medieval Kamrupi Authors in their works. "The Dakarnava" edited by Dr. N.N. Choudhury is another Vajryana text in the Apabhransa (derogatory) language, recovered from Nepal, which must have been compiled in Eastern India during the same time (eleventh century). The "Kamaratnatantra", another Vajrayana text, declining with the well known Sidhis, attributed to Gorakhnatha, the disciple of Minanatha, also most probably originated in Kamrupa, for an Assamese translation of this work was collected by Pandit Goswami in Assam.

The Gorkhas worship lord Gorakhnath. This may be the reason why they are called Gorkhas in the world. There is a Gorakhpur temple in Gorakkhpur town of Uttar Pradesh. The Gorakhnath episode has also been translated into the Assamese language.

Pandit Goswami's book "Hasta Muktabali" is found in Nepal Darbar (palace) library and Darvanga of Bihar. A copy of the same is also found in Assam and Mithila. The book also indicates a close relation that Kamrupa had with Nepal since time immemorial. The book left a great impact on the Assamese society.

The king named as Mahabhutvarman of Assam brought many Gorkhas (Bhramins) and made them settled in his area. The Gorkha Brahmins belonged to Kundil Gotra (elan) as well as Kanyakubja Gotra who were found in adequate number at Sadiya at the Kundil river basins. It is also believed that a Kundil Brahmin established the present Combodia.

Studying the Sadiya frontier of Assam, it is found that ever since the king Mahabhutvarman's rule in Kamrupa, Gorkhas were there in Sadiya. Similarly, Parsuram Kund (Hindu sacred place in the river Lohit) of the region is very popular among the Gorkhas. Regarding

Kundil Gotra, the work called "Were the Indian Colonialists from Assam in Indo-China" by Pandit Goswami has stated that "according to the Cambodian annals as well as Chinese history, compiled in about sixth century A.D., the kingdom of Kambaja (Founan) which comprised Cochin, China, Combodia and part of Sian and Laos, was founded by an Indian adventurer prior to third century A.D." This has been confirmed by the epigraphic evidence. The Mayson inscription of the king Prakasha Dharma-Virkanta-Verman, dated Saka 579 (657 A.D.), records that the founder of the kingdom was a Brahmin called Kaudinya (tantra Sthepitavachulam Kaundinyastad Dvijarsabhah). It is now claimed by some scholars that this Brahman named Kandiya, hailed from southern India and had sailed for Indo-China from Kalinga coast. It may, however, be pointed out the Kundina was the name of the place where Bhismak, the father of Rukmini is said to have ruled, and rightly or wrongly, the extensive ruins near Sadiya and close-by the river Kundin or Kundil are to this day, pointed out as an ancient city of Kundila. This has also been pointed out by *Gait* (History of Assam) and also by Pandit Vidyavinod in his *Kamarupa-Sasanavali*, wherein it is further stated that according to tradition a colony of Brahmins was there at this place made by Parsurama (Kamrupa-Sasanavali); can it not, therefore, be claimed that Kaudinya, the reputed founder of the kingdom of Kamboja belonged to this Brahman colony of Kundin and that he was called Kaudinya as he originally belonged to Kundin (Kundil) of Sadiya of Assam.

On the other hand, it may also be pointed out that Kaudinya was the name of a Gotra of the Nagar-Brahmans. According to the Nagarotpalta, Kaundinya is one of 72 Gotras of Nagar-Brahmans. Of the 33 Gotras of Nagar Brahmans as mentioned in the Nagar Pushanjali, Kaudinya is one. According to Precyavidyarnava, N.N. Vasu Kaundinya and Kaundiya Kausika are among the Gotras of Vaidika- Brahmans of Bengal, Sylhat and Kamarupa. Judged by their surnames, most of the donees of the land grant of Mahabhutavarman of Kamrupa of the fifth century A.D. were Nagar-Brahmans and some of them belonged to the Kaudinya Gotra. It is therefore a pertinent fact that Nagar Brahmans were numerous and influential in Assam during the early centuries of the Christian era. The settlement of a colony of these Brahmans near the Kundin or the river Kundil in Upper Assam in early days cannot therefore be regarded as impossible nor can we reject it as impossible on theory that a Brahman from

Assam belonging to the Kaundinya Gotra was the adventurer who founded the Kamobja kingdom in far off Indo-China.

It is again found in the Two Newly Discovered Ancient Inscriptions in Assam that "the fact that this very king (Bhutivarman alias Mahabhutavarman) of Assam granted lands on the bank of river Kosi within perhaps the tract that was known as Morang, to a large number of Brahmans which was the grant to his descendents of Bhaskarvarman that had to confirm by the well known Nodhanpur chapter that goes to show that the Kamrupa extended at that time from the Purnea district of Bihar to the extreme border of the Nowgaong district in the Assam valley."

In his article, "Indian Oil Presses and Oil Extraction in the Journal of Anthropological Institute (Kolkata), Vol. No.142", Prof. K.C. Chattopadhaya pointed out that oil compressor machine as found in Assam was also found in other parts of northern India of the country and Nepal. This was a primitive type of oil compressor machine ever discovered.

According to the opinion of Bipin Dungel (Editor of Himal Chuli), in 1200 A.D., a Darpusidha Lama of Bhutan brought Gurung, Kirati, Murmi (Tamang), Manger, Khas, Lepcha, Koch and Mech for his army which defeated Waktiyar Khilgi of Delhi in Kumrikata of Kamrupa. So, the Waktiyar Khilgi could not attack Kamrupa according to his programme. Therefore, all the Bhutanese soldiers were the Gorkhalis.

All these studies indicate that the Gorkhas were there in Upper Assam as well as Sadiya (universe of the study) from the days of Lord Krishna. It is claimed that the Pandits of Kundil Gotra among other Brahmans were very famous there at the Vishnu temple of Rukmini of Bismaknagar (Roing-Arunachal Pradesh). These Brahman Pandits had been claimed to belong to Kundil Gotra. They are all described to be the Himalayan Pandits. By "Himalayan", it is, of course, logically as well as rationally presumed to be the Gorkha Pandits as then no other Himalayan castes and tribes could dwell on Hindu priesthood job. Therefore, it can be safely said that Kundil river banks were the actual habitation of earlier Gorkhas. It was only after the conflict between the present Chulikata Mismis and Lord Krishna, the Gorkhas left Rukmini Nagar (Arunachal Pradesh) for Sadiya villages to settle down permanently. The name "Chulikata Mismis" were called after the Lord Krishna had cut their hairs when they were very badly defeated near the river Kundil. The Lord Krishna taken away Rukmini from the river banks of Kundil. It is also known from the field-work at Bismaknagar (capital of king Bismak) – the father of Rukmini that Krishna had brought lot of Gorkha Gwalas (milk suppliers)—grazers who had been left there itself at the time of departure of Lord Krishna from Bismaknagar with Rukmini. Presently, it is believed by Kundil Gorkha Brahmans that they are the descendents of those left out Gwalas of Lord Krishna. This is fully proved by the fact that Lord Krishna was fond of cows and always used to enjoy playing with the Gwalas (cow boys). However, the beautiful Kundil river banks were destroyed by the great earthquake of 1950 when the entire Sadiya-Kundil region was completely destroyed.

Objectives of the Study

The cardinal objective of the study of present section is to highlight the fact that Gorkhas were there in Sadiya ever since the days of Lord Krishna, Rama and other Hindu religious gods and goddesses. Secondly, the contribution of Gorkhas in the consolidation of North East wilderness Frontiers has been assessed with a case study of Sadiya which was and still falls on North Eastern Frontiers of India. Thirdly, the Gorkha Ekrupta (Unity) at Choonpura of Sadiya as a case study will throw some lights on the creativity, stubbornness, sincerity and devotion of Gorkhas to the soil of North Eastern Frontiers of India. Finally, the present socio-political dynamics of Gorkhas will also be analyzed at the closet quarters.

Scope of the Study

In spite of the historical significance of Gorkhas in the eastern frontier, there is no detailed discussion on the Gorkhas in either the books written by the British colonial authors or Indian scholars till today specially on the Sadiya Gorkhas. Although manifold notes have been made on the role of Assam Rifles or other battalions of Sadiya which used to be consisted of mainly the Gorkhas (Shakespear:2011), no specific account has been found till today on the Gorkhas of North Eastern Frontiers of Sadiya and also of the Choonpura. However, Dr. Khemraj Sharma (2012) has studied the Gorkhas of Changlang district of Arunachal Pradesh. The study shows that the Changlang Gorkhas are in the primitive stage of economic development. Very recently, books (in Nepali/Gorkha language) by Shri Debi Pd. Gautam and

Shri Trailokyanath Gautam entitled *Sadiya Ko Darpan* (Mirror of Sadiya) and *Sadiya Ko Jhalak* (Sadiya at a Glance) as well as *Sadiya Ko Itihas* (History of Sadiya) respectively have been published that have indicated the contribution of Sadiya wilderness Gorkhas for the socio-economic consolidation of Sadiya Frontier of North East India.

The Sadiya Gorkhas

Talking about the official records on the Gorkhas of Assam, it is found that prior to 1780, Gorkhas were there in Assam. The Gorkhas as grazers and cultivators had penetrated deep into Assam in early 16th century. However, officially, majority of Gorkhas came to Assam after the British East India Company and British army came to Assam immediately after the Treaty of Soguwli (1815) between Nepal and British Indian Government. In Shylet operation of 1817, the Gorkha force was used to surpass the Burmese Singpoo force. Thus, the emergence of Gorkhas in Assam is wrongly considered to be the people who came here in Assam after 1824-1826 (Indo-Burmese War). In fact, to be very specific and unbiased, the Gorkhas were already there in Lower Assam and also up to Dibrugargh area of Upper Assam. The emergence of Gorkhas in North Eastern Frontier is found to have been taken place after 1817 when for the first time British officers started surveying the frontier region. All the spies of British Government were Gorkhas who used to procure information about the possibility of penetrating into the hills of present Arunachal Pradesh. Of course, the presence of Gorkhas in Assam army needs specific discussion in order to know details about Gorkha penetration into the region.

In Sadiya of North Eastern Frontier, the Gorkhas mainly the Matwalis had come from Indian plains of Bihar and Uttar Pradesh during 6th century. It is said that the Matwalis of Gorkha community like Kiratas, Murmis, Chettris (Matwali Chettris of Nepal: Thapa Manger:1990) came to Sadiya due to the existence of adequate forest, Chars and barren land (Sharma:2012). With the installation of two companies of British force consisting of Gorkha Sepoys (Pemberton: 2000) of about 500 in numbers in Sadiya in 1818 started the Gorkhas to settle down in villages like Chandmari,Titakhori, Gormura, Kundil, Pensioners' Busty, Gorkhe Busty, Panch Mayal, Bagbelli, Balijan, Padmaful Busty, Bhawala Busty, Beng Gaon, Dram Pather, Sonowal Gaon,Tera Mile etc. (Gautam:1985). There was about five thousand population in Sadiya villages in early 1820 mainly consisting of Gorkha Matwali cultivators. In fact, the history of Sadiya starts from 1818 when the Burmese Thilura attacked Assam (North Eastern Frontier) and that was followed by the attack of Burmese Bondola in 1822 (Pemberton:2000). This has been elaborately discussed by Lieutenant Burnet in his report of March 1828. The then Khamptis of Sadiya had to pay Rs.50,000 to Poorinder Singh—the king of Upper Assam and Poorinder Singh used to pay tax to the tune of Rs. 20,000 only to the British Government in turn (*Ibid.*). The Khamtis had been concentrated in present Choonpura, Chapakhawa and Balijan areas of Sadiya. Stating the paramount position of Khamptis in the area, Pemberton (*Ibid.*) has stated that "the Khamptis of Sadiya who originally emigrated from the hills on the east and obtained permission from the Rajah (Poorinder Singh) of upper Assam to settle in the plains, established themselves on the banks of Tengapani (east of Choonpura) from where they made successful interruption into Sadiya during the troubled region of Raja Gopinath of Assam in 1794 and reducing the Assamese inhabitants to slavery, their chief assumed the title of Sadiya Khawa Gohain which he had ever since retained". The historian Prof. M.L. Bose (1997) has of the similar opinion on the Khamptis. Prof Bose has further stated that "Tai Khamptis had migrated from Thailand via river Irrawady of Myanmar. The Khamptis being the well-wishers of the British Government in the beginning prior to 1838, were allowed to keep 200 men armed with British arms. The observation made it clear that the Khamptis had been concentrated on the land between Sadiya and river Kundil and also at Choonpura. The Khamptis had a saw mill in Balijan Gaon (Choonpura) which was found there itself till the recent past. It was found at that time a population of 4142 in the land between Sadiya and Choonpura. The military force stationed at Sadiya from 1818 had been considered to overcome the numerous powerful and restless tribes like Khamptis, Singpoos, Mismis, Abors and Miris by which the post of Sadiya was surrounded, and who until our (British) occupations of the province had been accustomed to carry on a war of extermination against the more peaceable inhabitants (Gorkhas) of Brahmaputra valley. Two companies of the Assam Light Infantry under a British officer were constantly stationed at this Sadiya post with a couple of gun boats, each carrying a 12-pound carronade and managed by Khampti golundauz. This force of Sadiya was quite sufficient to preserve the province from the internal tumult and from the doubtful fidelity of our Singpoo, Moamanees and Khampti allies (of the British Government)". This proves the fact that all the tribes of the region were not in confidence structure of the British Government. It is because of the non-confidence of the British Government on the Khampti tribe of Sadiya, most of the soldiers of Assam Light Infantry on the one hand and Gorkha settlement on the other in Chandmari, Ghormura, Titakhari and other villages were managed by the Gorkha community under the British Government ever since 1818.

Pemberton (2000) has given the statistics of military force in Sadiya in 1832-33. They were as follows:

Assam Light Infantry	=	900
Ditto Mounted Rifles	=	24
Bridge of Artillery	=	60
Assam Subandy Corps	=	720
Total	=	1704 at Sadiya
Assiliaries		
Bura Senapati (Maomanees) Contingent	=	300
Khampti Militia	=	200
Gun Boats at Sadiya	=	20
Besa Gam (Singpoo) Contingent	=	80
Upper Assam Militia under Poorinder Singh, commanded by Hindustani Commisioned Officers	=	500
Total	=	2904

In 1917, all the military force was converted into a single force called Assam Rifles (Jaisi: 1990). It is found that Sadiya besides Balipara and Lakhimpur was the post to control, tame and administer the hill and foothill tribes of North Eastern Frontiers of India (Sharma:2012). This is the period (1818-1947) which was very significant considering the settlement history of Gorkhas in the region.

According to the Trailokyanath Gautam (1985), Sadiya-Saikhawa was a big town on both sides of the river Brahmaputra. There was

Miri Thapari (land of Miri tribe) which was also called Miri Pather (now in Dhola of Assam). Here at Sadiya, it is found that most of the Sepoys of Assam Light Infantry were Gorkha Matwalis (Manger, Gurung, Rai, Limbu and Tamang) while most of the grazers of Sadiya, Ghormura, Titakhori, 13th Mile etc. villages were absolutely having Tagadhari Gorkhas who in fact, since the Lord Krishna days were grazers. In Kundil-Sadiya area also only the Gorkhas were grazers. At that time, Sadiya Army Headquarters of Eastern Frontiers was the recruiting place for Jawans (Soldiers). There was also an airport and railway line from Calcutta up to the Dibang river of Sadiya which was also the place where Political Officer-in-charge of North Eastern Frontiers of India used to stay on. All the civil amenities like hospital, road construction department, reservation directorate, lad reforms office etc. were located at Sadiya only.

By the term "Sadiya", it was understood to be "blessing" or desert flower which was much like Jasmine. In Assamese term, it was known as the place of king of Sutiya tribe, may be the present Chutia caste—a prominent caste of Upper Assam. Among the villages of Sadiya, Chandmari, Padaful and Titakhor were completely inhabited by the Gorkha grazers and cultivators.

There was 13th Mile village on the east of Sadiya town where Miris and Gorkhas used to stay quite comfortably pursuing on grazing and cultivating sugarcane and rice. Among the Gorkhas of 13th Mile Gaon, Shri Bhawani Prasad Pokhrel and another Gorkha family (Visnu Bhattarai) used to stay at the bank of the river Kundil. Further, there was a dakbungalow at 15th Mile Gaon. Again, further to 15th Mile, there was Choonpura on the bank of river Balijan. But this Choonpura was exclusively under the possession of Khamptis ever since they were thrown out from Sadiya in 1839 by the Birtish. By "Choonpura", it is understood to be the place having lime furnace of Khamptis and this lime furnace was there prior to the arrival of Gorkhas in Choonpura. There was a Marwari family beyond the river Balijan. A health centre had also been made in Choonpura by the British Government. A small army post was also established there since 1882 at Choonpura (Balijan) during those days.

During 1902, Shri Damber Bahadur Tamang constructed a house at Dhania busty of Choonpura. He was selected to be the Gaon Bura (village headman) of Dhania Busty by the British Government and he was also given a gun in recognition to be elevated to the post of Gaon Bura. The Gaon Bura was responsible for the collection of taxes, administering the village and to induct more and more Gorkhas there. The Gaon Bura was also called as Kalu Gaon Bura. The Kalu Gaon Bura had six Tamang households in Dhania Busty of Sadiya. He had two wives living in the same village. Shri Amber Bahadur Tamang (Son of Gaon Bura) was the first person of the village who was sent to school and it is the reason why he is still called "Schoolee" Bura. This indicates the fact that in Dhania and other bustees of Sadiya, it was a few Matwali Gorkhas who settled down first. In the later phases, the Matwalis invited a large number of Tagadharis in Choonpura as well as in other villages of Sadiya for grazing.

The whole discussion so far done in the above paragraphs indicate that Sadiya was the centre of British Raj in North Eastern Frontiers of India that included both the Upper Assam plains and present hills and foothills of Arunachal Pradesh. Except few villages, most of the areas of Sadiya were under the dense forest. The British Government was badly in search of Gorkhas who could make the forest cleared and pursued on grazing and cultivating the land for British economy.

Choonpura of Sadiya

Choonpura is the universe of this section of study. Talking about Choonpura, for the first time, Kalu Gaon Bura established the Dhania Busty in early 19th century. He had six Tamang families in Dhania busty from Tamang caste of the Gorkha community. He came from Eastern Nepal or the then Darjeeling of Nepal.

Later on in 1937, Shri Debi Prasad Gautam who had come to Parsuram Kund and Brahma Kund as the sacred places of Hindus met Shri Damber Bahadur Tamang, the Kalu Gaon Bura. The Gaon Bura, being encouraged by the British Government, lured and motivated Shri Debi Prasad Gautam to come to Dhania Busty of Choonpura and settle down permanently with his family from Nepal. The Gaon Bura also encouraged Mr. Gautam to come Choonpura with his relatives and friends. Mr. Gautam visited various villages of Sadiya but did not like the same. In Baradhania Busty, the Gaon Bura brought his relatives and also his family members and settled down. There was also a village of the Assamese people known as Dalapani. At Dalapani, only one Tamang family of one Gaphi by name was there. The Dalapani village was situated near the mighty Brahmaputra.

After Mr. Debi Prasad Gautam met Kalu Gaon Bura in early thirties of 19th century, the Gaon Bura asked him to see forests at

Baradhania forest range and clear the forests and settle down. The Kalu Gaon Bura had his family from his Chettri wife at Baradhania busty. The Kalu Gaon Bura had twelve Puras (1Pura=5 acres) of land there. So, he asked Mr. Gautam to purchase all the twelve Pura land with Rs. 2000. As mentioned above, there was a person called "Gaphi"— the son of younger brother of Damber Bahadur Tamang-the Gaon Bura. After visiting Baradhania forest range, Mr. Gautam confirmed to settle there. There were mango trees and bamboos of rich variety in sufficient numbers in Baradhania forest area. In this way, to aid Mr. Gautam, a Pokhrel family by name from Nepal had brought to clear the dense forests at Baradhania forest range so as to construct huts and cultivate the land. Therefore, at Baradhania forests, Mr. Gautam along with six other families who were brought from Nepal started to live comfortably. At that juncture, Mr. Gautam also got a person called Rangalal who came from Saikhawa (Assam). Again, there was another person to aid him, called as Kaviraj Thapa (Manger) and his family in Choonpura. After the great political revolution of Nepal in 1950, altogether another 25 Brahman families arrived at Choonpura from Nepal Himalayas.

It is observed from the above discussion that there were altogether 22 Ghars (houses) at Baradhania Busty till 1950 great earthquake in Sadiya. However, following were the persons who settled with their families in Baradhania Busty till 1948-1949:

1. Damber Bahadur Tamang
2. Punya Prasad Pokhrel
3. Lekhnath Limboo
4. Debi Prasad Gautam
5. Rangalal Gautam
6. Debi Prasad Dahal
7. Madhusudan Dungana
8. Kaviraj Thapa (Manger)

The families of above persons constituted twenty two houses. They were all Tagadharis except a Manger, a Tamang and a Limboo family respectively in Baradhania busty of Sadiya. There was a Gorkha Dakwala (postman) in this area. In fact, it was the story of early 1940s. In this way, the Baradhania Busty became very famous for wet rice cultivation and grazing ground (Chapari) or Khuttis (cow-buffalo sheds) of the Gorkhas.

Sadiya and the Great Earthquake

On 15th August, 1950, the great earthquake occurred at Sadiya-Saikhawa area when everything had been destroyed (Gautam: 2009). All the government offices, army headquarters, Chandmari, Titakhori, Ghormura, 13th Mile,15th Mile, Kundil Busty, 5th Mile, 8th Mile, 7th Mile, Baradhania, Sonowal Gaon, Balijan (Khampti Gaon of present Choonpura), etc. were totally filled up with the Brahmaputra river water and also full of debris brought down by the river Brahmaputra. All the areas of Sadiya-Saikhawa had been submerged under the mighty Brahmaputra river. The villages of the lower region and the people living there at the Brahmaputra banks became fearful and therefore they went to the higher altitude forests, mainly at Mismi hills of Arunachal Pradesh to save themselves. Lot of foothills felt down on the Brahmaputra river and thus the river bed was filled up with debris being brought down from the hills of Arunachal Pradesh. In this way, the river level increased to almost hundred feet above the earlier base. The Baradhania busty along with all the village dwellers of Sadiya became victims of the earthquake. The village cattlestocks and wild animals of jungle all died in the earthquake. That time, the present Sadiya was under the North East Frontier Agency (NEFA) up to Makum of present Tinsukia district of Assam. At that juncture, all the government offices of Sadiya including Army Headquarters had been shifted to Tezu of Arunachal Pradesh. Again, many government offices had been shifted to Tinsukia of Assam many of course, temporarily and many others permanently. At first, most of the offices had been shifted to Sat Mile area of Sadiya. But most of the important civil amenities providing offices were shifted to Tezu. The NEFA border had been changed from Sadiya bordering up to Makum of Tinsukia, Assam to Balijan river of Choonpura. The post office, police station etc, were shifted to Tezu. In his book entitled "Sadiya Ko Jgalak", Shri Debi Prasad Gautam (2009) has stated the importance of villages like Titakhori, Baggholi, Bhawala Gaon, Potia, Balijan, Basagaon, Dumpather, Sonowal Gaon, Angkabusty, Hillaguri,13th Mile etc. where Gorkhas were the predominant population but they all became deserted with the river sand and debris.

At first, the people of those villages shifted themselves to 8th Mile and 7th Mile villages. The river Kundil also destroyed all its basin villages. The Barmura Gaon of Dhalla (Saikhawa of Assam) had been completely submerged under the Brahmaputra river. The then Saikhawa town came under the river bed. All the roads of Sadiya including roads towards Abor- Mismi hills that lead to Parsuram Kund and Brahma Kund were completely destroyed. "Save us—save us" was found to be uttered by the villagers at that juncture. To survive from the consequences of the great earthquake became the emotional upsurge of the people of Sadiya. All the debris so brought down from the hills by the Brahmaputra river accumulated at the foothills of Sadiya. All village terraces made for wet rice cultivation had been completely destroyed by the earthquake. In fact, after the earthquake of 1950, Tezu became the next headquarters of the British Government for North East frontiers. In Lohitpur, Gorkhas were asked to establish villages. In fact, many Gorkhas, while coming to the sacred Hindu places like Parsuram Kund and Brahma Kund had been settled down since time immemorial at places like Lohitpur, Wakro, Medo, Hayluiang, Walong, Pasighat, Anini etc. of North Eastern Frontiers of India. But Sadiya was the gateway to go to these places from the point of view of transportation, road and market facilities. On the extreme eastern end, Lohitpur became the centre of NEFA administration. A small airport was temporarily made at the bank of river Digaru (near Tezu of the Lohit district of Arunachal Pradesh). The river Digaru is also called river Mismi in the area (one of the tributaries of great river Brahmaputra).

The office of Political Officer of Sadiya had been shifted temporarily to Na-Sadiya. The Sadiya Bajar had been shifted to 7th Mile, Kundil Busty and Choonpura. The Sadiya Hospital was shifted to Tezu. At that time (1950), the Lohit district of Arunachal Pradesh emerged and in this way, Sadiya became the part of Lakhimpur district of Assam. The place like Chapakhawa (a village compressed by other villages of Khampti tribes) and the village called Shantipur ware established by the Gorkhas of Sadiya. The Deopani also emerged after clearing the dense forests. At that time, Shri Dalbir Singh Lohar (Digboi) as the nominated Member of Assam Legislative Assembly of Government of Assam became the central towering personality to aid flood/earthquake affected Gorkhas of Sadiya. At that moment, Shri Amber Bahadur Tamang—the son of Damber Bahadur Tamang (Gaon Bura of Dhania Busty of Choonpura) called as "Schoolee" assisted Shri Debi Prasad Gautam, Debi Prasad Dahal, Punya Prasad Pokhrel, Kaviraj Thapa and others to rebuild Sadiya Choonpura and make the area habitable. Thousands of Sisne Beteni Gorkhas had been shifted elsewhere beyond Dhalla of Assam. Altogether 500

Gorkha families of Saikhawa had been shifted to rehabilitate at Lekhapani and finally at Jagun of Assam. The Burmura Gorkhas (Dhalla) had been shifted to Hahakati, Tinsukia, Dibrugargh etc. At that time, present Choonpura had also been fall under the river debris and water. In this earthquake, the Gorkhas lost everything and became homeless. So, there was no other alternative except to go on Basai Sarnu— shifting habitation (Sharma: 2012) to new places or jungles to be cleared and settled down. The Baradhania Busty became desert and Shri Debi Prasad Gautam and his 21 other families started to see the appropriate land in Choonpura forest. They all sold out their land of Baradhania busty which became completely desert at that time. Therefore, they sold out all their land of Baradhania Busty at lower price than they purchased. After that under the leadership of Shri Debi Prasad Gautam, they decided to clear the forest and debris at Choonpura into three parts. At the north of Choonpura village, there was Nao-Potia, on the south, there was village named Nao-Gaon, on the west, there was Bagal Gaon etc. Combining seven Gaons of Choonpura, the whole Balijan Gaon emerged and named Balijan Gaon which is one of the Gaons of present Choonpura Gaon Panchayat today. After that a small road started to be made. A lower primary school was also constructed. All these lands were purchased from the Khampti tribes of the area. The Khamptis after their land being sold out to the Gorkhas, left for Tezu, Chowkham and other parts of foothills of Lohit district of Arunachal Pradesh. Shri Debi Prasad Gautam, out of his foresightedness, made land deeds of all the Gorkhas of 22 households who were shifted from Baradhania Busty to Balijan. Subsequently, he also helped to make the land deeds for those Gorkhas who came later on from Sadiya and other villages to Choonpura for future safety and security. Thus, Choonpura became the main centre of socio-economic, cultural, political and Hindu religious dynamics of Sadiya. Shri Debi Prasad Gautam had the clear vision which helped or contributed other Gorkhas of Choonpura to establish the Gorkha identity at Choonpura later on especially after seventies of 19th century when under All Assam Students Union (AASU) headed by Assam Gana Parishad Movement for foreigners escalation from Assam started in Assam (1979-1982) as a whole.

Present Choonpura

In order to consolidate the Choonpura Gorkhas at the parlence of socio-economic, political and cultural dynamics, Shri Debi Prasad Gautam and Shri Debi Prasad Dahal started Hari Kirtan Mandali in every ward of Choonpura which is now consisting of the following villages:

1. 1 No. Natun Balijan Gaon
2. 2 No. Balijan Gaon
3. 3 No. Balijan Gaon
4. 4 No. Balijan Gaon
5. Danabai Gaon
6. Nadikinar Gaon
7. 1 No. Toribari Gaon
8. 2 No. Toribari Gaon
9. Samaj Kalyan Gaon
10. Udaipur Gaon

There are 28,000 Gorkha voters in Choonpura, Ambikapur, Hootibill, 13th Mile, 5th Mile, 8th Mile, Na-Sadiya, Chapakhawa, Ghormura, Dhania and other villages of Sadiya. Chapakhawa is one of the sub-divisional towns of Tinsukia district of Assam. After 1954, up to 1972, Sadiya was under Lakhimpur district and after 1972 to 1987, Sadiya was under Dibrugargh district and finally after 1987, Sadiya became one of the sub-divisions of Tinsukia district of Upper Assam.

Today, in every ward of the Choonpura Gaon Panchayat, there is a Hari Kirtan Mandali which organizes Hari Kirtan session every day. The Kirtan Mandali helps the Gorkhas to be disciplined, sincere and committed to their duties and responsibilities. Even some Matwalis of the descendents of Dharma Limbu, Kaviraj Thapa (Manger), Damber Singh Tamang, Mac Mohan Gurung, etc. hardly pursue themselves on alchools and other lot of hot drinks rather they all of them have been maintaining absolute discipline in the villages of Choonpura.

Academically, today Choonpura is very prosperous. There are 3 High Schools, 12 lower primary schools and 3 middle primary schools. A degree college is also there at Chapakhawa. Therefore, educationally Choonpura is very famous. Lot of students from choonpura are going out for higher education in big cities of the country and job thereof.

Presently, Choonpura has altogether 7000 population having 46.7 square kilometers land under wet rice cultivation and having Khuttis—

cow sheds in significant number. However, the Gorkhas of Choonpura do not have buffaloes today. They have abandoned the buffaloe sheds. If we see the total Gorkha voters of Sadiya, it is 28,000 today while Assomiya voters are 32,000. Thus, second to Assomiyas, the Gorkhas are the main deciding factor for every candidate of the political parties to win the elections. There is a Siva Mandir and Kali Mandir near Choonpura. Besides, Gorkhas have very recently constructed a Visnu temple in Choonpura.

Altogether, there are 200 Khuttis at the bank of river Dibang of Sadiya. The Gorkhas had more than two thousand Khuttis till 1979 in Sisne (Sadiya), Roing and other areas of Arunachal Pradesh. Shri Thakur Prasad Gautam of Choonpura stated that he had 300 buffaloes at khuttis in Mismi hills of Arunachal Pradesh till the recent past but he had to abandon all the Khuttis there as the Arunachal tribals slaughtered his buffaloes. Now, in Mishmi and Abor hills of Arunachal Pradesh there are only about 1500 to 2000 Gorkha Khuttis at places like Bhuwan Khel (Dhalla), Jungali Jhora, Bhim Thapari, Musaldhare Tapu, Digaru (Arunachal Pradesh), Lalbill, Paglam, Hatigoli etc. of the Sadiya area. But most of the Gorkha Khuttis are not in good shape today due to the tribal domination and terrorist attacks.

The Gorkha Grazing Sites in Sadiya

As soon the British occupied Sadiya in early 1817, the Gorkha graziers were invited to clear the forests and start cattle rearing. In the process, the Gorkhas were given two Pura (1 Pura=5 Acres land) as free grant land (Sapcotta: 2009). Many areas emerged as the exclusive sites for cattle rearing or grazing. Altogether, in Upper Assam there were 79 sites under the Gorkha cattle grazing. At the Sadiya region, there were more than twenty such sites many of which are now in Arunachal Pradesh (Abor and Mishmi hills). In Sadiya, there were grazing sites in places like Dungbil, Bongibil, Sadiya, Saikhawa, Dhola, Malingeni Tapu, Mushaldari Tapu, Rangdoi Chapari, Lasune Chapari, Gorumuda Chapori, Miri Chapari, Sisou Chapari, Sisne Busti, Betini Chapori and Pagam Chapori. This is supplemented by the observation made by Dr. Deben Sapcotta (2009) that "Sadiya has been a milk-producing pocket since Pre- British era. There is no documentary evidence about the grazing and animal husbandry practices adopted here. However, it is said that the Gorkha settlers had been rearing buffaloes and other cattlestocks even before 1940. Due to the growing buffalo population, the then Deputy Commissioner of Sadiya issued an order for shifting of herds from Sadiya to a new place called Digaru (now Arunachal Pradesh—Lohit district). At the beginning, among the prominent graziers, Balabhadra Bhattarai had about two hundred heads of buffaloes. In British era, every grazier was given permission for mutation of 2 Bighas of land in his favour. Sisne Busti, a grazing land on river bank of the Brahmaputra was occupied by one Kirtiman Bhattarai in 1940. He had aroused one hundred heads of buffaloes. In 1940-45, at Saikhawa Ghat—another river bank, Narbahadur Thapa, Kul Bahadur Chettri and Pahalman Khandka had aroused one hundred and fifty eight heads of buffalo respectively. Among the graziers, Ravilal Nirola was most prominent with two hundred and fifty heads of buffaloes at Saikhawa Ghat. He migrated from Mohmara area of Sadiya in 1940. He also traded in milk and milk products. The demand for milk being insignificant, graziers made butter from milk by churning. However, World War-II brought about an upward swing in the price of milk, which was fixed at Rs. 2 per seer, similarly ghee fetched Rs.1.25 per seer. The separated milk had no takers and often it was disposed of in the river or fed to animals". This is supplemented by my observation at Sadiya that in fact, there were Gorkha graziers ever since the Lord Krishna days. It is because of the fact, since time immemorial, that the Gorkhas mainly Tagadharis (Bahuns and Chhetris) used to visit Parsuramkund and Brahmakund and settled down in these areas as graziers and later on as cultivators by clearing the jungles or dense forests.

Over the years especially after the Assam Movement, lot of Gorkha grazier lands have been encroached through different means by the local tribals. However, D.B Chetry (2009) has noted that there were in 1998, at least 149 sites in Tinsukia district with 35,657 acres of land under village grazing reserve. But interestingly, I observed that of the above sites in Tinsukia district, most of the reserves have been discontinued and shifted to the Arunachal foothills of Abor and Mishmi dominated region. Except a few places adjacent to the Brahmaputra river, most of the graziers are now found in foothills of Lohit and Lower Dibang valley districts of Arunachal Pradesh. These foothills are located near Sadiya of Upper Assam. There are about two hundred Khuttis near Dibang river on the opposite side of Dhalla of Saikhawa block of Tinsukia district. The milk so produced at Bogibil, Musaldhare Tapu, Paglam Tapu etc. on the Arunachal foothills are brought to the Dhalla Bajar and Tinsukia town through steamer over the Brahmaputra river. Many residents of Dhalla have Gai Ghots (cow sheds) at Musaldhare Tapu, Paglam Tapu and Bogibi Tapu. At Dhalla, the entire traditional Gorkha grazing lands have been encroached by Bangladeshi refugees and Arunachal Miris. Whatever, the grazing lands were there of the Gorkhas, almost all the grazing reserves have been on the verge of extinction in Sadiya of North Eastern frontier of India. This may the reason why we do not find any grazing land at Choonpura. Only a few families domesticate cows. I did not find a single buffalo with the Gorkhas of Choonpura or Chapakhawa of Sadiya frontier region. All the Gorkha Khutti lands have been occupied by the Deoris, Miris and other tribes of the frontier region. Here the government of Assam is virtually silent.

The Gorkha Brahmans of Choonpura

The Kanyakubji Gorkha Brahmans of Choonpura had a great stake at the present Bismaknagar of Arunachal Pradesh and Sadiya of Assam. They were the people who helped the British colonialists to survey areas in Mismi and Abor hills of Arunachal Pradesh and Sadiya frontiers of Assam to reach China (Hamilton: 2003; Cooper: 1995). In fact, Bismaknagar was the place where the British troops had completely defeated the Mismis to consolidate the area under NEFA. In this venture, the Gorkha Sepoys contributed a lot both as fighters and spies (Pemberton: 2000). Unlike other villages of Sadiya, Choonpura is the village where mostly Brahmans and Chhetris (Tagadharis) of the Gorkha community have established their hegemony entailing Hindu fundamentalism. While in other villages including Chapakhawa, Matwalis of the Gorkha community have been found with their complete dominance. Ritually, they are called drinking castes while Tagadharis are ritually the non-drinking castes of the Gorkha community ever since time immemorial.

All the Gorkha ex-servicemen have been settled down either at Lohitpur or Chapakhawa after they retired from the Assam Rifles. Only a small area of Alloobari of Lohit district is there at Chowkham of Namsai sub-division of Arunachal Pradesh where the Gorkha ex-servicemen are given land by the Khampti tribe. In fact, the Khamptis looking upon the agrarian perseverance of the Gorkhas have left the land to the Gorkhas at places like Choonpura (Balijan), Alloobari and Lohitpur. But the present Gorkha ex-servicemen are not given the land deeds by the Government of tribal Arunachal Pradesh.

There are 2000 households in Choonpura today consisting of 7000 voters and population of 4500 belonging to the Gorkha community. There are at least 5000 cattle stocks in Choonpura. Lot of Hindu religious festivals like Durga Puja, Kali Puja, Sivaratri Puja, Bhanujayanti (famous Gorkha Poet who wrote Ramayana in Nepali/ Gorkha language) etc., are organized and celebrated by the central committee of Hari Kirtan Mandali of Choonpura. The Sadiya Gorkha Bhasa Samity has also been formed very recently at Choonpura. The Bhasa Samity has made alliance with the Assam Sahitya Sabha and lot of conferences are being held to unite the Gorkhas of Sadiya. A small Bajar is also there at Na-Sadiya, Goomtibill and Choonpura of Sadiya today. Many good school teachers are there from the Gorkha community of Choonpura. But interestingly, almost all the schools are having Assamese as the medium of instruction.

Very recently, after the emergence of Arunachal Pradesh as a full-fledged state in 1987, lot of Deoris and Miris are coming down to Assam and the Assam Government through her tribal rehabilitation programmes, is encouraging the tribals to purchase as much land as possible from the Gorkhas. So, lot of lands of Gorkhas have been purchased by the tribals. For example, the son of Shri Amber Bahadur Tamang (earlier Gaon Bura of Dhania Busty) of Choonpura has sold out his parental land to Deoris and Sonowals resulting which a friction emerged and court cases are going on today between the son of Amber Bahadur Tamang and Mr. Tamang himself. In fact, this process of Gorkha escalation from the land of their centurion living started in early 1980 by the Government of Assam is being followed by the Government of Arunachal Pradesh (Sharma: 2012) and it has been increasing very rapidly today.

Officially, Ambikapur, Amarpur, Borjiah, Buraburi, Chapakhawa, Hollowgaon, Kundil, Na-Gaon, Na-Sadiya, Rajgargh, Santipur and Choonpura are the villages of present Sadiya sub-division of Tinsukia district. About 67.50 square miles are the area of the Sadiya sub-division of Tinsukia district where the Gorkhas are staying in the villages pursuing themselves on cultivation and in very small numbers of Gorkhas are with Khuttis. In fact, at Sadiya, ever since the time of British Political Agent named Francis Jack Nidham who asked, lured and motivated the Gorkhas to establish the villages (Website:2012) in Sadiya. Although the Gorkhas are given living right in Sadiya frontier of North East India, unlike Arunachal Pradesh, they are trying to be on minority so as not to enable the Gorkhas to realize their ethnic identity in the region by fabricating the State Census reports. Day by day, they are trying to make Gorkhas in minority in the region. The Gorkha Bhasa Samity of Assam has been given rupees one crore by the Assam Sahitya Sabha to rejuvenate the Gorkha culture in Assam. The Khuttis of Gorkhas have been encouraged at Guwahati by the Tarun Gogoi Government with land deeds. But now only those Gorkhas have been given land deeds in Assam who came prior to March, 1969. The present generation of Gorkhas are in most cases devoid of the status of Indian citizenship in Assam as well as other North Eastern region of India. Considering the present situation, the Gorkhas who had shed their blood and sweats, have found to have very bleak future. This uncertainty has led them all to be in close touch with Siliguri (Darjeeling) and even the Terai belt of Nepal (Ibid: 2012).

After the Indo-China war, 1962, lot of Arunachal Gorkhas have came down to Sadiya (Choonpura) and settled down. This has helped the Gorkhas to be in greater numbers in the region. They are allowed to stay here in order to make the land cultivated, nurtured and flourished properly. So, they out of Dukha (Hut: 2007) were forced to live here and still living in isolated places and jungles. The high adaptability of Gorkhas has enabled them to live in jungles of Sadiya with Khuttis, Khet and Gothala jobs since time immemorial (Sharma: 2012). Dukha is characteristic feature of the Gorkhas. It is always found in entire North East Frontiers with Gorkhas. In fact, Gorkhas are born to serve others and died by serving others. While they are looked down upon for their bravery, stubbornness, sincerity and open-heartedness. These have generated jealous eyes among other people of North East India (Sinha: 2007).

In fact, we being the Gorkhas do not have any conviction against any caste or community of the region. But whenever the local Gorkhas are forced to go for the escalation from North East India, we too feel very bad and neglected both by the tribal people and government of North Eastern states of India. Our history of many centuries has been belied, rejected and given less significance both by the historians and government agencies. Wherever in North East India, you go, you will find the Gorkhas, of course, on Dukha (Hut: 2007) but these days they are evolving complete assertiveness (Nath: 2007) as they believe on Dhawa—constant struggle (Sharma: 2012) which means that they do always believe on struggling hard for their survival.

Talk about the white revolution in Assam or Arunachal Pradesh or other North Eastern states, it is found the Gorkhas and Gorkhas only who helped the state governments. All these jobs done by Gorkhas have become meaningless, redundant and unaccounted to the concerned people and government of North East India. Unfortunately, they do not left the habit of designating the Gorkhas as foreigners, outsiders and explicators. But if we see elsewhere in the country, Gorkhas have not heard of exploiting others including the tribals of North East Frontiers. The Sadiya Frontier Gorkhas did not left the place even after the great earthquake of 1950 but struggled hard to rebuild the barren desert of Sadiya into rich wet rice cultivated area on which the Government of Assam realizes good revenue. At least, one crore of rupees have been recovered as tax by the government of Assam from the Sadiya Gorkhas every year.

The holistic development approach of (Constructionist Approach) Gorkhas of the Choonpura have helped the entire Sadiya to go ahead consistently over generations. Even the famous composer, singer and writer named Bhupen Hajarika who was an Asomiya from Tezpur of Assam sang many songs on Sadiya Gorkhas. He learnt to wear Gorkha cap (black Gorkha Topi) from his childhood at Tezpur and he put the same on his head till his last breath (2011) with the Khukuri as given by his well-wishers in Nepal.

The above discussion makes it very clear that there would have been no village in Arunachal Pradesh today if the Gorkhas would not have given their blood, sweat and lives. This may be the apparent reason why the Gorkhas do not mind to give his life for the cause of others but in vain. This is spectacularly seen from the point of view of services rendered by all the Gorkhas both in militia and jungles of North East frontiers wilderness. In fact, prior to the coming of British, Assam as a whole used to be called as "forbidden land of backward people". No other community except Gorkha, wanted to come to Assam, as the Gorkhas with all vigour and vitality used to call Assam as "Achaam", for they wanted to come here for future prosperity till 1979.

Writing in "History of the Assam Rifles" (1924), N.N. Acharya stated that "in a graphic and detailed manner, Colonial Shakespear has recorded how very courageously the military leaders in those days tried to infiltrate into Assam which was then known as a forbidden land of backward people. In this matter, some trustworthy survey spies (Gorkhas) had greatly aided the soldiers by providing them with valuable information on the historic, strategic, cartographic as well as economic fields". Again, W.J. Reeds (*Ibid.*) has further stated that "the economic growth of Assam has been threatened with peculiar danger—that of trans-frontier forays—forays into the low lands have been checked the development of the tea industry would have been impossible". At that time, the local tribes were men hunters. A tribal family would be considered most prosperous provided it had largest number of men skulls being hanged on the house walls. To check this, military police force had been established in Assam. The military police force had converted into five battalions of Assam Rifles. Here in this context, Shakespear (1924) wrote that "the task of pacifying and humanizing these primitive hill people would have been impossible had there not been at the command of the civil government, a trained and armed forces which could be employed in small detachments, could be rapidly set in movement and could make shift with a minimum of transport. These have been amongst the distinctive features of the Assam Military Police".

Jaisi (1990) has stated that in 1833, there was already a police post in Choonpura, Sadiya, Makum, Joipur etc. in the eastern frontiers of North East India. This indicates Sadiya as well as Choonpura were already there in the political map of British administration. All military police force of Assam had to wear Khukuri as the emblem in their dress as also the symbol of bravery shown to the British Government. Although other communities were also recruited in Assam Military Police Force but finally the Gorkhas only had come under the zone of confidence of British Government for their sincerity, bravery and stubbornness in North Eastern Frontiers of India.

With the incorporation of Bengal province to East India Company in 1765, the British came to Assam. For example, David Scot (first Agent of Governor-General) came to Assam (Meghalaya) with 7 Gorkha soldiers to establish the British Raj at Shillong (Meghalaya). The Gorkha force helped the British Government to establish Bengal-Assam Railways in 1902. All coolies in road construction had hail from the Gorkha community. In 1824, 10th Native Infantry was formed and in 1928, 7th Gorkha Rifles was also established. In 1928, again, the 8th Gorkha Rifles was established. In fact, in all battalions, Gorkhas were prominent. It indicates that all the soldiers of Sadiya military station comprising of three companies were consisting of Gorkhas. A road had been made from Sadiya to Choonpura in early 1828 only.

However, at that time, the Nepal Government had imposed

restriction to recruit soldiers in the Indian British army. This may be the reason why Sardars and Gallawalas (Sharma: 2000) used to be sent to various places of India and Nepal to lure the fellow caste people who were to be recruited in Indian army and village jobs. In this contaxt, Jaisi (1990) has rightly pointed out that since generations together, Gorkhas used to stay in Indian plains (Bihar, U.P., M.P., Kashmir etc) up to Assam. In this regard, a report of Ramse (Hussain: 1977) also stated that "the Durbar is, and always has been, averse to its subjects entering the British service, and orders have been existed to prevent their doing so without the ministers' previous permission and a few years ago Maharaja Jung Bahadur Rana went so far as to declare that no Sepahees in the British army, Native to Nepal, on leave only from their Regiments should be allowed to re-enter the country and visit their families, an order which he only withdrew after I had strongly remonstrated against it, and had reported the particular instance that occasioned it for the consideration and orders of the Governor-General". The statement indicates that there were Gorkhas at that time in India as Indian citizens. Even after the king Jung Bahadur Rana, Gorkhas of Nepal were not allowed to go on Gorkha Regiment of the British Government. This is adequately proved by the report of Goldesten (Hussain: 1977). It is stated in the report that "...any person who is detached in an attempt to leave the country for this purpose will be imprisoned, and that the goods, house and lands of any person so enlisting will be confiscated. It is also believed that any person who on their return to Gorkhas' territory, are suspected of having served in a British regiment will be severely dealt with". Thus, whoever the Gorkhas from Nepal used to come to join the British Regiment in India, they came with their family permanently. Their sons afterwards were ensured to be recruited in the British Regiments. Asad Hussain (1977) stated that "it also conceived the idea that if the Gorkhas who were serving in the Indian army were to bring their families to India, in the long run past of the recruits who were needed could be obtained by enlisting their children. In this way, the British Government had become less dependent on Nepal for the Gorkha recruits" in India.

It was the year 1824 when David Scot wrote to the British Government about the dominance of Burmese in Upper Assam that they must be escalated and accordingly in 1824 itself a war taken place between the British Gorkhas and Burmese soldiers. The Burmese force surrendered and the treaty known as Treaty of Yandabo entertained between the British and Burmese governments. In this way, Assam was liberated from the hands of Burmese and Singpoos. After that, entire Upper Assam came under the sovereignty of the British Government.

In 1871, all the soldiers from North India in Assam Rifles were escalated and only the Gorkhas and Garwalis were recruited. Here Huxford (1952) wrote that "in 1871, the Government of India ordered that Poorbeah element should be deleted from the Assam Regiments and that the vacancies occasioned thereby should be filled up by the Gorkhas, Nepalese and Garwalis". This may be the reason why till 1950, the entire Sadiya battalions were consisting of Gorkhas only.

It is also found that Sadiya till 1890 had no specific border. This was the reason why Abors and Mismis used to loot the Sadiya village very frequently. To tame the Abors of Sadiya, in 1893, December, about 400 Gorkha riflemen had a tough fight at Dumko (present Arunachal Pradesh). All the 400 Jawans were Gorkhas. For the symbol of bravery, Havildar Goma Basnet got Order of Merit Award. Huxford (1952) has described the gallantry of Gorkhas in Dumko conflict with Abors. He stated that as an example of sort of fighting that might be expected when in conflict with Abors, the following account by an officer of the regiment is reproduced:

"The first engagement with the Abors began in a somewhat unusual manner. We had marched for some miles through the forest in which underground was so dense that one could not see 20 yards on either side of the narrow path and so full of thorny canebrake that flanking was almost impossible, yet the enemy made no attempt to molest us, even in the few places where it was more open owing to the bamboos there was no sign of life. In many parts of overhanging branches had to be cleared away to enable the elephants which carried some of the baggages to get along, so the advance was very slow. The column then comes on some open cultivated ground (possibly by the Gorkhas) where a halt was made to enable everyone to close up. Soon after the next advance, a few Abor scouts were seen and fired upon and then the point of the advanced guard bumped into a stockade ten of twelve feet high, built of trunks of trees right across the path, in the thickest bit of forest yet encountered. It was 'crowned' with frieze of bamboo spikes and the ground in front was covered with more spikes driven into the earth which looked almost like grass and were so sharp they penetrated the sole of a boot if traded on.

The next came the Mismi hills in the process of frontier

consolidation. Two companies of 44th and one company of 43rd Regiment consisting of the Gorkha Riflemen surveyed the entire Mismi hills under Leutenant Colonel E.H Molesworth. The basic objective of that survey was to find out route to reach Tibet or China for trade and commerce. In 1903, the 43rd and 44th Regiments of Assam became 7th and 8th Gorkha Rifles".

Among the tribes, Abors were more dangerous at that time. They used to loot the property of Gorkha villagers in Sadiya region. Lot of Gorkhas died fighting with the Abors. Considering this, in 1911, English force had to fight with Abors at Kobo. Here in this context, Huxford (1952) in his "History of the 8th Assam Rifles" has stated that "Kobo, on the right bank of Brahmaputra, where the river Dibang flows into it, was the base for the operations. This place was a name only, no village and dense forest or jungle. In Assam due to wet weather, the work entails in transforming this terrain into a base camp can be imagined. The Dibang valley was the line of advance. So dense was the jungle and so bad the Abor paths that only about an average of one mile a day was made. It is not possible in the history of Assam Infantry march and camp procedure in jungle warfare of this sort, but the official does this, and in extremely revelation of the trails endured in jungle warfare. The 8th Gorkha Rifles had done this sort of thing for some ninety years. No doubt young readers had a test of it in the Burmese operation (in the past) i.e., 1842-1845 but there were no mechanical side to road making and jungle clearing in 1911, the Khukuri and Dao had to do it unaided". It was therefore Khukuri which helped to clear jungles, make road and converted jungles into human habitation at that time in Mismi and Abor hills of present Arunachal Pradesh. In Abor expedition, Subedar Major Nawal Singh Rana received 1st Class Order of British India award. Jamadar Makan Singh Gurung of "A Company" received I.D.S.M. award. Lance Naik, Chitrabir Rana of "B Company" and Rifleman Kalia Pun of "B Company" got Indian Service Medals for Abor expedition and exploration (Jaisi:1990).

On the other hand, under the four Gorkha officers with the leadership of A.L.M. Wordsworth having 144 Gorkha Riflemen of Sappers and Minero Company had started constructing road from Sadiya towards Tibet-China border in 1912 and May 1913. Here Mismis were friendly and there was no fighting. By 1911-1912, there was Puccka a road up to Choonpura and from Choonpura to Digaru, Medhaghat and finally up to Walong under the leadership of

Comandant C. Bliss and Captain Bycurse. From Choonpura up to Pion, another road was constructed as well as a road was also made from Choonpura via Chorpani up to Denin in 1912-1913. In 1912, Lakhimpur battalion surveyed Abor and Mismi hills. Finally, in 1917, all the Assam battalions were converted into Assam Rifles.

In Bismaknagar, reminisces were recovered by the Assam Rifles in 1912-1913 under Major Hannay. The Tamsari Mai temple and Bhuri-Bhuri temple were also recovered under Major Hannay. The Kundil areas were also explored and he found the Kundil villages with Gorkhas as grazers and cultivators. The Tamsari Mai temple is located at the distance of 8 miles from Choonpura. The temple has been appeared to be the prototype of Kamakhya Mai at Guwahati (Assam). The Bhuri-Bhuri temple is located at the distance of 15 miles from Sadiya and the temple is meant for the worship of lord Siva (Jaisi: 1990). In this context, Prof. L.N. Chakraborty (2005), the historian stated "it was decided in 1967 to take up excavations at Bhismaknagar during early part of 1967 and accordingly a party under the Historical Research Officer reached there in early February, 1967. On reaching there, they started reconnoitering the area covered by thick jungle mainly very big trees, cane, bamboo, creepers and infested by elephants, tigers etc. The most disgusting thing was the presence of innumerable blood sucking leeches. In course of their movement, a few feet of brick work located in between the two gates, it was decided to start the work there.

After some progress it became quite clear that we took the right decision in selecting the site for excavation. But due to paucity of labourers we could not make as much progress as we desired, even then from what we saw it became quite clear that it was a well planned as well as protected city inhabited by people who reached a high degree of culture and civilization. However, it was too early to say anything definitely about the date of the ruins as well as the ruling dynasty and the particular ruler responsible for the construction of the palace/fort.

The findings from the area excavated during the first phase were also not sufficient in number and variety to offer any clue in this regard but it goes without saying that there were expert artisans who knew these works quite well. In addition to this, there were people with advanced engineering skill who could initiate the plan and execute the construction of the building and such other works quite successfully to meet the requirement of time.

Now, we have heard of two such people ruling in the area viz. (a) the Kalita and (b) the Chutiyas. About the original home of the Kalitas there are mainly two views current among the scholars. From Dr. B.K. Barua's "A Cultural History of Assam", we learn as follows: "In a biography of Bhavanipuriya Gopala Ata (1541-1611), a disciple of Sankaradeva it is said that Gopala with his mother came to Acadadesa from Kalitadesa. The same text records that the Kalita country was located at the north-east of Acama and near the region inhabited by hill tribes, such as Miris and Abors." The account is corroborated by other writers. Captain Hohn Bryan Neufville writing on geography and population of Assam in 1928, stated "the country to eastward of Bhot and northward of Sadiya extending on the plain beyond the mountains is Sadi to be possessed by a powerful nation called Kalitas or Kultas, who are described as having attained a high degree of advancement and civilization equal to any of the nations of the East. The power, domination and resources of the Kalta Raja are sated to have been kept up between the estates, now long ago discontinued. To this nation are attributed the implements of husbandry and domestic life washed down by the flood of Dihang".

Dr. Barua further says "According to the popular belief the Kalitas were Ksatriyas who fled from the wrath of Parsurama who was determined to exterminate the Kshatriyas. They fled from home and concealed themselves in the forests of Assam so they are Kula (caste) Lupta (gone) or Kalita (degraded caste)". But this seems to be a bit of false etymology.

The general belief is that the Kalitas came to Assam from outside. In this connection, it is interesting to note that among the people inhabiting the north of India as per the Markendeya Purana were Kulta along with Darada, Gana etc. Dalton considers them to be Aryans of pure descent, who came to the province before the formation of the existing professional castes. Baden Powell is of opinion that they were formerly Buddhists and were dispersed from Mid-India by the subsequent Brahmanic revivalists. He refers to the tradition that the oppressed Buddhists sought refuge in the hills, and remarks that there are shattered remnants of those once ruling houses still existing under the name of Kulta or Kalita caste. The Kalitas of present day Assam, however, are good Hindus, and as said before, rank as a high caste. Martin on the other hand, refers to their orthodox character and says that they are independent of the Brahman priests.

"Bastian seeks to connect the name Kalita with Moggalana Kalita. It is clear that as a designation on the Maudgalayanputra Hiun Tsiang refers to the name of Kalita or Kolita. The Koliya also appears as one of the names of the ten republican states of Vrijian confederacy. The Koliyas of Ramagrama were Kshatriyas and were related to Buddha. By tradition, they were agriculturalists. The Koliya may be equated with Kalita. It may, therefore be suggested that the Dalitas whom Dalton praises as excellent cultivators having extensive holdings, well stocked farmyards, and comfortable houses, are the descendents of the Buddhist Kshatriyas of the Koliya tribe. Kalitas were thus the Aryan settlers of the Brahmaputra valley who once spread out to the eastern limit of the province".

The above contention is also supported by Dr. Kakati in his book "The Mother Goddess Kamakhya" and he furnished some additional information in the shape of the names of ancestors of Gopala Ata. He has stated thus, "That there was a colony of Vaisnavite settlers in north-east frontier is shown by the fact that the ancestors of Gopala Ata whose mother was migrated from the Kalita kingdom which bore Vaisnavite names and also Vasudeva, Harideva, Shankarsand, Kamadeva etc".

It will not be out of place to take notice of what has been stated by Shri R. M. Nath in his book "The Background of Assamese Culture". "The Tamil word Kallu means stone and Kalton means the stone mason. It appears to be most probable that Kalta and Kalita are distortions of Kal-Taton meaning firstly the stone-mason and then in general term, the artisans connected with temple building. The mason, the carpenter, the iron and coppersmith, the porter and the cobbler—all fall under the same category of Kalitas.

After the fall of the Pala dynasty—the most wealthy and powerful group of people in the country was that of the temple builders who came mostly from Deccan side and were settled in the country. They were comprised of the Holihoyas, the Andhra Kakatiyas, the Choliyas and the Duvarajas, but the majority of the society consists of artisan class who were called the Kaltatons. The people organized themselves under a leader who belonged perhaps to the family of the princes whom Purandara Pala married and established a kingdom in about 1132 A.D. in north-eastern part of the country. The city was named Bhishmaknagar in memory of the city of this name in Berar, mentioned in the Mahabharata. They carried the traditions of the epic period of their original homeland and attributed them to their newly established kingdom. Thus, the tradition of Rukmini, the daughter of Bhishmaka, the king of Vidarvha (Berar) who was kidnapped by Shri Krishna, came to be associated with this part of the country".

Next, from Mr. Gait's "History of Assam" and some other sources we have come to know about the Chutiyas to have ruled over the foothill areas; they were ultimately defeated by the Ahoms in the 16th century (1523). The same source tells us that after the final defeat of the Chutiyas in the hands of Ahoms under Suhungmung, the royal family with the leading men amongst the Chutiyas were deported to Pakariguri, while a number of Brahmins (possibly the Gorkha Brahmins) and some expert artisans (Gorkha Matwalis) were taken from Sadiya to the Ahom capital. The whole Chutiya country was then annexed and a few officers of the state known as the Sadiya Khawa Gohain was appointed to administer it.

On the other hand, we do not hear anything about the annexation of Kalita territory and so in the absence of any such definite proof about the annexation of the Kalita territories of the north-east corner of the country it will possibly be safer to presume at this stage that the ruins of Bhishmaknagar might have been connected with the Chutiyas.

From the references in Mr. Gait's "History of Assam" about the existence of Brahmins in the Chutiya kingdom, it may not be too much to presume that the Chutiyas had some link with the main body of the Aryans in the 'Aryavarta'. Otherwise, it appears difficult to explain as to how the Brahmins could be seen there. The only direction from which they could enter the Chutiya kingdom was the west because the north lies in the Himalayan ranges and Tibet, to the east lies Burma and to the south lies the upper Brahmaputra Valley where there were no settlements of the Aryans during those early days. Thus the direction through which they might have entered the Chutiya country cannot possibly be any other than the west. If the above contention is correct then it is quite likely that the Chutiyas of those days had some link with the region colonized by the Aryans and that to the west of the country, they brought not only the Brahmins to their country but also the religion professed by them. The existence of experts in that far off corner of the country possibly leads us to the same conclusion that the Chutiyas had very close connection with localities inhabited by the Aryans and could boast to have reached quite an advanced stage of civilization. The construction of the brick-built palace as well as the surrounding walls with massive gates and the ditch surrounding the whole thing speaks of lot about the experience and skill of the engineers and artisans responsible for those things. However, I am quite conscious about my limitations because the materials available up till now are extremely scanty and limited in nature. Anyway, I am hoping that future excavations may reveal some more helpful materials which may help us to offer our views about the ruins (Bhishmaknagar) in a better way.

The Nagas were then creating problems in North-Eastern Frontiers. So, to tame them, Subedhar Medha Thapa shown bravery and he was given 2nd Class Order of British India award and also Shri Bhuwan Singh Gurung, the lance Naik and Kalia Pun got Indian Distinguished Service Medals. To commemorate the great Gorkha soldiers, in 1928, 13th January, a Gorkha Memorial was established at Gorakhpur by Field Marshal William Wordsworth. In 1935, 2nd Gorkha battalion (Regiment) completed 100 years. A celebration was done at Quata. It is seen from the above historical account that by 1912-1913, entire North Eastern frontier hills were explored, surveyed and brought under the total British administration. It is also seen from the above description that Gorkha soldiers and also Gorkha grazers and cultivators contributed a lot to consolidate the North Eastern frontiers of India. After 1912-1913, the Gorkhas in much number of Choonpura started going to Mismi and Abor hills to pursue themselves on grazing and cultivating land. Prior to 1912, already Gorkhas had pursued themselves on cultivation by raising terraces in steep hills of Hayuliang, Walong and Lohitpur of Lohit district of Arunachal Pradesh. The Sapkota Gaon of Pasighat of East Siyang district of Arunachal Pradesh was a Gorkha Gaon (Sharma: 2012) prior to the arrival of British in the region. The Pasighat became quite developed immediately after the occupation of British Government at the Abor and Mismi hills of Arunachal Pradesh.

It is however found that the authors like Pemberton, Cooper and Hamilton have concentrated on their writings on North Eastern frontier tribes and not much is written on the Gorkha grazers and cultivators of the North Eastern frontiers. In fact, Gorkha villages taught tribes for settled and civilized life (*Ibid.*).

The Sadiya Gorkhas, in spite of having all sorts of wild animals, isolated niches having no road and attacks of Abors and Mismis made the Sadiya land fertile and with crops of rich variety. At that time, there were more than 3000 Khuttis in Sadiya alone while after 1950 earthquake, the Gorkhas concentrated on land cultivation. All sorts of crop had been grown in Choonpura.

Socio-economically, Choonpura had been developing like anything having dominant Tagadhari dominance which believes on constant socio-economic and cultural development (*Ibid.*). In this context, the role of Balkrishna Nirola, Kalu Gaon Bura named as Damber Bahadur Tamang, Kesev Prasad Timsina, Bisnubhakta Bhandari, Tulsiram Dahal, Narendra Prasad Dungana, Punya Prasad Pokhrel, Kalananda Dahal, Kamalnath Dahal, Kaviraj Thapa, Purna Bahadur Limbu, Deohang Limbu, Marki Limbu, Ekman Chhetri, Mandhoj Chhetri, Keseb Bahadur Chhetri, Debi Prasad Dahal, Debi Prasad Gautam and Ananta Narayan Gajurel is commendable. These were the personalities who made the present Choonpura. They had bent of thought for social welfare. In these welfare works, Mitralal Gautam (Gaon Bura), Trailokyanath Gautam and Rangalal Gautam were fully involved in Choonpura.

Among the above mentioned personalities, the role of Debi Prasad Dahal of Choonpura can not be forgotten. He was much concerned with the educational development of Choonpura. For the educational development of Choonpura, following contribution made by Mr. Dahal is worthy to be enumerated:

(1) In 1955, he took active part in the formation of Sanskrit school at the bank of river Brahmaputra;
(2) A Hindi school was established in 1956 and he became treasurer of the school committee;
(3) Saradha Sanskrit Pustakalaya at Danabari Gaon where he was an active member in 1960;
(4) The Choonpura Government Primary School was reestablished and there he donated land for the construction of school in 1956;
(5) He initiated for the establishment of Toribari Primary School as President as well as Treasurer of the school committee in 1957-1958;
(6) He assisted for the establishment of Danabari Primary School in 1960;
(7) He assisted for the formation of Choonpura Higher Secondary School in 1968;
(8) He assisted for the formation of Choonpura Madhyamik School in 1961;
(9) He established Lohityana Library in 1965. Later on in 1971 he renamed the library as "Lokpriya Library" at Choonpura.

Although Choonpura was inhibited by the Gorkhas since early 19th century, it was only after 1940, the Choonpura had been found to have the strong social structure with the formation of various social welfare organizations. But due to the unconsciousness for social solidarity today, the Gorkha unity is on the wane. In this respect, lot of sacrifices that had been done by Shri Debi Prasad Gautam and Shri Debi Prasad Dahal of Choonpura, Sadiya appeared to be of less importance to the present generation.

Concluding Remarks

Talking about the architects of Choonpura, Shri Debi Prasad Gautam is most important. He came to Choonpura in early 1940s and stayed at his in-law's house (Gajurel house). After that he decided to take the land of Kalu Gaon Bura named Damber Bahadur Tamang by paying Topi tax, i.e., tax to clear the forest and settled down there at the bank of river Brahamaputra. Here he got the support of Dakwali Amai (wife of one Dakwala) and Kaviraj Thapa (Manger). After some years his brother named Kamalnath Dahal came to Choonpura. He shifted to Toribari of Choonpura after 1950 by donating his land for school construction at the bank of river Brahmaputra. At Toribari, he had friends like Prasad Acharya, Nandalal Acharya, Abhinarayan Bhattarai, Ram Prasad Sharma etc. In 1956, L.W. Road between Choonpura and Tezu was constructed and the village was shifted on both sides of the road. In that venture, persons like Tikaram Bhattarai, Nirola, Luitel, Madhusudhan Dungana, Nunthala Tulsiram Dahal, Bisnu Prasad Gajurel, Anantha Narayan Gajurel, Debi Prasad Gautam, Khemnath Dahal, Chandranath Pokhrel, Narpati Dahal (from Digaru) etc. shifted to present Toribari. At that time, hardly the Gorkhas used to stress on children education; forget about their daughters' education. However, Pushpa Gautam—the daughter of Debi Prasad Gautam and Tilmaya Dahal, the daughter of Debi Prasad Dahal were the first two females who were sent to school for the first time in the history of Choonpura. At that time, Shri Amber Bahadur Tamang of Harudhania (old Dhania busty) of Choonpura donated land for the construction of Middle Primary School. In this respect, the contribution of Shri Amber Bahadur Tamang and Debi Prasad Gautam is quite memorable.

From the above observation, it is found that Choonpura became the dens of Tagadhari group of Gorkha community. This may be the reason why today the Hinduisation process is more or less complete at Choonpura while other villages of Sadiya are consisting of Matwali group of Gorkha community who have very little inclination towards the holistic development as well as the establishment of Hindu environment. It is because of the fact that Choonpura was most suitable place for Gorkha Tagadharis to cultivate land for crops and animal husbandry in a larger scale. It is because of all-round development of Choonpura, all the Gorkhas of Upper Assam have special regard and respect for Choonpura Gorkhas. In this way, the Gorkhas contributed a lot for the development of Sadiya Frontier of North East India. Sadiya is still operationally a frontier region although conceptually and politically it is in Assam (Tinsukia district). It is found that still the old or aged people call Sadiya as one of the frontier regions of the then NEFA and present Arunachal Pradesh. As mentioned in previous pages of the study that Sadiya is very much nearer to Arunachal Pradesh than Assam in so far as the topography and social relationship between Gorkhas and tribes are concerned. The Sadiya was part and parcel of Lohit frontier in the past and also today. It is also found that Sadiya provides lot of infrastructural amenities to Arunachal Pradesh. This is the basis of incorporating Sadiya Gorkhas among the frontiers Gorkhas of North East India. Like Gorkhas of Arunachal Pradesh, the Sadiya Gorkhas are having fearless ventures for overall socio-economic development of the region. The Sadiya rice is very popular not only in Upper Assam but also in eastern Arunachal Pradesh. The Gorkha Khuttis at the bank of river Dibang in Sadiya side provide sufficient milk to the people of the region. About 200 Gorkha Khuttis are still there on the bank of river Dibang but in the Sadiya side. Yet during the recent year, the number of Gorkha Khuttis (cattle sheds) has been constantly decreasing due to the torture accorded by the United Liberation Front of Assam (ULFA) and also due to the policy of the Government of Assam towards Gorkhas. This may be the reason why most of the Gorkhas of Choonpura have abandoned Khuttis in Assam and Arunachal Pradesh and rather engaged in land cultivation. Of course, each household has been found to have one or two cows along with bulls for ploughing the land. The so-called Pathari lands for cow grazing of Gorkhas have been converted into the sites for tribal rehabilitation programmes mostly for the Miris and Deoris. Lot of Deoris and Miris are being settled in such grazing sites of the Gorkhas during the recent years.

To face this crisis, what the Gorkhas are doing today is that they are trying to send out their children outside the Sadiya. Although

Marwaris have shown little inclination to Choonpura, Biharis are penetrating in Bajars like Na-Sadiya, Islampur, Goomtibill and Choonpura. Of course, many Marwaris are found at Chapakhawa—the sub-divisional town of Sadiya. Although Sadiya was once upon a time a big town next to Calcutta, today it is as good as a remote village of North Eastern Frontier of India. There is no difference between Sadiya villages and the Arunachal villages. However, the Gorkhas of Arunachal Pradesh have total uncertainty socio-politically while the Sadiya Gorkhas have restored their paramount position through their overall socio-economic, cultural and educational development. Culturally, lot of Gorkhas and Assamese have interwoven themselves on Mit (friendship) relationship ever since time immemorial. This along with inter-community marriages, the Gorkhas have restored a kind of socio-cultural symbiosis. Every Gorkha speaks Assamese and vice versa (Sharma: 2005; 2012) in the frontier region of Sadiya of North East India.

In fact, as Shakespear (1980) states that "after the occupation of Upper Burma, 1886-1887 and raising of new Burma Military Battalions, those in Assam Rifles began to suffer from numerous desertion to Burma, owing to men in that province receiving better pay as well as to the more attractive conditions of life and service there", mostly the deserted persons were Gorkhas. Along with the Gorkha soldiers of the Assam Rifles, common Gorkhas also went to settle in rural areas of Burma. This indicates the fact that Gorkhas had been settled in Burma (present Myanmar) ever since 1886-1887, If it is so, the Gorkhas were there in North Eastern Frontier including Sadiya frontier—the oidest British garrison and nearby Gorkha villages ever since 1826. Along with the men from Assam Rifles, the common Gorkhas who went to Burma in 1886-1887 had been hailed from the present Changlang and Tirap districts of Arunachal Pradesh (Sharma: 2012). In fact, it was the year 1826 when Sadiya was opened for the Gorkha grazers and cultivators. Here again, Shakespear (1980) states that "Sadiya was opened by the British on conclusion of first war with Burma (1825-1826) and was held by a regiment of the Native Infantry" consisting of mainly the Gorkha soldiers. One of the posts of Sadiya was also established at Choonpura since early 1882. The Gorkhas converted the dense forests into habitable land. This was the reason why Abors, Mismis and also Singpoos used to attack the Gorkha villages in Sadiya. In one of their attacks, Williamson, the commandant of Sadiya had been killed by the Khamptis in 1839.

Thousands of Gorkhas died in 53 different British expeditions in North Eastern Frontiers of India. Talk about the Abor, Mismi hills and Patkaibum hills expeditions, almost all-soldiers and survey teams were consisting of Gorkhas of 2nd Assam Light Infantry of Sadiya. Mainly the soldiers were hailing from Manger, Gurung, Chhetri and Gharti castes of the Gorkha community. Only in later stage of 19th century, the other Gorkha castes like Rai, Limbu, Murmi (Tamang) etc. were enrolled in the Assam Rifles. This has been proved by the account of Shakespear (1980). All the Gurungs, Mangers and Chettris were mainly Hindus and they used to belong to mainly the Indian plains and hills of Darjeeling-Sikkim-Bhutan Himalayas. If it is so, how and why the Gorkhas are called immigrants in North Eastern frontiers of India? Their holistic contributions are therefore yet to be properly rewarded by the Indian Government and Indian communities.

The Sadiya Gorkhas have not at all left the region in spite of all aberrations and disruptions created by the local government and people of Assam. Their commitment to the place indicates as a glaring instance showing the case study as to how the Gorkhas sacrifice everything of their own for the cause of land and economic development of the country. After 1950 earthquake, all other communities left Sadiya except the Gorkhas and Gorkhas only. All the devastated land by earthquake had been reconverted into the fertile agrarian niche in the region. Sadiya once famous for all-round development in the region has been equally made under total convergence to the country by the Gorkhas after the havocs created by the great earthquake. Whatever the description accounted for by Huxford, Shakespear and Hannay about the Gorkha soldiers, the similar description is to be accounted for the agrarian Gorkhas of Sadiya. Unfortunately, this has not been done either by the Gorkha scholars or the Government of Assam so far in the history of Sadiya Gorkhas. This is because of the fact that very little is written about the Gorkhas of North Eastern Frontier both during the British era and independent period. Did other communities face the agonies that were being faced by the Gorkhas of the region? No, never, as every other community left the place (Sadiya) for fear of another natural disaster. But the Gorkhas with all their boldness stayed there, faced the consequences of earthquake and helped the Indian government to expand the province of Assam up to the China border like Walong and further up to the extreme east of North East region of the country. While today the Gorkhas of Mismi hills, Abor hills and Daphla hills along with Sadiya Gorkhas are looked with the spackle of all suspicions, doubts and what not, by following all sorts of eviction techniques against the Gorkhas of the region. This is what I found to be the apparent outcome of tribal development policy of the Government of Arunachal Pradesh. Tribalism and development are found to be the two opposite orientations. It is Gorkhas who can in any geographical niche develop the region putting hard work with blood and sweat and not the indolent nature of the tribes of the region. The tribes simply want to lead leisure life designating themselves as "Maliks" of the tribal land but doing nothing for agrarian development. In fact, in this Sadiya-Lohit region also all the agrarian people belong to the Gorkha community. Even in steep hill like Anini of Abor hills only the Gorkhas have been pursued on dry land agrarian economy. Other communities of the region are simply the service holders and businessmen.

Interestingly, unlike Choonpura, most of the Gorkha castes in Abor hills and Mismi hills are Rai, Limbu, Gurung and Manger along with Tamang who have been well adjusted and adapted to the hill ecology of the tribes. The tribes are carefree, careless and simply pleasure loving human stocks. This may be the reason why even the most developed Khampti tribes of the region (Lohit district) have leased out their land to the Gorkhas. The area like Choonpura, Alloobari and Lohitpur (Tezu) are completely given to the Gorkhas for agrarian economy by the Khamptis. In Lohitpur (Tezu) there are mainly Tamang Busty, Gairi Gaon and Lohitpur (ever since 1912), the Gorkhas are contributing terrace cultivation up to Bismaknagar (Lower Dibang Valley district of Arunachal Pradesh). The Mismis did not know to raise terraces in hills and foothills of Arunachal Pradesh. But interestingly, everywhere we find Visnu Mandirs constructed by the Gorkhas in Sadiya and Mismi hills of Arunachal Pradesh. In spite of frequent disturbances done by Mismis and Abors, still the Gorkhas have Khuttis there. The tribals are found to kill buffaloes and cows of the Gorkhas. They forcefully confiscate their cattle and kill and finally eaten away. Nobody, neither the Government of Arunachal Pradesh nor any tribal organization dares to counter such mischievous acts of the tribals done against the Gorkhas.

On the other hand, what we found in case of the Gorkhas that such acts of the tribals as natural and normal process of living as the Gorkhas still believe that this is legal on the part of the tribals as tribals are considered to be the sole owners of the land. The government has provided land to other outside communities like

Chakmas (Changlang district), Deoris (Lohit district) and Bengalis (Lohit district) but the Gorkhas are branded as immigrants, foreigners and what not, apparently blame for once and ever since the last 200 years in the region. Although the ex-soldiers of Assam Rifles are allowed to stay at Alloobari, Tezu, Lohitpur, Chapakhawa, Santipur etc. of the region, but they have not been issued land deeds in their name. What is the most important point that we noted here with the Gorkhas is that they look for today only and thereby they do not have clear future vision. It is because of this, they have been undergoing loss of ethnic identity. In course of our field-work, we talked to many Gorkhas about their future security. All of them told us that they will go elsewhere on Basai Sarnu process (Sharma: 2012) if they are evicted from the land. By attitude, we found the tribals of the region who want to keep Gorkhas as their slaves only although the Gorkhas are given right to cast votes in elections. This is because of the historical background of the tribals who used to keep slaves under their slavery system in the past. They called Gorkhas as Khuttiwalas only. The Gorkhas once upon a time were Khuttiwalas and still they are considered by people of North East as Khuttiwalas. So, they are having the status of Khuttiwalas. The tribals knowing fully this fact, made the Gorkhas slaves and the Gorkha community as an uprooted community does not have any protector or people having soft corner of their living and for contributing to the regional economy. This is the reason why Gorkha exodus is there to Siliguri and Nepal Terai these days. In fact, now Siliguri of West Bengal and Nepal Terai are the ultimate destinations of the North Eastern Indian Gorkhas.

On the other hand, as mentioned by Sharma (2012), the government is already in duality. The duality is being reflected through the agrarian economy. Who will do agriculture and allied pursuits if all the Gorkhas are escalated from North East India? In reality, the problem is being faced by all the governments of North Eastern states and people thereof. Even if the tribals do not by heart favour the Gorkhas, but due to their necessity, the Gorkhas are given the land as tribals get rent or in some cases Bhaghi (share) from share-cropping (*Ibid.*) land. The Government duality is responsible factor for the uncertainty of the Gorkhas in the region. So, what we intend to suggest from our part is that the government should officially evacuate the Gorkhas or give proper credentials to the Gorkhas as the citizens of North Eastern states. Further, what we do suggest through this academic work is that Gorkhas should dwell with complete assertiveness (Nath: 2007). If the Gorkhas become assertive then other communities like Bengali, Bihari and Marwari communities in the region will also be secured. The tribal tenacity to comfortability leads the government forcefully to allow the Gorkhas in the tribal agrarian soils. The trends appeared to increase further in future days. This may be the stimulus for the Gorkhas to be on the defensive side of their living in North Eastern Frontiers of India. But the habitation of the Gorkhas is always located in far off places of the region in inaccessible villages consisting of forests and thereby the life becomes very tough. Whenever the Gorkhas become worthy to lead modern life, the local tribals or communities cast their jealous eyes and evict the Gorkhas for far flung areas in hills or forests or "Chars" and backward locations (Sharma: 2012) to make a new history in the new region. Except in the Gorkha dominated regions, almost all the Gorkhas having minority status appears to be ready to be evicted from the land that they nurtured, monitored and developed over the years or may be centuries. This is the historical background of the Gorkha eviction from North East India in general and eastern tribal frontiers in particular.

It is found that Sadiya (Choonpura) is the contact zone between Assam and Arunachal Pradesh because the river Balijan of Choonpura is the borderline between Assam and Arunachal Pradesh. Once upon a time Balijan Gaon, now one of the Gaons of Choonpura Gaon Panchayat was on the Arunachal Pradesh till 1954, This may be the reason why operationally there is no difference between Balijan Gaon of Assam and Arunachal Pradesh. Almost all the Lohit, Lower Dibang Valley, Mismi and Abor hills vehicles of Arunachal Pradesh go to Tezu or Roing via Choonpura of Assam. Tinsukia is the main Bajar of eastern frontier of Arunachal Pradesh and Upper Assam. This is the reason why the Gorkhas of Tezu and Choonpura have very close relationship. This social relationship is found even among the Gorkhas of Lohitpur (Arunachal Pradesh) and Sadiya (Choonpura) of Assam. For Arunachalis, Sadiya was the centre of attraction both for friends and foes during the British rule with the Gorkhas. In fact, Arunachal Pradesh during the earlier British rule in the region was unexplored land being mostly inhabited by tribals and Gorkhas. For tribals, the Gorkhas were the first preference than other communities of the country. This is found from the Lord Krishna days in the region. The erection of Visnu Mandir at Bismaknagar was due to the Gorkhas as the Gorkha community had deep conviction for constructing Lord

Visnu Mandir everywhere in North East India. The Gorkhas mostly worship Lord Siva and Lord Visnu in every region of the Himalayas and the same is also found in north-east India. The Gorkhas of Arunachal Pradesh and Assam have either Lord Siva or Lord Visnu temples. This is the area of their socio-cultural continuity in the region (Sharma: 2012). The temples devoting to the worship of Lord Siva or Lord Visnu are the central places where the Gorkhas of the respective area gather together in different festivals and also organize the Gorkha cultural programmes. Thus, it is found in north-east India that every ethnic community has its own temple which in reality represents the ethnic solidarity of the respective community. For example, Biharis have their own temples, Gorkhas have either Visnu temple or Siva temple, Assamese have Namghars and Bengalis have Kali Mandir. For all the communities, temples or Namghars are the centres of excellence to portray their respective socio-religious and cultural symbiosis in the region. Lot of festivals and ceremonies are being organized under the guidance of temple-Namghar committees. The temples are the centre of respect and veneration to all ethnic communities. Even the tribal communities pay due regard and respect to temples and Namghars.

In spite of such socio-economic, cultural and religious symbiosis on the soil of North Eastern Frontiers, there are some fissiparous forces operating today against the Gorkha living in the region. In fact, over the last few decades ever since the Assam Agitation from 1979-1982, the Gorkhas have been dwelling with complete sense of insecurity on their living both in Assam and Arunachal Pradesh along with the other north-eastern states of India.

The Gorkhas are not only found in agrarian belts of Assam and Arunachal Pradesh but it is also observed that lot of Gorkhas have been pursued themselves on dry land cultivation in far off hill dense forests of Arunachal Pradesh where the owners of the land do exclusively belong to tribal communities. It is heard from the reliable source during our field work that the agriculture with hazes, Gaja etc. (drugs) are being produced and supplied internationally by many tribal mafia gangs in Arunachal Pradesh. Nobody can go there in the dense forests to interrupt the mafia gangs from pursuing such drug producing plantations. Mostly, such plantation agriculture is done in the Indo-Myanmar and Indo- China borders. The Government of Arunachal Pradesh knows it very well but it is a helpless child as the mafia tribal owners of drug plantations have upper hand in the regional politics of the Government of Arunachal Pradesh. The Patkaibum Range (India) and Hookoon valley of Myanmar are having full of such drug related plantations. Here in this respect, Verier Elwin (1959) has categorically stated that "talking of opium, which under the tolerant laissez-faire policy of the former regime, gained almost a stranglehold over certain tribes, is another custom in which Government obviously has to interfere. For its curse, lies heavily on the border villages of Arunachal Pradesh, it is an astonishing experience to travel along the Patkoi Range from Raho to Havi and see the fields of poppy surpassing food-crops in the Jhums and the little opium-gardens behind almost every house. Without seeing it, it is not easy to imagine the extent of this cultivation, the energy expended on it and the care with which it is cherished. Opium is almost a form of currency; it may be part of girl's bride-price; it may be used to pay a fine, it is perhaps the most valuable of all tribal products for export or local trade. Some villages, like Wakka, cultivate opium only for sale: its hardy virile men scorn its enervating pleasures; but they grow it on a fairly large scale for their weaker neighbours. It was agreed everywhere that opium-addiction as on the increase; it is now taken in the dormitories, where the young men have no longer to be alert in the new era of peace. Dr. R. N. Chopra, who is our chief authority on opium addiction in India, found among patients examined by him that the habit had been contracted in 50 per cent of the cases by association with other smokers for its euphoric effects, with 33 per cent for relief of pain and sickness and in 17 per cent to overcome worry and nerve strain. Mishmis of the Khamlang valley with whom I discussed the matter, laid chief emphasis on the spread of the habit through imitation: a group would be sitting round the fire, and one or two of the older men would have their pipes. It was only natural that the younger men would have a try, and having tried to be seduced by the pleasurable effect.

I think, however, that the cold and gloom of the climate must play its part, and it is significant that the highest incidence of opium-smoking occurs in those tribal groups whose culture is in the greatest state of decay. Life is dull, hard and the pipe offers all too easy an escape into a land of dreams.

Efforts have already been made, especially in the Singphoo area and in the Boduria (Bordumsa of Changlang district of Arunachal Pradesh) villages to wean the people from the habit on it and some success has been achieved so far. But the time has come to have a determined and comprehensive programme to bring it to an end throughout NEFA.

The fear is sometimes expressed that vigorous action may have political repercussions. There was also the danger of political repercussion when head-hunting was stopped. But, in my opinion, opium addiction is a greater evil even than head-hunting, which did not in practice lead to the loss of many lives (it recorded, for examples, that during sixteen years, in which two villages were in a constant state of war, only four heads were taken). Head-hunting fostered the martial virtues, it maintained a high degree of discipline, it was the inspiration of carving and weaving, the dance and song. But opium is the destruction of all these things. No art can flourish, no virtue or discipline can be maintained and no plan for development will be successful in the areas where this problem remains unsolved. The Noctes, Tangsas, Singpoos and Mishmis addicted to opium are poor, thin, miserable, caught in vicious circle so that the poorer they grow the more they turn to opium for relief, and the more they smoke the poorer they become. The narcotic drugs, says De Ropo, 'do not necessarily destroy life or impair intellect. They do reduce ambition, reduce sexual desire almost to vanishing point, produce a feeling of lethargy and encourage idleness. Above all they enslave, and the slavery they impose is absolute'.

At one time during the British period there was some attempt to solve the problem by wholesale destruction of the poppy-crop. This policy was not successful and it is not being tried today, though in a few places the people have destroyed the poppies of their own accord and planted food-crops instead. In all these matters propaganda is proving far more effective than the giving of orders or the use of force. The tribesmen are responsible people, surprisingly reasonable, and they have a great respect for the Political Officers (NE Frontiers) who hold meetings of the village councils and ask the members themselves to make suggestions, thus leading them to feel that the programme is theirs. The general tribal view is that, while the older men must be permitted to continue their opium smoking, for otherwise the loss of "this disease which cures all diseases" will be intolerable, the younger men should at all costs be saved from it, and that poppy-cultivation should be gradually reduced and its introduction into areas where it is not known such as Dibang Valley, should be prohibited.

The ultimate solution will through a vigorous positive programme to bring prosperity and happiness to the affected villages, so that a new interest may drive out the old.

However, here also at the poppy cultivated areas, the Gorkhas are employed as the daily rated labourers. They are motivated to earn handsome income from the poppy plantation sector and in the process many of them have been normally coming out with huge income and settle in either Assam or other parts of the country or even the Nepal Terai belts.

VIII

Gorkhas in the Lohit Frontier Wilderness

During 2002-2003, the scholar had opportunity to do the academic work with the Gorkha tea plantation workers at Gunnanagar (Chowkham) of Namsai sub-division of Lohit frontier district on the socio-economic life of the Gorkha tea plantation workers. Thus, in the present section of study, I will dwell on the tea plantation workers and also find out the consequences of the industrialization process of the Government of Arunachal Pradesh.

The emergence of tea industry in the state of Arunachal Pradesh of North East India is a saga of Arunachal Pradesh Government process of industrialization of the state in the late eighties of 19th century. For the first time in 1977, Arunachal Pradesh Forest Development Corporation Ltd. was established by the Government of Arunachal Pradesh to streamline the process of industrialization so as to regularize and systematize the then wood cutting process in the state forests. The idea behind that was to continue the then wood based industry of the state more and more scientifically (Bose: 1997). Exploring the plantation potentials of the territory (North East Frontier Agency), the Arunachal Forest Development Corporation Ltd. could successfully venture to open tea plantations in eastern districts (Das:1995) of the state. It started two tea plantations one at Kanubari and another at Medo of Tirap and Lohit districts respectively in the state of Arunachal Pradesh in 1991. Similarly, during the period, two private tea estates emerged, viz., M/s Siang Tea and Industries (P) Ltd. and M/s Namshum Tea Company (P) Ltd. in Changlang and Lohit districts respectively in the state of Arunachal Pradesh. It is observed that the altitude, climatic conditions and topography of the eastern districts of state mainly the East Siang, Upper Dibang Valley, Lower Dibang Valley, Lohit, Changlang and Tirap are very congenial for the introduction and development of tea industry. The introduction of tea industry in these districts of the state was strongly endorsed by various expert committees (Das: 1994) appointed earlier for the purpose. But due to non-acceptance of the proposal of the committees by the Government of Arunachal Pradesh during the eighties of 19th century, tea industry could not be introduced successfully before 1991 in the state. This might be obvious reason why tea plantations under the Arunachal Pradesh Forest Development Corporation Ltd. are presently running at tremendous loss. Although private tea plantations of the state are flourishing day by day, there are number of inherent constraints of their expansion. The main constraint is that the land policy of the state government does not allow outside corporate houses on tea to enter or to make an easy access into this aspect of state sponsored industrialization process. It is because of the fact that most of the land in Arunachal Pradesh is community based or community (*Ibid.*) owned land and these lands cannot be leased out to any outsider (Mukhiml : 2012). Due to this reason, banks have also not shown much interest to remit loans to such community owned landowners of the state for want of mortgages.

It has become an established fact that the Government of Arunachal Pradesh cannot really force the community based lands owners to lease out their land for tea cultivation (*Ibid.*). Secondly, there is an acute problem of labour shortage at the plantations due to the restriction imposed on the import of outside labourers as per the Inner Line Permit policy of Government of India (*Ibid.*). The local tribal people do not prefer to work as tea plantation labour (unskilled, manual jobs) for they are the owners of rich (fertile) cultivable wet land (*Ibid.*) and other natural resources of the region. Due to that, many new projects on tea plantation had been shut down in the state during 2001-2002 A.D.

According to the reports of Consultative Committee of Plantation Associations, Calcutta, there were seventeen tea estates in Arunachal Pradesh in 1996 having 11,559 hectares of land under tea area. About 325 thousand kilograms of tea had been produced by those seventeen tea estates in the state during the period. The average daily employment of labourers as per the Muster Roll was 1,329 and another 450 labourers were employed on casual basis during the peak plucking season. It has been mentioned in the reports of CCPA that though a small tea estate of twenty hectares was established in 1981, its real expansion could take place in the state only after 1987. There were sufficient amount of land available from Jhum (slash and burn) areas of about 70,000 hectares as per the report of North East Council. The Consultative Committee of Plantation Associations, Calcutta (1996) has also categorically projected that by the year 2006 A.D. there will be an additional 6,325 hectares of land under tea with 9,225 kilograms of tea having 1,459 kilograms yield per hectare. The Tea Board of India has also projected that there will be an additional 13,932 kilograms of tea with another 8,225 hectares of land under the tea bushes having 1,694 kilograms yield per hectare by the year, 2006 A.D.

After 1995, a large number of local tribal entrepreneurs entered into tea plantation industry as an alternative to wood based industry due to the prohibition for deforestation imposed by the Government of Arunachal Pradesh. But unlike other manufacturing or processing units, the plantation sector requires large number of stable labour force within the territory. In view of her sparse population (*Ibid.*) of tribal origins and their utter reluctance to join the private sector industries during the nineties of 19th century, the Arunachal Pradesh Government started widely to accommodate a huge labour force from outside required for the development (*Ibid.*) of tea plantations in the region. Because of this step being taken by the government, the number of tea estate has reached to more than twenty today with three thousand workers and another one thousand casuals in the plantations of Arunachal Pradesh. Almost 42,000 workers are working in medium and small scale industries (Bose: 1997) of the state.

The North Eastern Enclaves

As stated above, the tea plantations of Arunchal Pradesh are located at her eastern most districts. It has been proved over the last two decades that the eastern districts of the state appeared to have been increasingly the safety enclaves for the government on the ground that the location of tea plantations is either at the Myanmar (Burma) border or near the Chinese (Mac Mohan Line) mainland. The introduction of tea industry here has a historical relevance (*Ibid.*). Excepting two tea plantations under the Arunachal Pradesh Forest Development Corporation Ltd., all the eighteen tea estates located at the eastern most districts are under the ownership of local tribal elites to support the tribal based development policy (Das:1995) of the state government. For example, Mr. Chowkhamoon Gohain, ex-Member of Indian Parliament from Khamti tribe of Lohit district, Mrs. Yapang of East Siyang, Mrs. W.A. Rajkumar, the speaker of Legislative Assembly of Arunachal Pradesh state from Khonsa (Tirap District), Mr.Gore Pertin, Member of Legislative Assembly from Upper Dibang Valley district, Mr. Aken Lege of Roing (Lower Dibang Valley district) etc. have owned tea plantations in the eastern enclaves of the Arunachal state of North East India. Thus, elites associated with politics and administration have entered accurately into tea plantations (Mishra: 1994) of the state of Arunachal Pradesh.

Except the two tea estates, one each in Upper Dibang Valley and another in East Siyang districts, all the eighteen tea estates are located at Lohit, Changlang and Tirap districts of the state. There are certain pertinent historical antecedents as mentioned above for such enclave formation. These locations are either at the foothills of Arunachal Pradesh or at the Myanmar border being fully encircled by dense forests. Till 1995, all tea leaves so plucked at the Arunachal plantations had to be sent to the Assam factories for manufacturing. But due to the increasing sense of regionalism and communal terrorism in the Assamese plantations, separate factories had to start in Arunachal plantations only after 1995. In this venture, they got sufficient loans from Tea Board of India with handsome subsidy being provided to the tribal tea garden owners of the tribal state of North East India. Take for instance, in 1996, Tea Board of India provided Rs. 292.90 lakhs as loans and Rs. 160.10 lakhs as subsidy to the tribal tea plantation owners of Arunachal Pradesh.

This development process helped the tribal planters to make respective areas as complete enclaves as the British planters used to convert the plantations into their Plantocracy (Devi: 1989) or Planters' Raj (Guha: 1977) or Sahib-Coolie Raj (Sharma: 2003) in Assam and West Bengal. The onslaught of Liberalization, Privatization and Globalization policy of Indian Government for Indian industries in general (Ratnam: 2001) and tea plantation industry in particular (Bhowmik: 1996) after 1991, has further encouraged the tribal tea planters (owners) to convert the plantations into their absolute sovereignty. For example, Mr. Chowkhamoon Gohain of Chowkham, the owner of Gunna Tea Industries (P) Ltd. has named the area as Gunnanagar after the name of his late son 'Gunna'. Secondly, such enclave formation process appears to have been officially approved by the Government of Arunachal Pradesh due to two most primordial reasons, viz., to keep strategically strong base or strategical safety of the eastern most enchanted frontiers of the state and also to get good revenue by the government as the cost of production of tea is very low of Rs. 20 only per kilogram of made tea while the Arunachal tea fetches Rs. 70 to Rs.80 per kilogram of made tea in national and international markets due to its high quality of tea leaves being plucked from the young tea bushes of hardly fifteen years old. Except the wage of Rs. 35 per day per worker, no other extra welfare benefits or incentives are given to the workers. This is possible for the tribal planters as all the workers are either Gorkhas from Nepal Himalayas or Adivasis from the Assamese plain tea plantations. The Adivasis had been migrated here in the Arunachal tea plantations as they were reported to have been covertly involved in anti-social activities or terrorism of course under the banner of United Liberation Front of Assam (ULFA) in the plantations. Though these Adivasis are scheduled tribes in West Bengal tea plantations, here in North East Indian tea plantations they as "Tea Tribes" are treated as non-tribals along with the Gorkha workers. Thus, Tribal-Non- Tribal polarization of the society has been sensed quite sufficiently in the plantations of Arunachal Pradesh. The enclaves have been persisting safely as the local tribal planters have so far received solid support from their own tribes on the one hand and state political elites of the government on the other. Such eventuality has been further enunciated well by the fact that non-tribal tea plantation workers have very weak social foundation as they were recent migrants from Nepal, Assam and other parts of the country. Historically, they were brought there with temporary Inner Line Permits the period of which has in most cases already lapsed. Most of them do not go for renewal of their Inner Line Permits anticipating legal complicacies (Das: 1995). This fact is well known to all the tribal planters and local tribal population as well. As a result of this, their stay at the plantations is inherently considered to be totally illegal. Due to this reason, non-tribal tea plantation workers do not have courage enough to raise their voice against the exploitation of the tribal-planter-owners. Because of this weakness, they are easily succumbed to any threat or coercion (*Ibid.*). This is the actual reason why the local tribal people do not want to join tea plantation jobs especially at the unskilled category. Therefore, it is presumed that such enclaves would not have been emerged if the local tribal people of the region would have joined the plantation jobs. It is also conjectured that among the Gorkha workers, there is no upper caste Hindus such as Brahmins or priestly doubled born castes in the Anula Shagun T.E. as an integral part of the unskilled working force. In Gorkha society, Brahmins or Bahuns are very talented castes among others both in Nepal and the Eastern Himalayas (Sharma: 2000). It is not that the skilled industrial workers migrated to tea plantations of Arunachal Pradesh because of low wages, the story supplements that unskilled non-tribal reserve army have migrated to the plantations in search of their livelihood.

The unskilled labour forces are mostly illiterates or semi-literates and therefore, they do not know the terms and conditions of work or services. This has further enabled the tea planters to convert the Arunachal frontiers into strong enclaves.

Problem of the Study

This is a sociological study on Gorkha tea plantation workers in Arunachal Pradesh of North East India. For the sake of analytical convenience, the Anula Shagun T.E. of Lohit district of Arunachal Pradesh has been selected for the study. There are 150 households of Gorkha community of 300 workers. Besides, there are another 100 Adivasi workers in the plantation. Therefore, the study of Gorkha tea plantation workers in Arunachal Pradesh invites an interesting Sociological proposition. They are working under a tribal planter-owner from the Khamti tribe. The Khamti owner was once a Member of Parliament from Namsai area of Lohit district of Arunachal Pradesh. So far, hardly any study has been conducted on tea plantation workers of Arunachal Pradesh. The tribal planter as the owner of Anula Shagun T.E. along with other two tea estates in Tirap and Changlang districts belongs to the elite group of the state who does not allow any outsider to penetrate into his gardens. The migration of Gorkha tea plantation workers at Anula Shagun T.E. has portrayed the fact that the industrialization process has evolved in the eastern most enchanted frontiers of the state. The Anula Shagun T.E. is a garden of a Khamti family. The pull factors behind the migration of Gorkha as tea plantation workers were due to manifold reasons as delineated below:

Firstly, the Gorkhas can have their permanent settlement in the plantation environment which is perfectly an agro-based industry. Unlike other industries, tea industry possesses both the agricultural and industrial characters (Xaxa: 1997) in real sense of the term.

Secondly, the agrarian environment of tea plantation enabled the agrarian Gorkhas of the Nepal Himalayas having landless occupational category of the past, to adapt the industrial environment of Anula Shagun T.E. of Arunachal Pradesh quite easily (Sharma: 2000).

Thirdly, the Gorkhas by tradition, not only cultivate land for crops of variety but they are also the staunch practitioners of animal husbandry and floriculture. The plantation industry provides them with ample opportunity for animal husbandry, horticulture and agriculture.

Fourthly, in spite of having tribal-non-tribal differences in Arunachal Pradesh, the Gorkhas, due to their perseverance to work, could help to pay good revenue to the Government of Arunachal Pradesh because the jhum (shifting—slash and burn) cultivation of tribals, as the major constraint for development process of the state, could not at all provide such handsome revenue to the government.

Fifthly, basically the Gorkhas have deep resemblances in respect of their physical appearance (Parmer: 1990) and way of living with rest of the Arunachal tribes. For instance, the Khamtis of Namsai sub-division of Arunachal Pradesh have some physical appearance as of the Gorkhas. This might be one of the apparent reasons why most of the Khamti agrarian elites of Chowkham block where Anula Shagun T.E. is located, have given their land on share cropping to the Gorkhas (Dubey:1975). This has given prior stimulus for complete comprehension and integration of the Gorkhas into the tribal way of life in the region.

However, in spite of above mentioned area of integration of Gorkhas with the Khamti tribes of the region, the Gorkhas have retained their distinct ethnic identity (Subba: 1990) in respect of language, marriage and culture by internalizing some of the cultural traits of dominant Khamti tribe of the region. This has become possible for the Gorkhas as traditionally they were mainly tribes or sub-tribes in Nepal Himalayas (Sharma: 2003). The most glaring instance of their cultural integration as encouraged by the Government of Arunachal Pradesh or the Government of India in Arunachal Pradesh (Das: 1995) is language. The wide spoken Assamese language of the region has been totally internalized in day to day life by the Gorkhas. Besides the Assamese language, the tribal language/dialects are also fluently spoken by the Gorkhas in Arunachal Pradesh in general and the garden universe in particular. This is the main reason why Arunachal tribes prefer Gorkhas than Hindustanis in the plantation. This has been proved over the centuries that though Gorkhas have curse to be called migrants, their ingenuity and agrarian versatility have been positively ascertained by the Government of Arunachal Pradesh in general and people thereof. The sincere endeavours of Gorkhas have been profusely applauded by the tribes of North East India including Arunachal Pradesh. This caliber as cultivated by the Gorkhas has contributed a lot to the state economy (Sarkar and Lama: 1986) of Arunachal Pradesh. The government efforts to convert jhum cultivation into the settled ones have been amply supported by the culture of terrace cultivation as it used to be done extensively by the Gorkhas in the Himalayas. Therefore, Gorkhas proved themselves to be the protagonists of wet rice cultivation in Arunachal Pradesh also (Sharma: 2000). Even the rough terraces for tea cultivation appeared to have been made following the Gorkha instances of agrarian terracing in the Himalayan or sub-Himalayan regions of Arunachal Pradesh. The perseverance to work has designated the Gorkhas as 'Khati Khane Manchees/Jati' meaning thereby the community that survives by hard work and hard work alone. The same thing happened in case of the Anula Shagun T.E. also where Mr. Chowkhamoon Gohain, the Khamti owner of the plantation had to accept the Gorkhas as plantation workers for his own tribesmen did not accept the plantation jobs for the two simple most reasons, viz., most of the Khamti tribes were the owners of wet rice land (Pather) and jhum land at that time at Chowkham and secondly, the Khamtis are basically commercial minded tribe today among the other tribes (*Ibid.*) of Arunachal Pradesh. They always endeavour to have some sorts of trade and business in the region (Bose: 1997).

From the above discussion, it is very transparent that although the Gorkhas have been fully integrated into the plantation environment, they very often feel unsafe of their living in the plantation due to the increasing communal terrorism in North Eastern Frontiers of the country. This has enforced them to be in close touch or contact with Nepal (Sharma: 2012) or their places of origin as the Khamtis being the sons of the tribal soil of Arunachal Pradesh may also one day ask them to evacuate their land at Chowkham.

Heterogeneity, low wages, coercion and isolation were the characteristic features of the plantation system (Bhowmik: 1981).

Historically, such heterogeneity was completely sustained by the isolated enclaves all-over the plantation world. The same characteristic features have also been noted at the Anula Shagun T.E. today. Though there are Adivasi workers in the plantation, the Gorkha workers have been kept in a separate labour line known as Gorkha Labour Dhura. This has generated a kind of interesting sociological proposition in so far as their socio-economic relationship is concerned.

Most scholars while defining plantation system do normally overlook the socio-economic conditions of the workers. They have either elucidated the production relations or described the production unit itself (Sharma: 1994).

The International Labour Organization (1950) notes the term 'plantation' at first as a group of settlers or the political units formed by it under the British colonialism especially in North America and West Indies (ILO: 1950). Prof. Hla Myint (1973) has distinguished the plantation from peasant agriculture by its large scale enterprise which normally requires more labour per unit of land. Again, William O. Jones (1968) defines the plantation as an economic unit of land producing relatively large number of unskilled labourers whose activities are to be closely supervised. Therefore, defining plantation and conceptualizing relationship as a whole, mere elucidation of the economic characters and economic benefits of the owners of the industry is not at all adequate. The social relationship at the interpersonal and intercommunity levels are also to be taken into due consideration (Sharma: 2000) with thorough caution (Sharma: 1997).

From the above discussion, certain pertinent questions may be administered here as to whether there is really a point of difference between tribal and non-tribal groups at the Anula Shagun T.E.? How the Gorkhas have retained their distinct socio-economic-cum-cultural existence with the local Khamti tribes including the owner of the plantation? Responding these questions, it is very much comprehended that the Gorkhas are not only the protagonists of terraced cultivation but also the exponents of industrial development (Sharma: 2003) suitable to the Arunachal ecology.

The Gorkha tea plantation workers of the Anula Shagun T.E. have no high caste background. Most of them belong to Matwali group of Gorkha society of Nepal. Historically, the Gorkha Matwalis were toiling mass of Nepal Himalayas (Pradhan: 1991). They were very much prone to the Tribalization (Matwalization) process both in Nepal and Eastern Himalayas (Sharma: 1997). Whether such proneness to the Tribalization or Matwalization process has helped themselves to adapt well with the local tribal (Khamti) industrial environment of Anula Shagun T.E.? This is another aspect of the study. The interactions between the Hinayana Buddhist Khamti tribes and Hindu Gorkha castes in regard to their day to day economic activities have shaped to the tune of industrial environment in a loose form of the term having specified organizational hierarchy with specific goals of the organization in the plantation. The management hierarchy is completely dominated by the Khamti tribe as even ninety-nine per cent of supervisory and office staffs are Khamtis by ethnicity. It has been observed that except wages and house building materials for constructing labour huts, no other industrial incentives or facilities are given to the workers. This might be the obvious reason why the Gorkha workers always remain busy with non-plantation and animal husbandry jobs. This has been amply conceptualized by the fact that the Gorkhas are very popular for cow milk supplying job not only in Assam but also in Arunachal Pradesh. The major towns of Assam like Guwahati, Tezpur, Lakhimpur, Tinsukia, Jorhat, Dibrugargh etc. and Teju, Itanagar, Bomdila, Namsai etc. of Arunachal Pradesh get cow milk from the Gorkha populace. It is also overtly observed that of 300 Gorkha workers of the Anula Shagun T.E., 280 of them have animal husbandry along with agriculture in neighbouring Khamti villages of Chowkham.

Although the Anula Shagun T.E. is an agro-based industry formed after the abandonment of Namshum Saw and Veneer Mills (P) Ltd., the workers feel that they do not by and large bother about its future as they have deep confidence on Mr. Chowkhamoon Gohain, the owner of the plantation, as god father of the area, who will definitely save them in bad days as he did the same in case of the closure of Namshum Saw and Veneer Mills (P) Ltd. at Gunnanagar (Chowkham) in 1987.

In this way, they are unorganized workers as no labour legislation of Government of India has been implemented at the garden so far of its fifteen years of establishment. The workers do not have earned any consciousness for the formation of trade unions in the plantation. It means that whatever the owner of the plantation provides them they have to accept it forcefully. This shows that the workers are in the colonial system of production relations. A kind of industrial autocracy has taken place between the workers and management hailing from the family of Mr. Gohain. In this way, the plantation workers of Anula Shagun T.E. have been hardly come across the concept of trade union movement and working class solidarity. The industrial relation between the workers and management is the relation of Master-Servant in nexus (Bhowmik: 1996). The workers being migrants have been made scared of ousting from the plantation by the management in spite of their boarding at the plantation for more than fifteen years or so of its existence. This is the reason why they always remain silent of their exploitation by the management system which is autocratic in form as Chief Managing Director, Directors etc. of the plantation belong to the same Khamti family. Even most of the supervisory and office staffs of the plantation hail from the Khamti tribe of the region. In this way, management hierarchy of the plantation is ethnically organized.

Another reason for the complete sustenance of such technique of taming the Coolies in the colonial fashion is due to the fact that the state government is guided by a Khamti Member of Legislative Assembly of Arunachal Pradesh from the Namsai constituency.

It is therefore transparent from the above description that the tribal ownership of tea industry being fully patronized by the Government of Arunachal Pradesh is as good as a British colonial enclave in the state to encourage to flourish the community based industrial development (Das: 1995) process and local's participation in the process. All the contracts regarding the supply of necessary goods and articles for the plantation are given to the local Khamti youngsters. Thus, coercion of the workers as exercised by the management (Bhowmik: 1995) is widely supported by the Khamti population of the region. Historically, the Khamtis had been migrated from Upper Burma (Myanmar) to Sadiya of Assam and later on from Sadiya to Chowkham area of the Arunachal foothills; after residing for over fifty years at Choonpura of Sadiya (Gautam: 1985; Gogoi: 1971). Thus, Chowkham is the den of Khamtis due to the existing dense forests and fertile wet rice field since the British days (Bose: 1997) so as to lease out their land for share cropping to the Gorkhas of Nepal Himalayas.

Operationalisation of the Concept of Study

There is hardly any study ever done on the tea plantation workers of Arunachal Pradesh except a few stray reports that are available at the Directorate of Commerce and Industries, Government of

Arunachal Pradesh. Therefore, there is an absolute dearth of published materials on tea industry of the state. Hence, the Anula Shagun T.E is also not an exception in this regard. Reports of the Directorate of Commerce and Industries, Government of Arunachal Pradesh reveal some ideas about the production figure, target, marketing situation etc. Not a single report of the Directorate of Commerce and Industries of Government of Arunachal Pradesh has categorically stated anything about the socio-economic conditions of work force of tea plantations of the state. The reports available with Tea Board of India revealed information about the quantum of subsidy provided to the tribal tea plantation owners along with the total loans sanctioned for extension and expansion of tea industry in the state. This may be accurate reason why Mr. Gohain of Anula Shagun T.E. had only thirty hectares of land under tea in the year, 2000 A.D. but during my survey period (2002-2004), land area had been expanded to the tune of 219 hectares under tea bushes with three lakh and fifty thousand kilograms of made tea per year. Being the sole landowner of most of the villages of Gunnanagar (Chowkham), it is known that he is going to expand the plantation land under tea bushes to the tune of 700 hectares by the year, 2006 A.D. While the tea plantations under the Arunachal Pradesh Forest Development Corporation Ltd. (two in number) are in very deplorable condition due to non-availability of land for expansion as the neighbouring tribal and forest lands cannot be brought under tea cultivation. Moreover, the cost of production is very high of Rs. 70 per kilogram of made tea while it is as mentioned above even less than Rs. 20 per kilogram of made tea in private sector tea plantations because the workers are devoid of any industrial incentives except the wage and house building materials. Above all, age of tea bushes is very young of hardly fifteen years old and the labour productivity is very high of 250 kilograms of made tea per worker per year.

The theoretical approach adopted in the study is Social Anthropological ones as the society of Anula Shagun T.E. is neither purely Hindu caste oriented nor perfectly a tribal in nature. In fact, it is a Hindu-Buddhist integrated zone of Arunachal Pradesh.

Historically, the area was directly under the Assamese influence since the days of Ahom Kings (Dutta Choudhury: 1978; Bose: 1997). The Assamese society is predominantly a Hindu one. The three major communities of Anula Shagun T.E. viz. Khamti, Gorkha and Adivasi have common industrial habitation with separate labour lines for the workers and independent land holdings for the Khamtis. A kind of social stratification has been emerged between the tribals and non-tribals here. Former claimed themselves as 'sons of the soil' of Arunachal Pradesh while later is considered as 'migrants' or unskilled enchanted Coolies from outside the Arunachal Pradesh.

Under the situation as stated above, it is wholly agreed by all Gorkha castes that industrialization process of Anula Shagun T.E. is an extra stimulus for their living. For them, agriculture minus industry is not a misnomer while industry minus agriculture is completely myth (Sharma: 2003) for their living here. This is the inherent reason why they have been attached to the industry with all commitments in spite of their complete exploitation by the management system.

The present study focuses not only on the socio-economic life of tea plantation workers but also on health dimension, nature of Hindu-Buddhist relationship, changing social structure of Gorkha society, family, marriage, education, religious structure, caste-tribe diffusion and integration processes etc. in various chapters of the study. In regard to the economic life of the workers, landholding pattern, animal husbandry, occupational structure, migration pattern, place of birth of the workers, income, borrowing etc. have been analyzed thoroughly. The migration history of Khamtis has also been incorporated in the present study.

Methodology of the Study

For the first time, I visited the Anula Shagun T.E. in June, 2002 to acquaint myself with the workers, management and other important personnel of the plantation. Being a Gorkha by ethnicity, I was thoroughly accepted by the Gorkha tea plantation workers of the plantation. At first, Mr. Chowkhamoon Gohain, the Chief Managing Director of the Gunna Tea Industries (P) Ltd. was found to be little bit indifferent to me when I explained the cardinal objectives of my research project. But later on during my survey (field-work) period (November, 2002 to October, 2003) he was convinced to such a extent that he not only supported me morally but also provided me with the literature that was available with him about the emergence and growth of tea industry in Arunachal Pradesh. Besides this, the Government Gaon Bura of Gunnanagar Gram Panchayat, a few old Khamti village chiefs and other influential people were also interviewed thoroughly on the historicity of the plantation and recruitment of workers in the plantation.

The Anula Shagun T.E. represents the emergence of tea industry in Arunachal Pradesh as a whole on the logic that it is located at the eastern most frontier of not only Arunachal Pradesh but also of the country adjoining Myanmar. In fact, the Lohit district where the Anula Shagun T.E. is located is one of the frontier districts of Arunachal Pradesh. Secondly, the plantation has accommodated 300 Gorkha and 100 Adivasi workers. No other tea plantations of the state have employed such a large percentage of Gorkhas as manual (unskilled) workers. All 150 households of the Gorkha community with 300 workers were covered under the study. The present study does not exclusively rely on theoretical sophistications but on the empirical data collected from the Anula Shagun T.E. of Arunachal Pradesh during 2002 to 2003.

Methods of Data Collection

Considering the problem of the study, following sample questionnaire had been prepared. The first section deals with household census:

1. Name of the Respondent
2. Relation with the head of the family
3. Age structure of the family members
4. Sex structure of the family members
5. Place of birth of the family members
6. Educational standards of the family members
7. Religious structure of the family
8. Occupational structure of the family
9. Landholding pattern of the family
10. Cattle stocks of the family
11. Modern equipments of the family
12. Wage structure of the workers
13. Number of working persons in the family
14. The name of the festivals observed in the family
15. The name of festivals/rituals attended in other households
16. Name of languages known to the workers.

The above questionnaire were administered for the pilot study to frame the following semi-structured questionnaire for conducting field survey at the Anula Shagun T.E. on socio-economic as well as cultural aspects of the workers:

1. Why did you migrate to Anula Shagun T.E.?
2. Who brought you to the plantation?
3. Where did you work before joining the Anula Shagun T.E.?
4. What did you do in your place of origin?
5. How much wage that you get in the plantation?
6. What are the other incentives you get from the plantation?
7. How many hours you work in a day at the plantation?
8. What are the main duties during the twelve months in a year?
9. How your management recruits workers in the plantation?
10. What type of industrial relation is there in your plantation between the workers and management?
11. Is there any social organization in the plantation?
12. Which community is most dominant in the plantation?
13. Whether the Gunnanagar Gram Panchayat has any role in the plantation?
14. What is the relationship between the Gorkhas and Khamtis at the plantation?
15. What kinds of marriages have taken place in your family?
16. Number of marriages within the castes and communities
17. Number of marriages with other castes and communities
18. Do you accept Pucca foods from other communities?
19. Do you accept Kuccha foods from other communities?
20. Do your management personnel attend marriage and death rituals in your house if they are called for?
21. Do you sacrifice animals' blood in your household rituals?
22. What are the common festivals in your plantation?
23. Do you invite other communities in celebrating your family festivals?
24. What are the major food items that you use in celebrating festivals and rituals?
25. Do you offer wine and meat to a Brahmin (Bahun)?
26. Do you accept inter-community marriages?
27. Do you think that there are inter-ethnic conflicts between tribals and non-tribals in the plantation?
28. Do you celebrate communal festivals? If yes, why? If no, why?
29. Do you invite Shaman (Jhankris) in celebrating festivals or rituals?

30. Where do you go first if any member of your family falls sick? to a Jhankri or to a Doctor, Why? If to a Jhankri, Why?
31. Does one community helps others in time of emergency? If yes, how? If no, Why?
32. Do you think that there should be a trade union or workers organization in the plantation?
33. Is there any Bhatti (liquor furnace) at the plantation?
34. Do tribal neighbours invite you in their festivals? If yes, how? If no, why?
35. Do you cast votes? If yes since when? If no, Why?
36. Whether you share crops with the tribal owner? If yes, how much per year?
37. Do you pay land tax? If yes, to whom—landowners or the Government of Aruanchal Pradesh?
38. Do you have to pay anything for keeping cattle stocks? If yes, to whom?
39. Whether you visit your place of origin once in a year/two or so? If no, Why? If yes, Why?
40. Whether there was any communal riot here between tribes and non-tribes in the past years?
41. Whether you face threats from the terrorist organizations?
42. How the government officers treat you?
43. Whether you can avail forest resources as enjoyed by the tribals of the region?
44. Do you left the plantation if your owner of the plantation asks you to leave any time? If yes, why? If No, why?
45. What are the divisions of roles among the family members?
46. How many new babies were born in your family during the last ten years?
47. How many members died in your family during the last ten years?
48. Do you have heard anything about family planning? If yes, have any member of your family undergone vasectomy or tubectomy operations?
49. Do you believe on "Small Family Norms"? If Yes, Why? If no, Why?
50. Whether the local Khamti tribes (Buddhists) try to convert Gorkhas or other communities into the Buddhist religion?

IX

The Anula Shagun T.E.

The Anula Shagun T.E. is located at Chowkham block of Namsai sub-division of Lohit district of Arunachal Pradesh. It is situated near the Indo-Myanmar border. The actual area where the plantation is located is locally known as Gunnanagar. The Gunnanagar is named after the name of late son "Gunna" of Mr. Chowkhamoon Gohain, the Khampti owner of the Anula Shagun T.E. In fact, the real name of tea industry is known as "Gunna Tea Industries (P) Ltd."

The Anula Shagun T.E. is named after the name of grand daughter of Mr. Gohain who was a Member of Parliament from Arunachal Pradesh at the time of Jawaharlal Nehru, the first Prime Minister of independent India. Then, the Arunachal Pradesh was known as North East Frontier Agency (NEFA) under the administration of the Government of Assam (Bose: 1997) from Shillong. The Anula Shagun T.E. was established in 1987. Prior to 1987, there was a wood based industry of Mr. Gohain in Gunnanagar where about five hundred workers of mainly Assamese origin used to work as wage labourers. It was known as Namshum Saw and Veneer Mills (P) Ltd., Gunnanagar (Chowkham) of Arunachal Pradesh.

Following the example set forth by Mr. Gohain, another saw mill was also established by a Marwari from Tinsukia (Assam) at Gunnanagar of Chowkham. It is still there in Gunnanagar. Before 1987, Mr. Gohain had a tea estate known as Lallung T.E. in Bordumsa (Changlang district) where tea leaves of the Anula Shagun T.E. used to be sent for manufacturing etc. Considering the cost effectiveness of production, a separate factory had been established at the Anula Shagun T.E. only in 1999. Under the prohibition of the Government of Arunachal Pradesh for deforestation, the Namshum Saw and Veneer Mills (P) Ltd. had to be completely abandoned by 1987 at Gunnanagar.

To begin with, there were only thirty hectares of land under tea in the Anula Shagun T.E. till 1996 (CCPA). With the increasing popularity of Arunachal tea in the national and international market, the area under tea had to be expanded very fastly since 1995 and today there are 219 hectares of land under tea in the Anula Shagun T.E. On the east of the Anula Shagun T.E., there is river Dehing, on the west, there is Chowkham town, on the north, there is a Chakma village and on the south, there are Gunnanagar Bajar and Stakilu village.

The Labour: An Inherent Constraint

One of the major objectives behind the introduction of tea industry at Gunnanagar was to industrialize the local Khamti tribes and then to discontinue the then prevalent Jhum (slash and burn shifting) cultivation in the area under the industrial policy of the Government of Arunachal Pradesh (Das: 1995). Being one of the prominent political elites of the area, Mr. Gohain introduced the tea plantation. The tea plantation is unlike other sophisticated industries involving high level of technology (Bhowmik: 1981), an agro-based industry which is also a society of permanent nature (Bhowmik: 1996) employing a large number of resident manual labourers.

Opening the plantation, Mr. Gohain apparently thought that he would be easily procured his Khamti neighbours as labours at his plantation. But as Eric Wolf (1959) stated that the introduction of an industry would 'destroy the local culture', the Khamtis also felt that their culture of Jhum cultivation that designated the cultural tradition of their society was going to extinct. That caused a type of terrible commotion in the minds of Khamtis and thus they became all of a sudden deeply antagonized. That resulted into their denial for joining the plantation jobs. Again, they did not vote in favour of Mr. Gohain in 1988 election for his membership to the Indian Parliament. In this way, not a single Khamti including their previous slaves (Bose: 1997) joined the plantation manual or unskilled jobs. That problem was immediately raised in the state Legislative Assembly session that decided to allow the outside labours for the planters by issuing the workers with temporary Inner Line Permits (*Ibid.*). However, it was stated in the resolution taken in the Legislative Assembly session that the owners of the plantations had to soldier the responsibility of renewal of Inner Line Permits of the workers before the expiry of renewal dates. But subsequently, the planters did no venture to renew the Inner Line Permits of the workers. Instead, they enrolled the names of workers in the voter list schedule of Chowkham constituency. That could help the planters in two ways, viz., the procurement of cheap labour force and victory in elections. This might be the apparent reason why Mr. Kung Inju (son of Mr. Gohain) of the Anula Shagun T.E. won elections for two consecutive periods (1987-1991 and 1992 to 1997) as a Member of Parliament from Arunachal Pradesh. Even the daughter-in-law of Mr. Gohain also won election in 1998 as a Member of Legislative Assembly of Arunachal Pradesh.

After 1999, the policy of industrialization of Union Government through her integration rather than assimilation (Das: 1995) process as introduced by the British administration in Arunachal Pradesh, helped the tribal planters to import as many labourers as possible because the very efficacy of Inner Line Permit became less effective (*Ibid.*) in the state except in some places of national importance.

Following the integration process of Government of India, Mr. P.K. Thungon, the then Chief Minister of Arunachal Pradesh once stated, 'The policy of the government has been to encourage evolution into the modern world of traditional structure of every society of Arunachal Pradesh where aspects of the traditional structure are inconsistent with the modern needs or national policy, the aim is to reform them within and avoid any sudden or drastic abolition without adequate replacements (of emotional aptitudes relating to tribal culture: Government of Arunachal Pradesh: 1987). It also gave rise to the end of slavery system in the state' (Bose: 1997).

Considering the above contention and to appease the local Khampti educated unemployed youths, the owner of Anula Shagun T.E. appointed a few Khamti supervisory and office staffs at the plantation. However, to meet the labour shortage as an inherent problem of the plantation, Mr. Gohain, the Khamti owner, asked a few Rai, Mangar and Chettri workers who were under him since the establishment of Namshum Saw and Veneer Mills (P) Ltd. to bring workers for the plantation and therefore he appointed them as labour recruiters to entice respective caste/tribal members from Assam or Nepal or elsewhere the country for which the labour recruiters were promised to give some awards in the form of cash or kind during the Dashera (Dasai in Gorkha language) festival. Accordingly, a Rai labour recruiter went to Upper Assam and enticed as well as recruited ten workers from Lakhimpur of Assam. Similarly, the Mangar labour recruiter enticed and recruited 70 labourers from

Nepal from his own caste group. In the same way, a Chhetri labour recruiter enticed and recruited five workers from Upper Assam and 45 labourers from Nepal Himalayas. Again, a Rai labour recruiter enticed and recruited 42 labourers from Eastern Nepal. They could mostly entice and recruit their own caste members from their native villages. Thus, the caste affiliation of labour recruiters helped to entice the labourers otherwise the then Government of Nepal had imposed restriction on such labour recruitment from Nepal to Indian industries. The other Gorkha castes and tribes joined the plantation jobs following the Chhetri, Rai and Mangar workers who were close neighbours to them in Nepal or Upper Assam. Interestingly, it is also observed that most of the Gorkha migrant labourers belong to Western Nepal. The Gorkhas migrated to the plantation from Upper Assam were ousted selectively by the United Liberation Front of Assam (ULFA) mainly from Lakhimpur, Sadiya, Dibrugargh, Sibsagar and Tinsukia districts. All the Adivasi workers of the plantation were migrated prior to 1990 due to their involvement, of course, forcefully by the United Liberation Front of Assam (ULFA), in anti-social activities or terrorism in the Assamese tea plantations. They reported that now they are free from any terrorist threat. This is sufficiently supplemented by the fact that Arunachal Pradesh is free from terrorism except at Changlang and Tirap districts, both from within and outside the state. Secondly, the local Khamtis are the ardent believers of "Ahinsa Paramo Dharma" or non-violence is considered to be the greatest religious ethos in Buddhist philosophy of life. All the Khamtis are the believers of Hinayana sect of Buddhist religion (Bose: 1997).

The above discussion makes it very clear that in spite of complete exploitation by the management system, the workers of the Anula Shagun T.E. are silent as they normally feel that Mr. Gohain (owner) is their god father. In this way, Mr. Gohain appears to be the don of the plantation. One, Mr. Nagen Baruah (the senior most man of the plantation as vehicle driver) informed me that he has told Mr. Gohain that he will serve the plantation till Mr. Gohain is alive. Mr. Baruah as a vehicle driver has been working under Mr. Gohain since 1967 when the Namshum Saw and Veneer Mills (P) Ltd. had been established at the Namshum Gaon (present Gunnanagar).

After enticing and recruiting the workers from Upper Assam and Nepal Himalayas, all three hundred Gorkha workers staying in 150 households were kept at the Gorkha Labour Line or Gorkha

Labour Dhura near the present factory premises. But it is observed that all the Adivasi households are located in proper plantation area and the plantation is actually located at four kilometers away from the factory premises. The idea behind keeping the Gorkha and Adivasi workers in two separate labour lines is to avoid them to be freely mixing together so as to share their sorrows and melancholies openly which may lead them to the formation of trade union in the plantation. Secondly, the plantation has two divisions, viz., Anula and Gunna. All the Adivasi workers work at the Anula division while all the Gorkha workers work at the Gunna division. Thirdly, the Gorkhas are better educated and hence they have better quality of life than the Adivasis. Fourthly, Mr. Gohain has some Gorkha Mits and therefore he often visits the Gorkha households while he hardly visits the Adivasi households. A Mit means a friend with whose family members, no marriage relation should be taken place throughout life and a Mit has to observe death rituals at the demise of a member of his Mit's household. The Mit relationship is treated as good as blood relationship.

The Gorkhas have certain unique qualities. Firstly, the Gorkhas supply vegetables, milk, crops and other edible goods to the tribal planter due to the reason that in the Gorkha society, agriculture and animal husbandry always take place simultaneously while the Adivasis do not have much lust for Pather (wet rice field) and animal husbandry either at the plantations or in villages. The Gorkhas are also fond of floriculture. There are four nurseries of floriculture of Newar caste of the Gorkha community in Satkilu Gaon (village) of Chowkham.

Secondly, the Gorkhas are stubborn, sincere to their work and martial by characters (Northey and Morris: 1976). These might be the reasons why Mr. Gohain has constructed his bungalow near the Gorkha labour Dhura at the plantation. Here, an example has been cited to prove how the Gorkhas belong to a martial race. It relates to an incident that had taken place in the plantation in 1969 when the Bangladeshi Chakmas attacked the Khamtis in Chowkham. In the incident, Mr. Gohain was brutally attacked by the Chakmas as he was then the Member of Parliament. A Limbu bodyguard from the Gorkha community saved him and the bodyguard was butchered on the spot by the revolutionary Chakmas. The Bangladeshi Chakmas and Assamese Deoris had been creating acute problems (Das: 1995) then in the Lohit district of Arunachal Pradesh. However, the problem was later on sorted out amicably by rehabilitating them under the rehabilitation scheme of Government of India on the other side of river Dehing of Chowkham. The incident of Chakma attack on Mr. Gohain was reported to the Provincial Legislative Council of Arunachal Pradesh and Indian Parliament. This may be the apparent reason why Mr. Gohain has kept Gorkha driver, Gorkha cook and a Gorkha bodyguard even today. It is heard from the senior workers of the plantation that the Chakmas had been revolted against the Khamtis because the former were tried to make slaves of the later in Chowkham region.

Replying to the question of Khamti reactions regarding the import of Gorkha plantation workers in his plantations, Mr. Gohain categorically stated that he is the pioneer of industrialization in Chowkham who therefore does not at all believe on the domination of Khamti tribal culture in his industrial pursuits. He feels that an industrialist should always think about the spillover impacts of industrialization process on the society. Because of the opening of tea industry, towns like Gunnanagar, Chowkham, Wakro, Medo, Khonsa, Changlang etc. have emerged where sizeable population have got earning source by opening shops of variety. Again, industrialization through tea industry has helped to have a balanced ecology of the region as the local forests have been saved from rampant deforestation. At the same time, he has maintained shade trees at the plantations. In this way, tea industry is found to be mostly suited to the Arunachal ecology by maintaining environmental balance. Hence, it is also known that the Gorkhas have love for forests to have their good animal husbandry that requires sufficient cattle fodders from the forests. Thus, they collect cattle fodders from the branches of trees without destroying the trees as such. This is the main reason why even the Government of Arunachal Pradesh also encourages the Gorkhas to settle down in agrarian belts of the state. Similar picture is also found in Assam and West Bengal particularly in the hill areas of Darjeeling, Kalimpong and Kurseong sub-divisions of Darjeeling district and the state of Sikkim (Sharma: 2003). It is also explored from the study that the Gorkhas by nature are loyalists to their masters. Over the pages of Indian history, it is found that they were loyal to the Kauravas in Mahabharat war, the British and independent Indian government by serving in Gorkha Regiments, Assam Rifles etc. They were loyal to their masters both in Nepal and

India. Take for instance, Mr. Dil Bahadur Limbu, the cook of Mr. Gohain told me that he will left the plantation for Nepal or Assam aftermath of Mr. Gohain' demise. It shows that the upbringings of Mr. Gohain as tea planters are not acceptable even to the cook. The same thing is also found in case of many aged workers of the plantation.

Still another reason for the deployment of Gorkha workers was that the local Khamti tribe including their earlier slaves (Bose: 1997) tested the salt of industrialization process of the state government in such a way that they have started earning sufficient money from the plantations and forest resources of Chowkham. All the petty business/ contracts of the plantations and forests are given to the Khamtis. The supervisory (Mauri) and office staffs of the plantations are Khamtis. As reported by the Government Gaon Bura of Gunnanagar, there are about ten thousand Khamtis in Chowkham region of Lohit district of Arunachal Pradesh today. Their strength as non-workers is hardly one thousand at the Anula Shagun T.E. Rest of the Khamtis are staying outside the plantation in Gunnanagar, Chowkham, Wakro, Medo and other areas of the region as owners of fertile wet rice fields (Pather) and forests.

Evolution of Work Force in Arunachal Tea Plantations

The emergence of tea plantation workers in the state of Arunchal Pradesh is the creation of state sponsored tribal process of industrial development. Loosening the efficacy of Inner Line Permit of the Government of India, import of tea plantation workers started in Arunachal Pradesh after 1995. This is evident from Table 9.1.

Table 9.1: Evolution of Work Force in Arunachal Tea Estates

Year	*Male*	*Percentage*	*Female*	*Percentage*	*Total*
1995-1998	400	30.1	929	69.9	1329
1998-2001	500	31.0	1080	68.4	1580
2001-2003	726	24.2	2274	75.8	3000

Source: Directorate of Commerce and Industries: Government of Arunachal Pradesh: 2003.

Another 1000 casuals are estimated to have been employed in tea plantations in peak plucking season.

Table 9.1 indicates that throughout the origin and growth of tea plantation industry, the percentage of female workers went on increasing from 69.9 per cent to 75.8 per cent in 2003 A.D. The reasons for employing more female workers in the plantations have been described in later pages of the study.

The Structure of Work Force

To comprehend tea plantation as an agro-based industry, a peep on its structure of labour force is indespensible. In the following paragraphs, an attempt has been made to study the structure of labour force in Anula Shagun T.E. of Arunachal Pradesh.

On the whole, Table 9.2 indicates that the percentage of female tea plantation workers (61.3%) is almost double to the male (36.7%) counterpart in Anula Shagun T.E. It is also observed from the table that planter prefers female workers due to manifold reasons. Firstly, historically, the British planters established the fact that fingertips of female workers as tea pluckers are much more sensible (Sharma: 2003) than the male counterpart. Secondly, the females are simple minded and sincere enough in their work (Bhadra: 1992) than the males. Thirdly, the females tender similar care and attention as well as love for the tea leaves and bushes as they do in case of their own children (Sharma: 2003). The Caste-wise, Manger and Adivasi male workers (25.0% each) have highest percentage among other male plantation workers. Next to Manger and Adivasi, 12.9 per cent of Chettri males are workers. Similarly, 12.3 per cent of Rai males are the plantation workers. Among the workers 24.5 per cent of Adivasi female workers are very significant. Another 16.7 per cent of Rai and 16.3 per cent of Chettri females are workers in the plantation. The percentages of rest of caste workers are more or less same. Interestingly, it is also observed from Table 9.2 that all these castes of Gorkha and Adivasi communities were traditionally toiling mass in their places of origin (Sharma: 1997; Bhowmik: 1981) on agrarian habitations. They have to be satiated with the plantation system (Bhowmik: 1996) for the simple reason that they have settled here with permanent plantation job and they are living in calm and quiet industrial environment. The Assamese tea plantations are fully shattered by communal terrorism as led by the United Liberation Front of Assam (ULFA) with lack of tranquility and absence of freedom of living.

Table 9.2: Structure of Work Force (Coolies) in Anula Shagun T.E.

Sl. No.	Caste/ Community	Total Household	%	Male	%	Female	%	Total
I.	**Gorkha**							
1.	Chettri	30	15.0	20	12.9	40	16.3	60
2.	Manger	50	25.0	40	25.8	60	24.5	100
3.	Gurung	10	5.0	9	5.8	11	4.5	20
4.	Kami	12	6.0	15	9.7	9	3.7	24
5.	Tamang	6	3.0	6	3.9	6	2.4	12
6.	Rai	30	15.0	19	12.3	41	16.7	60
7.	Limbu	10	5.0	4	2.6	16	6.5	20
8.	Newar	1	0.5	1	0.6	1	0.4	2
9.	Thami	1	0.5	1	0.6	1	0.4	2
II.	**Adivasi**	50	25.0	40	25.8	60	24.5	100
	Total	200	100.0	155	38.7	245	61.3	400

Source: Field Work: 2003.

Age Structure of the Workers

In order to ascertain the working potentiality of workers, their age structure is very pertinent so as to arrive at a concrete empirical generalization. This will be clear if we see Table 9.3 of the study.

Table 9.3: Age Structure of Workers

Sl. No.	Caste/Community Gorkha = 300	18 to 27 Years	28 to 37 Years	38 to 47 Years	48 to 57 Years	58 Years Plus
1.	Chettri = 60	40(17.8%)	10(11.8%)	9(23.1%)	1(3.7%)	—
2.	Manger = 100	65(29.1%)	20(23.5%)	2(5.1%)	10(37.1%)	3(12.0%)
3.	Gurung = 20	8(3.6%)	4(4.7%)	2(5.1%)	3(11.1%)	3(12.0%)
4.	Kami = 24	10(4.5%)	6(7.1%)	5(12.8%)	2(7.4%)	1(4.0%)
5.	Tamang =12	2(0.9%)	1(1.2%)	7(17.9%)	1(3.7%)	1(4.0%)
6.	Rai = 60	31(13.8%)	10(11.8%)	8(20.5%)	3(11.1%)	8(32.0%)
7.	Limbu = 20	8(3.6%)	3(3.5%)	2(5.1%)	3(11.1%)	4(16.0%)
8.	Newar = 2	—	—	1(2.6%)	1(3.7%)	—
9.	Thami = 2	—	1(1.2%)	—	1(3.7%)	—
10.	Adivasi= 100	60(26.8%)	30(35.3%)	3(7.7%)	2(7.4%)	5(20.0%)
	Total = 400	224(54.0%)	85(21.2%)	39(9.7%)	27(6.7%)	25(6.2%)

Source: Field Work: 2003.

Table 9.3 portrays the fact that 54.0 per cent of the workers belong to the age group of 18 to 27 years; 21.3 per cent of them belong to 28 to 37 years; 9.7 per cent of them belong to 38 to 47 years; 6.7 per cent of them belong to the age group of 48 to 57 years and 6.2 per cent of them belong to 58 years and above. The workers belonging to 48 to 57 years and 58 years plus are employed having long term experience in the industrial job. They are working in the plantation because of their long association with Mr. Gohain ever since 1967. They stated that they will work as long as they can. It shows that there is no age bar for the plantation jobs as we found in agrarian Arunachal Pradesh. This is because of the fact that there is no labour legislation to regularize the terms and conditions of work or service for the plantation workers in Arunachal Pradesh. In this way, they are as good as unorganized sector workers because they do not have any organization or trade union of their own to fight for their just rights and responsibilities. The trade union movement as prevalent in other tea plantations of far and wide corners of the country has not yet penetrated (Sharma: 1991) into the Arunachal tea plantations in general and Anula Shagun T.E. in particular. In fact, there is no existing mechanism in the Department of Commerce and Industries, Government of Arunachal Pradesh to regulate various central labour legislations. This is overtly possible because no outside trade union leader is allowed to enter (Mamkotam: 1994) into the plantations and impart trade union education (Bhowmik: 1995) to the workers. Thus, the birth of working class consciousness in the state plantations is a distant dream (Sharma: 2000) for the workers.

Labour Migration in Arunachal Pradesh

Das (1995) observed "The emergence of non-agricultural labour force in Arunachal Pradesh economy is concomitant outcome of the externally thrust process of development in the post-independent period. The process of development not only needed flow of fund from the centre but also manpower from outside". Further, he observed that "not only skilled manpower had been recruited in different services but a large number of unskilled workers had also been brought". This is due to the non-participation of tribal people in the affairs of the enchanted plantation frontiers of Arunachal Pradesh. Thus, the process of transition of tribal labour force from Arunachal Pradesh belts (Mishra: 1994) to industrial sector with particular reference to the plantation frontiers is not at all significant in the state. The observation made by Das (1995) that money wages in different private sector industries in Arunachal Pradesh are by and large same to that of the plain workers of Assam and West Bengal is found to be contradictory here in case of tea plantations where each worker is simply paid Rs. 35 per day. In most of the cases, the plantation workers were unemployed or disguisedly employed at their places of origin. They moved to Arunachal Pradesh to join the unskilled labour force of the plantations. As a result, it is not that skilled labour force migrated because of the wage differentials, rather the fact is that the unskilled reserve army migrated to the enchanted plantation frontiers (enclaves) of Arunachal Pradesh in search of their livelihood.

In regard to health dimension of the workers, it is entirely left to the discretion of employer (planter) to or not to provide the incentives. It is observed that in case of minor injuries during the working hours, the workers are generally provided with little amount of money for medical treatment. Sometimes, they are sent to their homes for the same and generally reinstated later on when they come back. Thus, for all practical purposes, job security of the workers is under the mercy of the planters. All planters do not follow legal formalities while recruiting and employing the workers. The length of their service life continues till it is beneficial (*Ibid.*) to the management and workers.

Again, in regard to other welfare facilities like housing, fuel, recreation etc., the migration of workers to the plantation does not make much difference to that of their places of origin. Here, as in the past habitations, the nature of having sparsely populated territory, provides sanitary facilities. The river water is used for drinking purpose and jungles as the source of fuel and cattle fodders (*Ibid.*) to the workers.

The migrant tea plantation workers of other plantations have the same platitude that has been described above regarding their health and sanitation. The workers themselves have to maintain their homes and procure fuel from nearby forests for cooking food at home.

Place of Birth of the Workers

The foregone discussion has very categorically depicted the fact that all the tea plantation workers of Arunachal Pradesh are migrants from Nepal, Assam and other parts of the country. In the following paragraphs, an attempt has been made to study the places of birth of the workers with particular reference to the Anula Shagun T.E. of Arunachal Pradesh.

Table 9.4 transpired the fact that 74.7 per cent of the Gorkha tea plantation workers of Anula Shagun T.E. had migrated from Nepal Himalayas. Another 11.3 per cent of them had migrated from Assam plains particularly from Lakhimpur, Sadiya, Tinsukia and Sibsagar districts due to the communal riots there as led by the United Liberation Front of Assam (ULFA). Only 14.0 per cent of the Gorkha workers were born in the plantation. The parents of these 14.0 per cent workers were employed in Gunnanagar at Namshum Saw and Veneer Mills (P) Ltd. of Chowkham of Mr. Chowkhamoon Gohain ever since 1967. Among the Gorkha castes, 31.1 per cent of Manger, 20.1 per cent of Chettri and 18.7 per cent of Rai workers had migrated to the plantation after 1987 from Nepal Himalayas. They migrated here due to the Maoist movement in Nepal. Similarly, other castes like Gurung, Kami, Tamang, Limbu, Newar and Thami migrated to the plantation due to poverty (Regmi: 1971) and terrorism launched by the Maoists in Nepal. The workers stated that they are at least at peace here although they have been looked down upon by the Khampti tribes of the region. Table 9.4 shows that 47.6 per cent of Mangers, 23.8 per cent of Chettris and 19.1 per cent of Rais were born in the plantation. Not a single Brahmin (Bahun) as tea plantation worker is found at the Anula Shagun T.E. In the same way, 29.4 per cent of Manger, 19.4 per cent of Rai and 14.7 per cent of Chettri workers have been migrated to the plantation from Assam and other parts of the country. The percentage of labour migration from rest of the other Gorkha castes is by and large not so significant. Another reason for their migration to Arunachal Pradesh plantation is due to the existence of adequate forest resources to the agrarian Gorkhas (Sharma: 2000) of the Nepal Himalayas.

Workers, Connection with their Places of Origin

Exploring the recurrences of workers, contact with their places of origin, the following picture has been evolved at the Anula Shagun T.E.

Table 9.5 of the study indicates that 54.5 per cent of the workers do not at all visit their places of origin in Nepal and Assam. The workers visiting once in five years (4.0%), once in four years (3.2%) and once in three years (8.7%) may be treated as the people who do

Table 9.4: Place of Birth of the Workers

Sl. No.	Caste/ Community	Born in the Garden	Percentage	Born in Assam/ other parts of the country	Percentage	Born in Nepal	Percentage
	Gorkhas						
1.	Chettri=60	10	23.8 %	5	14.7 %	45	20.1%
2.	Manger=100	20	47.6%	10	29.4%	70	31.1%
3.	Gurung= 20	—	—	2	5.9%	18	8.1%
4.	Kami = 24	2	4.8%	3	8.8%	19	8.4%
5.	Tamang =12	1	2.4%	2	5.9%	9	4.1%
6.	Rai = 60	8	19.1%	10	19.4%	42	18.7%
7.	Limbu = 20	1	2.4%	2	5.9%	17	7.6%
8.	Newar= 2	—	—	—	—	2	0.9%
9.	Thami = 2	—	—	—	—	2	0.9%
	Total= 300	42	14.0%	34	11.3%	224	74.7%

Source: Field Work: 2003.

not have much touch or contact with Assam or Nepal and other parts of the country. However, 29.5 per cent of the workers who visit their places of origin can be conceptually considered as the first generation migrants to the plantation. But it is not totally wrong to brand the 70.5 per cent of the workers of Gorkha origin as migrants. It is rather a curse or myth in real sense of the term to call them migrants. They do not even know the actual places from where their grand-parents hailed. Their commitment and contribution to the state economy is much more than the local tribes. So, in view of the participative economic development approach or policy of the Government of Arunachal Pradesh (Das: 1995), the Gorkhas appeared to have been totally merged (Ratnam: 2001) as part and parcel of the Arunachal state population. To Mr. Chowkhamoon Gohain, the Gorkha people are firstly his loyal resident workers and then secondly the citizens of the state of Arunachal Pradesh Government. This indicates the fact that no more Gorkha tea plantation workers can be branded as migrants in the state of Arunachal Pradesh.

Education of the Workers

The concept of educational standard is very vague (Chakraborty: 1997) among the Gorkha tea plantation workers as they belong to

Table 9.5: Workers' Contact with their Places of Origin

Sl.No.	Caste/Community	Annual	In two years	In Three years	In four Years	In Five Years	No Contact
	Gorkhas						
1.	Chettri= 60	35(48.6%	15(32.6%)	3(8.6%)	1(7.7%)	1(6.2%)	5 (2.3%)
2.	Manger = 100	10(13.9%)	15(32.6%)	20(57.1%)	3(23.1%)	4(25.0%)	48(22.1%)
3.	Gurung = 20	2 (2.8%)	1(2.2%)	2(5.7%)	1 (7.7%)	1(6.2%)	13(6.0%)
4.	Kami = 24	3 (4.2%)	7(15.2%)	2(5.7%)	1 (7.7%)	2(12.5%)	9 (4.1%)
5.	Tamang= 12	1(1.4%)	1(2.2%)	2(5.7%)	1(7.7%)	1(6.2%)	6(2.8%)
6.	Rai= 60	10(13.9%)	3(6.5%)	3(8.6%)	2(15.4%)	1(6.2%)	41(18.8%)
7.	Limbu= 20	1(1.4%)	2(4.3%)	1(2.9%)	3(23.1%)	2(12.5%)	11(5.1%)
8.	Newar= 2	—	—	—	—	1(6.2%)	1(0.5%)
9.	Thami= 2	—	—	—	—	1(6.2%)	1(0.5%)
10.	Adivasi = 100	10(13.9%)	2(4.3%)	2(5.7%)	1(7.7%)	2(12.5%)	83(38.1%)
	Total= 400	72	46	35	13	16	218

Source: Field Work: 2003.

unskilled category in Anula Shagun T.E. However, in the following section, we will be able to roughly comprehend the educational standards of the workers.

It is transparent from Table 9.6 of the study that 62.0 per cent of the workers are illiterate. Interestingly, the table also shows that 27.3 per cent of them have V to X standard of education and 3.0 per cent of them have higher secondary level of education. Altogether, 38.0 per cent of tea plantation workers of Anula Shagun T.E. are literates.

Table 9.6: Educational Standard of the Workers

Sl. No.	*Caste/ Community*	*Illiterate*	*%*	*I-IV*	*%*	*V-X*	*%*	*XI-XII*	*%*
	Gorkhas								
1.	Chettri= 60	40	21.5	10	12.2	8	34.8	2	22.2
2.	Manger= 100	65	34.9	30	36.6	4	17.4	1	11.1
3.	Gurung= 20	18	9.7	2	2.4	—	—	—	—
4.	Kami = 24	15	8.1	7	8.5	1	4.3	1	11.1
5.	Tamang = 12	8	4.3	3	3.7	1	4.3	—	—
6.	Rai = 60	29	15.6	20	24.4	7	30.4	4	44.4
7.	Limbu = 20	11	5.9	7	8.5	1	4.3	1	11.1
8.	Newar = 2	—	—	2	2.4	—	—	—	—
9.	Thami = 2	—	—	1	1.2	1	4.3	—	—
	Total = 300	186	62.0	82	27.3	23	7.7	9	3.0

Source: Field Work: 2003.

Conceptually, such a high level of education of the Gorkha tea plantation workers in the Anula Shagun T.E. is due to reason that there are one higher secondary and three primary schools in Gunnanagar. Secondly, unlike in the past, the medium of instruction is in Hindi and English languages in Arunachal schools and colleges (Bose: 1997). The Gorkhas lingua franca is also based on Devnagari script as of the Hindi language. Thirdly, the Gorkhas prefer Hindi and pick up the Hindi language very promptly through conversation and other communication media like television, radio, newspapers, magazines etc. Also they prefer to send their children to Hindi and English medium schools. Having cosmopolitan characteristics (Northey and Morris: 1976), the Gorkhas adapt local languages, dialects and culture within a very short span of time. The Government of Arunachal Pradesh encourages Hindi and English languages in schools and colleges, as the medium of instruction. In the process, the Gorkhas have come up in much better way than the tribals and they write Hindi and English quite perfectly. Moreover, they express their feelings in Hindi and English languages in day to day life. Because of this inherent quality being possessed by the Gorkhas, many top most bureaucrats of Arunachal Pradesh hail from the Gorkha community. But interestingly, in spite of possessing such quality, most of the Gorkhas are not given even the supervisory and clerical posts in the state tea plantations.

Demography

Altogether, the Anula Shagun T.E. has population of one thousand today. They are directly or indirectly dependent on tea plantation economy. Considering the existing demography of the plantation, an attempt has been made in the following section to study the nature of mortality and fertility rates of the plantation workers.

Table 9.7: Fertility and Mortality Rates of the Workers (Last Ten Years)

Sl.No,	*Caste/ Community*	*Fertility*	*Percentage*	*Mortality*	*Percentage*
	Gorkhas				
1.	Chettri	18	10.8	4	3.6
2.	Manger	25	15.1	13	11.6
3.	Gurung	14	8.4	19	17.0
4.	Kami	10	6.1	7	6.2
5.	Tamang	29	17.5	19	17.0
6.	Rai	30	18.1	13	11.6
7.	Limbu	15	9.0	7	6.2
8.	Newar	2	1.2	1	0.9
9.	Thami	3	1.8	—	—
10.	Adivasis	20	11.0	29	25.9
	Total	166	—	112	—

Source: Field Work: 2003.

Table 9.7 transpires the fact that the fertility rate of Rai caste of the Gorkhas community is very high (18.1%) followed by the fertility rate of Tamang (17.5%) and Manger (15.1%) castes. The table also indicates that the fertility rate of Adivisis (11.0%), Chettri (10.8%) and Limbu (9.0%) is also quite significant. The fertility rate of Rai caste is very high as most densely populated caste is from the Rai group in not only North East India but also Darjeeling-Sikkim Himalayas (Dozey: 1989; Sharma: 2003). In fact, the Rais have highest trend of migration from the eastern Nepal known as Panthar. Traditionally, the Panthar was the native place of Rai (Pradhan: 1991) caste of the Gorkhas community.

Pondering on the mortality rate of various castes, it is observed in Table 9.7 that caste like Gurung (17.0%), Tamang (17.0%), Adivasi (25.9%), Rai (11.6%) and Manger (11.6%) have high mortality rate. Rest of the castes like Chettri (3.6%), Kami (6.2%) and Limbu (6.2%) have by and large similar mortality trend in the plantation. The Newar caste of the Gorkha community has lowest percentage (0.9%) of mortality rate. The Adivasis have highest mortality rate (Bhadra: 1997) because of the fact that they hardly bother about their health aspect of life. This may be the reason why their quality of life is very low compared to the Gorkha counterpart at the plantation. The Gorkha caste like Gurung, Rai, Tamang and Manger have higher mortality rate because they are habitually addicted to alcoholism in their day to day life. The caste like Chettri, Newar, Kami and Limbu appear to be more and more conscious about it as they do not normally indulge in alcoholism at the plantation or outside. The occurrence of tuberculosis disease is very high among the Adivasis as well as Rai, Tamang, Gurung and Manger castes of the Gorkha community in the plantation. This has been nicely supplemented by the reports of local hospital of Chowkham, Gunnanagar in Namsai sub-division of Arunachal Pradesh. The health services rendered by the Department of Public Health Services of the Government of Arunachal Pradesh (Bose: 1997) has not yet penetrated into the Anula Shagun T. E. of Gunnanagar (Chowkham).

X

Economic Life of the Workers

In the present section of the study, we shall discuss about the economic life of the plantation workers belonging to the Gorkha working class of the Anula Shagun T.E. How the heterogeneous working mass of the plantation has been categorized as the homogeneous work force as they all are the sellers of their physical labour (Bhowmik: 1995) power. Discussing the economic life, we shall deal with caste and landholding, caste and livestock population, caste and working population of the workers and caste and years of service at the Anula Shagun T.E. We shall also see the nature of secondary occupation and traditional occupational structure of the Gorkha castes and how the traditional occupational structure of the Gorkha castes has been transformed after their migration from the agrarian Nepal to the industrial environment of the plantation economy of the Anula Shagun T.E.?

The Organisational Structure of Anula Shagun T.E.

Unlike other tea plantations of Assam, West Bengal or any other tea plantations of North East India, the organizational structure of Arunachal Pradesh tea plantations in general and Anula Shagun T.E. in particular is very simple. It is because of the fact as mentioned in previous chapters of the study that the tribal family members occupy the top most management hierarchy. Take for instance of the Anula Shagun T.E. where Mr. Chowkhamoon Gohain, the owner of Gunna Tea Industrics (P) Ltd. is the Managing Director. Below him, his son (Rajen) is the Director In-charge of the plantation. Below the Director In-Charge, the daughter-in-law (Rupa) of Mr. Gohain is the Director of the plantation. No formal Manager or Assistant Manager has been appointed for the plantation. Below the Director, ten Khamti males and two Gorkhas (males) have been appointed as the supervisory staffs of the plantation. Locally, the supervisory staffs are called as "Mauris". There are only two Khamti clerks in the office of the plantation. Below the supervisory staffs, factory workers numbering about twenty have been employed from the Gorkha community. Four vehicle drivers one each from Assamese, Gorkha, Khamti and Bengali communities are there in the plantation. The tea plantation workers are at the bottom of the organizational hierarchy. By 'plantation workers', here we mean both the plantation and factory daily rated Coolies (workers). They work on 'No Work No Pay' basis (Ramaswamy: 1995). Although a Muster Roll is being maintained at the plantation for the workers, they are treated as daily rated 'regular' working force of the agro-based industry. In this way, they are as good as casual workers. It may be due to the introduction of Liberalization policy by Government of India because the Casualization of industrial workers and Liberalization of Indian industries are two sides of the same coin (Bhowmik: 1995).

Interestingly, it is observed that fifty per cent of names in the Muster Roll go on changing among the Adivasi workers every week. Thus, keeping a stable work force at the plantation is a very big problem for the tea garden management (Choudhury: 2000). The Adivasis as reported by the Mauris of the plantation, do not attend the work regularly and thus very frequently they remain absent in their duty. Again, some Adivasi workers are not found reporting Mauris almost throughout the month. If the wife of an Adivasi worker works today, then tomorrow, in her place his daughter comes for the work. This is due to the absence of welfare incentives like Provident Fund, Gratuity, Bonus etc. coupled with other industrial facilities as enshrined in various labour legislations of the Government of India. However, such problem is not found with the Gorkha tea plantation workers of the Anula Shagun T.E. This is evident from Table 10.1 of the study.

It is observed from Table 10.1 that 31.3 per cent of the workers have been working at the plantation for more than ten years. Again, another 34.7 per cent of them have been working for more than five years but less than ten years. Similarly, 34.0 per cent of the workers have been working at the plantation for less than five years. It is also found that 31.3 per cent of the workers are associated with the plantation since its inception (1987) while 68.7 per cent of them were

Table 10.1: Years of Service in Anula Shagun T.E.

Sl. No.	Caste/Community	1 to 5 Years	Percentage	6 to 10 Years	Percentage	10 Years Plus	Percentage
	Gorkha						
1.	Chettri = 60	40	29.4	15	10.8	5	4.0
2.	Manger = 100	30	22.1	40	28.7	30	24.0
3.	Gurung= 20	5	3.7	3	2.2	12	9.6
4.	Kami = 24	4	2.9	15	10.8	5	4.0
5.	Tamang = 12	1	0.7	2	14.4	9	7.2
6.	Rai = 60	20	14.7	10	7.2	30	24.0
7.	Limbu = 20	5	3.7	3	2.2	12	9.6
8.	Newar = 2	1	0.7	—	—	1	0.8
9.	Thami = 2	—	—	1	0.7	1	0.8
10.	Adivasi = 100	30	22.1	50	36.0	20	16.0
	Total = 400	136	34.0	139	34.7	125	31.3

Source: Field Work: 2003.

recruited in phased manner with the expansion of the plantation from thirty hectares (1987) to 219 hectares under tea bushes today (2003). Interestingly, in the beginning, more and more stress had been given to the recruitment of Adivasi workers from the neighbouring state of Assam but later on more and more Gorkha had to be recruited from Assam and Nepal Himalayas because the Adivasi workers did not ordain required commitment to the plantation jobs. This might be the apparent reason for employing 300 Gorkhas workers while only 100 Adivasi workers have been employed at the plantation today.

It is very much clear from the above discussion that Gorkhas have shown deep conviction to the industrial autocracy of a Khamti family of the Anula Shagun T.E. Interacting with Mr. Gohain, it is learnt that he has kept a Gorkha (Rai) Chowkidar with deep confidence at his bungalow. Even Mr. Gohain takes the Rai Chowkidar whenever he goes to Tinsukia or Teju to draw money from the bank for weekly wage payment of the workers. Thus, the Gorkhas have exhaustively proved their loyalty, perseverance and commitment to the cause of tribal industrialization process of the Government of Arunachal Pradesh. Adherence to such commitment for the landlords or planters (Thulo Manchees—big sorts) is a hereditary quality of the Gorkha community from their places of origin. In the traditional Gorkha society, each caste was to be fully committed to its masters by providing respective caste occupation. This is evident from Table 10.2 of the study.

Table 10.2: Traditional Occupation of Gorkha Castes

Sl. No.	*Caste*	*Traditional Occupation*
	Gorkhas	
1.	Chettri	Warriors
2.	Manger/Thami/ Limbu	Agriculturists
3.	Gurung	Shepherds
4.	Tamang	Horse/Traders/Cavalries
5.	Newar	Goldsmiths/Businessmen
6.	Thami	Porters/ Bodyguards
7.	Kami	Ironsmiths

Source: Sharma: 2000.

It is very apparent from Table 10.2 that traditionally, all the Gorkha castes were toiling mass (class) of Nepal (Pradhan: 1991) and Eastern Himalayas (Sharma: 1997). However, the Gorkha occupational structure had undergone a drastic or sea change in Nepal after 1926

(Haimendorf: 1966) with the abolition of slavery system. After that, the occupational structure of Gorkha castes became primarily agrarian in nature, The formation of new agrarian social structure in Nepal made those castes the 'landless' toiling mass for they were exposed to a new type of hierarchy into Pattadar (landowner) and Pakhurey (share cropper) groups. It is explored from the study that the workers who had been migrated from agrarian Nepal belong to Pakhurey group having various agrarian related manual jobs. The drastic change that has taken place in the plantation is that they are the owners of Kitchen gardens that have been provided by the plantation management and wet rice land (Pather) of Khamtis mainly at Satkilu Gaon (village) of Gunnanagar, Chowkham. Occupationally, they have dual characteristics (Xaxa: 1995), viz., agrarian and industrial. No more, they are purely Pakhureys by land ownership pattern. The nature of dual characteristics of the Gorkha castes can be distinctly understood if we see Table 10.3 of the study.

Table 10.3: Structure of Working Persons of the Workers

Sl. No.	*Caste/Community*	*Double*	*Triple*	*Four*	*Five*	*Total*
	Gorkha					
1.	Chettri= 102	60	3	—	—	63
2.	Manger= 180	100	20	—	—	120
3.	Gurung = 32	20	2	2	1	25
4.	Kami = 38	24	2	2	1	29
5.	Tamang =19	12	2	1	1	16
6.	Rai= 120	60	30	5	3	98
7.	Limbu = 37	20	3	1	1	25
8.	Newar = 4	2	—	1	—	3
9.	Thami= 4	2	—	—	1	3
10.	Adivasi= 170	100	39	10	5	154
	Total = 706	400	101	22	13	536
	Percentage	56.7	14.3	3.1	1.8	76.0

Source: Field Work: 2003.

Table 10.3 of the study indicates that 76.0 per cent of the families of plantation workers are engaged in different kind of jobs either in agriculture, petty business or in the government services also. Remaining members of the workers' families numbering about 170 are either school/college going kids, kids on mothers' laps, retired or old persons. It is also observed that these retired or old persons look after the smaller kids at homes and also they look after the cattle stocks in jungles and Khuttis. Therefore, occupationally, they are also to be treated as good as working population of the families of the workers. Again, it is very transparent from the table that 56.7 per cent of the families of the workers have double working persons. Still another 14.3 per cent of the families have triple working persons. Above all, 3.1 per cent of the families have four working persons and 1.8 per cent of families of the workers have five working persons.

The above discussion has portrayed an interesting fact that hardly any person except the smaller kids stays idle without work at the plantation. To the Gorkha workers, human survival is part and parcel of work and without work they cannot just survive. They also said that this is the high time to earn sufficient money to ascertain their future security. It is because of this fact that there is nothing unsure that they may be ousted from the plantation being non-tribal migrants from the Nepal Himalayas and various parts of the country. Hour-wise, they work for twelve to thirteen hours a day of which eight hours have been devoted to the plantation duty and five hours either in agrarian field or other agrarian related jobs and also pursuing themselves on Khutti culture. Each family devotes at least two to three hours everyday for rearing and dearing the cattle stocks. This will be clear if we see the possession of cattle stock population by the workers.

Table 10.4: Cattle stock Population of the Workers

Sl. No.	*Caste/Community*	*Cow*	*Goat*	*Bull*	*Hens*	*Total*
	Gorkha					
1.	Chettri= 30	60	10	2	—	72
2.	Manger = 50	120	30	4	20	174
3.	Gurung = 10	25	25	2	50	102
4.	Kami = 12	24	30	2	30	86
5.	Tamang = 8	13	15	2	35	65
6.	Rai = 30	30	20	4	46	100
7.	Limbu= 10	12	10	2	60	84
8.	Newar =1	1	—	—	30	31
9.	Thami = 1	1	—	—	25	26
	Total= 150	286	140	18	296	740
	Percentage	38.6	18.9	2.4	40.0	100.0

Source: Field Work: 2003.

Table 10.4 indicates that comparatively Chettri caste has highest number of cows considering their total number of households at the plantation. Next to Chettris, Mangers have significant number of cows. The remaining Gorkha castes do not have significant number of cows at their households. It is because of the fact that historically Chettri, Manger and Grurung castes were purely Gorkhas—the protectors of cow Dharma (religion) and hence they were considered as pure Hindus (Sharma:1997) in Nepal Himalayas (Pradhan: 1991; Haimendorf: 1966). Caplan (1970) has also made the same observation in Eastern Nepal. Interestingly, it is also observed in the Table 10.4 that Matwalis (Manger, Gurung, Rai, Limbu, Tamang, Newar, Thami and Kami) have large number of cattle stock population at their households (40.8%). They are Matwalis who are supposed to use wine and sacrifice animals' blood while performing their rituals whereas Chettri being a Tagadhari caste has to wear sacred threads. The Chettri is to be considered as double born Hindu caste along with the Brahmins (Sharma: 2000). This will be elaborately discussed in next chapter of the study. The Mangers and Gurungs being highly Hinduised (Srivastava: 1966) in the past in Nepal Himalayas, have the habit of keeping cow in large number at their homes. This is also very evident from Table 10.4. Another interesting point to note here is that not a single Matwali household has kept pig. Keeping of or rearing on piggery is prohibited by the plantation owner who has constructed/ maintained a Buddhist monastery (Gumpha) near the Gorkha labour Dhura of the plantation. Secondly, it has also prohibited by the Government of Arunachal Pradesh because in 1995, a malarial fever from the mosquitoes after biting the pigs ruptured the Lohit district of Arunachal Pradesh in an epidemic form. So, mainly the Gorkha workers are scared of domesticating pigs at their households. Again, it is seen from Table 10.4 that 2.4 per cent of bulls have been kept at their households because bulls are necessary animals to plough the wet rice fields and mating with the cows. The poultry chicken and cow milk are mainly sold for Gunnanagar and Chowkham dwellers who do not mostly rear and dear cows at their households. In fact, most of the Khamtis are not much accustomed to domesticate cows and other animals as they were Jhumers (slash and burn cultivators) in their own way till the recent past. Keeping goats is mainly meant for the household consumption. Altogether, on the average, each household has at least ten domesticated animals at its disposal. It shows that agriculture-cum-industrial economy of the plantation has enabled the agrarian Gorkhas to keep such a large number of cattle stock population at their households.

Landholding Pattern

The landless Gorkhas of the Nepal Himalayas migrated to Anula Shagun T.E. as they were assured of settled life with agrarian field both in and outside the plantation. In general, this was one of the pull factors for their migration to Arunachal Pradesh. Every household of the workers has been provided with the kitchen land or kitchen garden at the plantation. Historically, the plantation used to provide kitchen garden to the workers due to its isolated location or enclave where the workers could not get market to purchase vegetables. After joining the plantation jobs, they got ample opportunity to clear up the dense forests and do terracing for wet rice cultivation. The work relating to forest clearance had taken place in tune with the state policy for terminating Jhum (Shifting) cultivation by the local tribes in the area under reference.

Table 10.5 of the study shows that 286 acres of land are wet rice field being cultivated by the workers in Satkilu and other villages. It transpired the fact that every Gorkha caste has been engaged in cultivating the land for paddy, maize, wheat and vegetables. The field also provides cattle fodders such as straw and grass of variety for the agrarian Gorkhas. Only paddy has to be distributed equally with the Khampti landowners as the agrarian land holding right lies with the Khamptis only. But operationally, the Gorkhas are the real owners of wet rice land (Pather) known as Panikheti because the tribal landowners hardly visit the field and therefore they do not at all encroach upon the management right of the land being exclusively given to the Gorkha households.

Table 10.5: Caste and Landholding

Sl. No.	*Caste/ Community*	*Kitchen Garden (in Katha) **	*Percent-age*	*Wet Rice Land (Pather) in Bigha ***	*Percent-age*
	Gorkhas				
1.	Chettri= 30	150	20.6	60	21.0
2.	Manger= 50	250	34.4	100	35.0
3.	Gurung= 10	30	4.2	20	7.0
4.	Kami = 12	36	5.0	24	8.4
5.	Tamang = 6	18	2.5	20	7.0
6.	Rai = 30	180	24.8	40	14.0
7.	Limbu = 10	30	4.2	10	3.5
8.	Newar = 1	3	0.4	5	1.7
9.	Thami = 1	3	0.4	7	2.4
	Total = 150	700	—	286	—

* 1 Katha = 720 Sq. Feet ** 1 Bigha = 2 Acres

Source: Field Work: 2003.

In the plantation, 34.4 per cent of kitchen land is owned by the Mangers. Another 24.8 per cent of the kitchen land is owned by the Rai caste. Similarly, 20.6 per cent of the kitchen land is owned by the Chettris. The logic behind holding more kitchen land by Manger, Rai and Chhetri castes is associated with their migration and settlement history at the plantation. These castes of the Gorkha community were earlier migrants while the other castes were recent migrants to the plantation of Arunachal Pradesh. Again, in regard to holding of wet land of paddy field, these three castes have higher quantum of land in Satkilu Gaon and other villages of Chowkham, Gunnanagar. The percentage of agrarian landholding is lesser among other castes of the plantation as they are the recent migrants. The former migrants are called as "Raithanees" and later are considered as "Sukumbasis". The Sukumbasis have not yet been fully acquainted with the local Khamti landowners. On the whole, it is observed that Mangers are much better off than other castes in so far as the question of holding wet rice land is concerned.

Style of Life of the Workers

To operationalize the issue 'style of life' of the workers, holding valuable articles has been taken as the main parameter in the study. This is evident from Table 10.6 of the study.

The table shows that Manger, Rai and Chettri castes appeared to have been leading better quality of life than the other castes in the plantation. Holding modern equipments and mechanical goods is more with Rai, Manger and Limbu castes than other castes of the Gorkha community. This is evident from the ownership of scooters by Rai, Limbu and Manger castes. The Gurungs have also a good number of scooters at their own. Remaining castes have owned less number of such modern equipments at their homes. Interestingly, not a single worker's family has any vehicle. It is because of the fact that the location of plantation is as such that they cannot go to Teju or Tinsukia towns regularly for marketing and other works. Whenever they go to Teju (the district headquarters of Lohit district of Arunachal Pradesh) which is 30 kilometers away from the plantation, they go by bus only. They said that it is very difficult for them to keep vehicle as there is no servicing centre nearby to repair the same in case they go wrong.

Table 10.6: Possession of Valuable Articles by the Workers

Sl. No.	*Caste/ Community*	*Television*	*Radio*	*Sofa set*	*Watch*	*Clock*	*Cycle*	*Scooter*
	Gorkhas							
1.	Chettri = 30	20	8	2	19	25	20	2
2.	Manger = 50	45	4	45	40	50	35	12
3.	Gurung = 10	8	1	8	18	10	17	8
4.	Kami = 12	10	1	7	8	13	21	4
5.	Tamang = 6	5	2	4	9	7	2	3
6.	Rai = 30	25	10	28	52	32	21	19
7.	Limbu = 10	9	5	7	17	12	9	10
8.	Newar = 1	1	1	1	2	2	1	1
9.	Thami = 1	1	1	2	2	2	1	1
	Total = 150	124	33	104	167	153	127	60

Source: Field Work: 2003.

Moreover, they do not want to purchase vehicles because of their low level of living at the plantation. Owning such articles carry higher social status that reflect hierarchy, utility and attractiveness (Bose: 1997) which is absolutely absent among the plantation workers.

Working Hours of the Workers

With the garden siren at 7 A.M., the workers have to report to Mauri for work. The work starts sharp at 7 A.M. and continues till 11 A.M. At 11 A.M., they go home for lunch and come back to work places sharp at 12 Noon. From 12 Noon to 4 P.M., work continues for the workers. Each worker has to pluck 32 kilograms of tea leaves per day as Thicka and if extra tea leaves are plucked then one rupee is given to the workers per kilogram of plucked tea leaves. During the pruning season, each worker has to prun ten Tangs (tea tables) per day. Unlike other tea plantations of Assam and West Bengal, the workers have to work for full day (eight hours) in the pruning season also. At peak plucking season (April to October), every factory worker has to work for nine to ten hours per day with extra time allowance of Rs.10 per hour of work.

Benefits for the Workers

Excepting four days Puja holidays, 15th August and 26th January every year, no other holiday or leave is given to the workers in the plantation. There is no system of providing Annual Leave with wages to the plantation workers as we found in Assam and West Bengal as per the provisions of Plantation Labour Act, 1951 of the Government of India. The house building materials are provided to the workers by the plantation management. The constructing cost of the labour quarters is to be totally borned by the workers themselves from their own wallet.

There is neither the system of Employees Provident Fund deduction from the wage slips of the workers nor the contribution made from the plantation industry towards the Provident Fund for the workers as per the provisions of Provident Fund Act of the Government of India. Every labour Dhura (line) has been provided one tube well for drinking water. The workers have to collect fuel from the forests. There is no children education cess as we found in West Bengal and Assam tea plantations for the workers. No crèche facility has been provided for the workers' children below the age of six years as per the provisions of Plantation Labour Act, 1951. There is electricity supply to the workers' Dhuras but the workers themselves have to pay electricity bills. In the name of recreational facility, there is a labour club at Gunna division of the plantation without any recreational item. Even the Bonus and Gratuity are also not provided to the workers. In regard to the medical facility for the workers, the plantation management does not pay anything except one or two days leave without deducting the wages of the workers. All the medical expenses incurred on treatment at hospitals and nursing homes are to be beared by the workers themselves from their own purse. A cooperative ration shop has been opened at the plantation where the workers procure necessary edible goods costing to the tune of actual wages received from the plantation. A Ration Khata (copy) has been issued to the workers to draw the edible goods from the cooperative shop.

As there is no Badli (substitute) system of labour recruitment in the plantation as we found in Assam and West Bengal tea gardens, the workers are recruited as good as casual labourers (Bhowmik:1995) and they are employed on "No Work No Pay" basis. This may be the reason why the workers generally remain absent in the working days. Normally, in most of the cases, they remain absent in the plantation work every year with the commencement of agrarian sowing (June to August) and harvesting (October to December) seasons. The workers prefer jobs in the agrarian sector because they can earn more than in the plantation sector. If a worker holds a pair of bulls and if he tills the land of others for six months then he can earn the whole year's bread and butter for his family members. This might be the apparent reason why most of the Adivasis do not like to work at the plantation regularly throughout the year. Further, the Anula Shagun tea plantation workers stated that there is no prospect for their promotion onto the supervisory category. So, a worker joins as an ordinary worker and retires as an ordinary worker only at the plantation.

Therefore, the industrial casualization of the Indian workers as brought about by the policy of Liberalizaiton, Privatization and Globalization (Bhowmik: 1996) has also left perceptible impact on the enchanted plantation frontiers of Arunachal Pradesh. To cut down the legal incentives of the workers so as to make prospered the industrialization process of the state is observed to be the easy means to manage the tea industry in the state. The government intervention in the industrial relation scenario of tea industry is very much negligible especially in regard to welfare facilities of the workers as the plantation owners belong to local middle class elites (Mishra:1994) of the tribal society. In fact, the state sponsored industrialization process of Arunachal Pradesh is mainly meant for the local tribes of the tribal state of North East India.

The above cited illustration helps us to generalize that so-called industrialization process of Government of Arunachal Pradesh had hardly evolved an industrial society in the truest sense of the term. Rather, in the name of the protectionist approach of the Government of Arunachal Pradesh by patronizing the tribal way of industrialization process, the enchanted tea plantation frontiers have become the protected enclaves of the country in clear sense of the term. The tea industry is therefore appeared to have been the extension of agrarian economy of the state.

Housing Conditions of the Workers

All the Gorkha households of the plantation are of Pucca type with G.I. sheets roof and wooden walls. It is known from the workers that the houses provided to them are of Pucca type. The Pucca houses were constructed during the late sixties of 19th century when the Namshum Saw and Veneer Mills (P) Ltd. had been established in 1967. But now the workers themselves have to maintain and repair the same as the management of the plantation do not at all provide housing maintenance expenses and repair cost.

Interestingly, it is also observed that the houses made after the introduction of Gunna Tea Industries (P) Ltd. in 1987 are of Kuccha type. Most of the Adivasi houses are of Kuccha type with thatched roof and bamboo framed wet walls. It is learnt from the workers that the owner had constructed the Pucca houses in 1967 when Chowkham had full of forests that enabled him to construct the wooden quarters for the workers with G.I. sheets roof at low cost. The situation changed after 1987 when the Government of Arunachal Pradesh banned for deforestation in the state. This is the reason why the Adivasi households of about fifty in numbers are of purely Kuccha type till today because the cost of constructing a single Pucca house involves about sixty thousand rupees. No worker does launch complaint against the management for the construction of Pucca house because he does not dare so to approach the owner for obvious reasons as mentioned above in the study. If he does so, then he will be threatened to be ousted from the plantation stating him as a migrant without possessing the Inner Line Permit. So, the workers feel it better to keep themselves mum rather than inviting troubles for themselves. Therefore, the issue of new house construction does solely depend on the mercy of the plantation owner. The sizes of Kuccha houses are of 30' by 40' while the size of the Pucca houses are of 80' by 100'. It is because of the fact that in 1967, there was sufficient land available for the planter of the Anula Shagun T.E. in Gunnanagar area. It has also been observed that the size of Pucca household is quite sufficient to accommodate entire family members of the workers as population structure of the plantation is still not so high. Almost 30.0 per cent of the land in the plantation is still vacant. Even the whole Chowkham area does not have more than two thousand households. Almost ten thousand Khamti tribal population (Mishra: 1994) have occupied the village lands on both sides of 52 National Highway in Chowkham that destines to the Hindu pilgrimage ever known as Parsuram Kund.

Caste and Income of the Workers

It is transparent from Table 10.7 of the study that the annual income of the workers is quite good. The gross income of the workers has been calculated from all the sources like plantation (wages), agriculture, animal husbandry and allied services including the government services.

Table 10.7: Caste and Income Structure of the Workers

Sl.No.	Caste/ Community	Monthly Income (In Rupees)	Annual Income (in Rupees)
1.	Chettri = 30	63,000	7,56,000
2.	Manger = 50	1,26,000	15,12,000
3.	Gurung = 10	30,450	3,65,400
4.	Kami = 12	30,450	3,65,400
5.	Tamang = 6	16,800	2,01,600
6.	Rai = 30	1,02,900	12,34,800
7.	Limbu = 10	26,250	3,15,000
8.	Newar = 1	3,150	37,800
9.	Thami= 1	3,150	37,800
10.	Adivasis = 50	1,61,700	1,94,000
	Total = 200	5,63,850	50,19,800 *

* Gross income from all sources

Source: Field Work: 2003.

Among the Gorkha castes, Rai, Tamang, Manger and Kami are much better off than other castes in so far as their income structure is concerned. They are proficient because they owned good amount of agricultural land. Moreover, they are earlier migrants to the plantation. Though Adivasis earn equally at par with the Gorkhas counterpart, their level of living is comparatively much lower than the Gorkha workers. This relates to the historical background of Adivasis who had little inclination towards descent living with the income they used to earn from various sources of their economy at their places of origin.

Quite interestingly, all the workers stated that 40.0 per cent of their income is spent in maintaining their houses. Again, a substantial amount of money of the workers is being spent for medical treatment of their family members every year in Teju, Tinsukia, Dibrugargh or Guwahati hospitals and nursing homes.

Caste and Borrowings

It is comprehended from the discussion that plantation workers hardly borrow from others except on emergency. An analysis has been made in the study to understand the nature of borrowing. This will be evident from Table 10.8 of the study.

Table 10.8: Caste/Community and Borrowing

Sl. No.	*Caste/ Community*	*Community*
1.	Gorkhas	Gorkhas/Khamti/Marwari
2.	Adivasis	Adivasi/Khamti/Gorkhas/Marwari

Source: Field Work: 2003.

Interestingly, it is observed from Table 10.8 that the Gorkhas borrow from their own community. They go for loans to the Khamtis who are their masters at the plantation and if they do not get loans from the Khamtis as their masters then they go to Marwaris for the same. Similar picture is also noted among the Adivasis. But Adivasis go for loans to Marwaris if they do not get loans from their own community, Khamtis and Gorkhas. It indicates that Marwaris are not much preferred by the workers except under some compulsions. The sole reason for giving secondary option to the Marwaris for loans is due to high interest rate incurred of almost eighteen per cent per thousand per month. It shows that on the whole, Marwaris have good source of income from the interests incurred for loans from the workers. Borrowing and its nature indicates the area of cultural integration among the ethnic communities of the workers in the plantation. The workers feel that Adivasis, Gorkhas and Khamtis are the actual permanent neighbours while the Marwaris, Biharis and other Indians have been temporarily settled here in Gunnanagar for trade and business. If their business is dwindled down then they at any point of time will leave the place for elsewhere. Borrowing is therefore found to be a strong thread for cultural integration in the Anula Shagun T.E. among the Gorkhas, Adivasis and Khamtis.

Plantation Workers and Trade Union Movement

The study revealed that there is no sign of trade union movement in tea industry of Arunachal Pradesh. Whatever the trade unions are there, they are mainly centred around the Itanagar Printers, construction, Public Works Department and in two wood based industries (Das: 1995) of the state. The tea plantation workers of the state are mainly migrants under the short term Inner Line Permits. They are scared to talk about the formation of trade unions or unionization of tea plantation (Bhowmik: 1995) workers. Whatever the social problems emerge at the plantation of the state they have to be solved by the Government Gaon Bura (village headman) of the area. The Government Gaon Bura has been paid an honorarium of Rs. 1000 per month by the Government of Arunachal Pradesh. He looks after the problems of the society.

In the Anula Shagun T.E., there is a Khamti Gaon Bura who tries to solve the social problems of the workers. But interestingly, it is found that recently, a rift has taken place between the Government Gaon Bura and the owner of the plantation. It has been found that the Government Gaon Bura belongs to another clan of the Khamti society while the planter belongs to Namshum clan which was considered to be historically the ruling class or superior clan than other clans of the Khamti society (Mishra: 1994). The Government Gaon Bura wants to make conscious the workers about their rights and responsibilities at the plantation industry. This is in fact highly against the vested interest of the plantation owner who, by heart and soul, wants to keep the workers in darkness so that his profit margin is always high. He thinks himself as the lion of Chowkham and God father of the workers. Even the Government schemes which are not liked by him, can hardly be implemented here at the area. If he does not like any government scheme, he then straightway rejects the same. Nobody except his pet persons can penetrate the plantations. Thus, the plantation is his personal colony, of course, an enchanted ones and the society is an enclave society of Arunachal frontier.

In this way, from the point of the Government legislations, the tea plantation workers of the Anula Shagun T.E. can be termed as an unorganized sector workers. They are unorganized as the owner of the plantation has fully owned the tea industry but he has nothing to own the labour force both in industrial as well as social life of the workers (Mamkottam: 1994). Thus, there is every doubt as to whether any trade union movement as we found in neighbouring Assam tea plantations, can have an access (Seth: 1994) to the Anula Shagun T.E. in future. The same platitude is noted (Sampath: 1994; Dubey: 1994) in case of other tea plantations of Arunachal Pradesh in so far as the unionization (Sinha: 1994) of tea plantation workers is concerned.

Labour Commitment to Tea Industry

In spite of complete exploitation of tea plantation workers in the Anula Shagun T.E., the workers are found to be fully committed to the industry as no work remains pending or undone right from plucking of green tea leaves to packaging of made tea. Even they work for eight hours a day during the pruning season. It is called Ek Bela Kam or half a day work in West Bangal and Assam tea plantations. This really supplements the hypothesis that the Gorkha are hard working people. Had there been any other dominant working community, then the Anula Shagun T.E. had to be abandoned long back for ever. This may be the background reason why Mr. Gohain has also started another tea plantation in Medo area by recruiting the Gorkha workers from his Bordumsa tea estate and also a few Gorkha workers from the Anula Shagun T.E. The commitments of the Gorkha workers along with the young tea bushes of hardly fifteen years old and low cost of production (Rs. 20 per kilogram of made tea) has given encouraging direction to the tribal tea plantation owner. The high rate of Tea Board's subsidy schemes for introducing new factories and field has given further stimuli to the tea plantation tribal planters (owners) of the state. The tea plantations of the state are paying handsome revenue to the Government of Arunachal Pradesh by fetching the selling price of Rs. 70 to Rs. 80 per kilogram of tea on the average in the markets. To supplement the above statement, here a concrete instance has been cited regarding the price that Arunachal Pradesh tea plantations got in 1999 in the market that portrayed the fact that tea industry of the Arunachal Pradesh has a promising or bright future.

Table 10.9: Tea Price for Arunachal Pradesh (1999)

Sl. No.	*Garden*	*C.T. Leaf (Qty. in Thousand Kg.)*	*Average Price(per kilogram)*	*Orthodox (Qty. in Kg.)*	*Price per Kg.*	*Dust Qty. In Kg.*	*Price*
1.	Ganesh Tea Tayang	2039.1	45.77	—	—	—	—
2.	Shreenanda	28982.4	74.88	—	—	17980.2	61.20
3	Tayang	830.0	32.16	—	—	—	—
4.	Total	31841.5	67.02	—		17980.2	61.20
5.	Excise Zone II	—	—	—	—	—	—
	Total	4938051.1	67.02	1448696.0	78.65	1183904.4	53.42
	Grand Total	13651351.6	70.84	4978633.4	69.85	6518000.4	58.91

Source: Assam Tea Review and News: 1999 (May, 35).

Table 10.9 indicates that on the average, the Arunachal tea of C.T.C variety got Rs. 70.84 in 1999-2000 per kilogram of made tea.

The price level of Arunachal tea is higher than any other tea of Assam and West Bengal plantations in so far as the C.T.C. variety is concerned. The apparent reason besides cheap labour for getting such a higher level of price in the market is due to its higher quality tea procured from the young tea bushes. It indicates that the plantation industry is quite lucrative to the state economy of Arunachal Pradesh.

XI

Social Life of the Workers

In this chapter, we will discuss about the social life of the workers. Discussing the social life, changing social structure of the Gorkha castes, caste and family structure, caste and marriage and caste and commensal relations will be highlighted elaborately. Again, a special stress will be given to the relationship between the Gorkha and Adivasis as well as the Gorkha and Khamti communities of the plantation. Highlighting the changing social relationship, we will see the traditional social structure of the Gorkha and how the traditional social structure of the Gorkha society based on hierarchical divisions has been transforming into a new type of social stratification in the plantation—industrial environment of the Anula Shagun T.E.

The Anula Shagun T.E.: Land of Migrants

Historically, the local dominant Khamti tribe had migrated from Bor Khamti country of Myanmar (Burma) at the source of river Irrawady in early 18th century (Gogoi: 1971). First, they settled down at Tengapani area of Tinsukia district of Assam where they were badly defeated and ousted by the Singpoo tribe (*Ibid.*). After being ousted by the Singpoos from Tengapani, the Khamti tribe moved towards Sadiya of Assam (Das: 1995) and settled down there by defeating the local Assmese people. Prof. M. L. Bose (1997), the historian, has very lucidly described the origin and settlement of the Khamti tribes in Arunachal Pradesh. He described. "The British came into contact with the Khamti tribe when they came to Assam during the Anglo-Burmese War of 1824 to 1826. The Khamtis were immigrants from the land called Bor Khamti between the eastern extremity of Assam and river Irrawady. At first, they had settled around the Tengapani in

Upper Assam. During 1799 to 1800, the Barasiringio (the dominant Assamese people) revolted in Sadiya, the Khamtis along with other tribes joined the Assamese Governor of Sadiya (Bhuyan: 1947). The Tung Khangia Burangi records that they occupied Sadiya in 1797 and the title and dignity of Ahom Governor were assumed by the Khamti tribal chief (*Ibid.*:1947). The Ahom kings had no formal relations with the Khamtis nor had any of the Ahom kings granted any Posa (tax) on them. The Khamti chief ruled like an independent prince.

Further, Bose observed, "He has succeeded in keeping his Sadiya free from this Anglo-Assamese turmoil when Scot, the first British Agent to the Governor-General came to Upper Assam in 1824, the Khamtis of Chowkham had rendered him good service. Therefore, Scot recognized the Khamti chief as 'Chousalan Sadiya Khowa Gohain' as the chief and permitted him to collect taxes from the Assamese people within his jurisdiction. The Khamti chief himself did not pay any tax and instead undertook to maintain a contingent of 200 men to be armed by the British as per the term of an agreement entered to obey orders of the British Government sent through the Political Officer of Upper Assam to whom they were to bring all serious crimes for trial. The relation between the Khamti and British remained friendly and peaceful till 1839 though rumours of Khamti intrigue were reported occasionally. As late as 1838, Captain White, the Political Agent of Sadiya, wrote that they were faithful to their engagements and no cause for anxiety though a report of the year shows that the Khamtis had become disgusted at the long continuance of the British supremacy over Sadiya which they considered to be their own territory. In 1835, a fresh batch of immigrants from Bor Khamti land entered Assam and sought the permission to settle under the British Government. They asked for the remission of taxes for ten years and fire arms. The British were very anxious to settle them as a barrier between Assam and Burma because still they were haunted by a dread of fresh Burmese invasion. Therefore, the Khamtis were allowed to settle without paying taxes for three years but no fire arms were supplied to them. In 1838, a dispute arose between the Khamti chief of Sadiya and Bor Senapati of Muttack, the Moamaria chief of Upper Assam in regard to the tract of land on the south bank of Brahmaputra. The Political Agent (Officer) of Sadiya asked both the parties to appear before him. The Khamti chief took possession of the land in defiance of the order whereupon the Political Agent in vindication of his authority attacked the land in dispute. He ordered first the suspension and then removal of the Khamti chief from the post of Khawa Gohain. The Khawa Gohain was therefore removed to a distant station down the river out of reach of easy intrigue and his post was abolished. His territory was brought under the administration of the British officer of Sadiya who collected taxes from the Assamese people and administered justice to them. But the Khamtis and Singpoos of this territory left under their own chiefs, no tax was levied upon them. Apparently, the Khamtis seemed contend and during the Singpoo rising in 1838, along with the Khamtis of Chowkham rendered good service to the British. The ex-Khawa Gohain was allowed to return to Sadiya in his private capacity in recognition of the Khamti service. But this hatred of the British and fear of losing being brought under regular jurisdiction of the British administration resulted premeditated outbreak on 19th January, 1839 when about 500 Khamtis in arms attacked the British post at Sadiya, butchered Col. White and his men and burnt down the lines in the ground. The Khamtis on the south bank of Brahmaputra (Chowkham) also rose but they were put down by the British troops. The successful Khamtis on the north bank of Brahmaputra, however, retreated with their adherents and took refuge among the Dibang Mishmis. Compelled by distress in their jungle refuge, one chief named Chonking Gohain, surrendered and then led a British force to compel others to follow him. In 1839 to 1840, more expeditions were sent to disperse the Khamtis from the hills and finally in 1843, all the Khamtis surrendered to the British under an agreement of good behaviour. After that the Khamtis were divided into four groups as suggested by Captain Vetch who suppressed the Khamti rebellion. With a view to weakening them they were dispersed by the British in four divisions. One group of Khamtis had settled at Choonpura above Sadiya under the captain Gohain, cousin of late Khawa Gohain. Another division which was formerly near Tengapani had settled near Saikhawa to the south of river Brahmaputra. The third party under Chowtang Gohain had been settled at Dhemaji and fourth group to Bhodia, west of Lakhimpur under the son of late Khawa Gohain. Since then they could not be united and as a result they failed to acquire any political importance. They took agricultural pursuits. Those who settled in Choonpura and below Saikhawa i.e. in Chowkham of Arunachal Pradesh did not pay any revenue, the rest in Bhodia and Dhemaji paid regular taxes to the government. The British relation with the

Khamtis did not face any strain thereafter. Rather, henceforth, the Khamtis and their chiefs always acted as regular guides to the British officers in their tour in Mishmis and Singpoos hills. Needham, Williamson and Dundas took Khamti Gohains in their tours. The Khamti chief of Chowkham was granted a pension and gun in recognition of British favour to him. As late as 1916, he claimed restitution of his independence and title. Though the request was turned down, his pension was increased to Rs. 50 from Rs. 30 and his people was exempted from taxation when the poll taxes began to be levied in the central and eastern districts of North East frontier in which some Khamtis were included after 1814". Today, the other Khamtis as dispersed by the British appeared to have been completely assimilated with other tribes of the places of their settlement. This may be the reason why the Khamtis are found to be mostly concentrated in Chowkham area of Lohit district of Arunachal Pradesh. The Khamtis who had there in Choonpura left forever after disposing their land to the Gorkhas in 1950—after the great earthquake in Sadiya-Saikhawa areas of north-east India.

After their settlement in Chowkham area in 1785 (Mishra: 1994), the Khamtis started settled cultivation along with Jhum. They also engaged themselves for petty business on the tribal arts and crafts. Their settled cultivation was supported by the institution of village chieftainship. Their "Lungi" making profession has become very prominent in the state. The traditional dormitory system which they inherited from their tradition has been on vogue in mainly the distant villages only. According to Khamti custom, the village chief used to allot the common land to the individual villagers. With the abandonment of any land by the individuals, it automatically reverted to the common village land (Das: 1995; Mishra: 1994).

The institution of Chieftainship among the Khamtis had been instrumental in dividing their societies into two main classes viz., the patricians and plebeians. In the Hinayana Buddhist Khamti society, chiefs occupied the highest position and they were followed by priests. Below them, there was a class of freemen. At the bottom, there were slaves. The chiefs, priests and patricians being the leisured class were largely dependent on the labour of the commoners—plebeians as well as slaves (Mishra: 1983).

Such system was supported by the British colonialists so as to keep the tribal Arunachal isolated under their policy of "Excluded

Areas" and "Partially Excluded Areas". Things underwent a sea change after 1947 when the Government of India started to follow the policy of integration in Arunachal Pradesh as elsewhere the country so as to keep the tribal identity in tact. Doing this, the development process through industrialization started in Arunachal Pradesh and at Chowkham also. With the formation of a full-fledged state in 1987, Arunachal Government officially abolished the slavery system (Bose: 1997). This gave a new social structure in Arunachal Pradesh, viz., landowners and landless categories in rural areas of the state. Along with the introduction of Panchayati Raj system in village Arunachal Pradesh ever since 1967 (*Ibid*.), the whole social structure started changing. All the slaves became free citizens of the state. The impacts of change also affected the industrially developed Lohit district of Arunachal wilderness (frontiers). Broadly, three tier class ridden societies emerged after that in the state viz., village chief/Gaon Bura, Middle class elites and low class Khamtis. Interestingly, it is observed that the village chief and Gaon Bura have formal power being delegated by the government while the real power lies at the hands of middle class Khamti elites (Mishra: 1994) in the villages of Chowkham (Gogoi: 1971) while the lower class Khamtis are purely agrarian people today which to them is more lucrative than working in tea plantation industry of the region. This really called for the import of tea plantation labourers from Assam and Nepal Himalayas in the eastern most districts of Arunachal frontiers. The above discussion makes it very distinct that Khamtis along with Noctes, Tangsas and Singpoos were mainly earlier migrants to the eastern most districts of the state from Myanmar (Burma) mainland (Baruah: 2000)). The question of survival made them more proactive in agriculture, Jhum cultivation and business from the beginning (Gogoi: 1971) in Chowkham (Mishra: 1994).

It is observed that the power and authority of Gaon Bura is secondary in the Khamti society of Chowkham as the newly emerged middle class of educated elites (*Ibid*.) among the Khamtis are now moulding the society, polity and economy (Das:1995) of the region. Almost all the land of Satkilu Gaon near the Anula Shagun T.E. is owned by the Khamtis. The Gohain family of the Anula Shagun T.E. has two more tea plantations one each in Medo and Bordumsa of Lohit and Changlang districts respectively of the Arunachal Pradesh.

TRADITIONAL SOCIAL STRUCTURE OF THE GORKHAS

Studying the present social dynamics of the Gorkha community, a pondering on its traditional structure is very important. In the traditional Gorkha society, the whole population was divided into three groups, viz., Tagadhari, Matwali and Untouchable in Nepal (Haimendorf: 1966) and even in Darjeeling—Sikkim Himalayas (Sharma: 2000) of Indian sub-continent. The caste falling in each category had specific occupation. Thus, prior to their migration to the Anula Shagun T.E., the Gorkha castes had their specific occupations. The society typically was an agrarian in nature. This will be very clear if we see Table 11.1.

Table 11.1: Traditional Gorkha Caste System (1769)

Sl. No.	*Varna*	*Castes*
1.	Brahmin	Upadhaya, Kumai, Jaisi, Deb Bhaju (Newar)
2.	Kshatriya	Thakuri, Chettri, Khatri
3.	Double Order*	Gurung, Mangar
4.	Shudra	Rai, Limbu, Low caste Newars,Sunuwars, Sherpa, Murmis, Thamis, Tamangs etc.
5.	Vaisya	Newar High Castes
6.	Untouchables	Kami, Damai, Sarki, Chyme, Jyapu, Pore (Newar)

* Converted into Hindu Religion from Buddhist Animism.
Source: Nepali: 1965.

The above Gorkha caste system emerged after 1769 (Unification of Nepal by Prithivinarayan Shah) in Nepal underwent a sea change afterwards. The five-fold classification of the Gorkha society underwent a drastic change later on. Haimendorf (1966) has classified the Gorkha society into three-fold viz., Tagadhari, Matwali and Untouchable. Caplan (1970) has also classified the Gorkha society into three groups, viz., Tagadhari, Matwali and Untouchable considering the overt changes occurring in Nepal after 1926—the year of the abolition of slavery system by the Government of Nepal.

The traditional Gorkha caste system was associated with the specific occupation of each and every caste. This is evident from Table 11.2 of the study.

It is very much transparent from Table 11.2 that most of the Gorkha castes were toiling mass of Nepal as well as Eastern Himalayas. They were mainly concentrated in agrarian belts of Nepal, Darjeeling, Sikkim as well as the Bhutan Himalayas.

Table 11.2: Occupational Structure of the Gorkha Society

Sl. No.	*Caste*	*Traditional Occupation*
1.	Bahuns	Priests
2.	Chettris	Warriors
3.	Thakuris	Aristocrats
4.	Newars	Businessmen
5.	Rais, Limbus,Yakhas, Mangers	Agriculturists
6.	Thamis, Sunuwars, Gurungs	Shepherds
7.	Tamangs	Horse Traders/Cavaliers
8.	Bhujels	Beaten Rice Makers
9.	Jogis	Ascetics
10.	Sherpas	Porters
11.	Yolmus	Paper Makers
12.	Lepchas	Shifting cultivators (Jhum cultivators) in eastern Nepal, Darjeeling-Sikkim Himalayas
13.	Bhutias	Petty Businessmen
14.	Kamis	Iron Smiths
15.	Damais	Tailors/ Musicians
16.	Sarkis	Cobblers

Source: Sharma: 2000.

The Gorkha caste like Bahun, Chettri and Thakuri belonged to Tagadhari group. The Tagadhari meant those castes which had to compulsorily wear the sacred threads and they were to be purely vegetarians by food habit. The caste like Manger and Gurung were partially Hindu and again partially Buddhist because they used to practice Buddhist rituals along with Hindu cultural (Matwali) ceremonies. The Mangers, Gurungs along with Rais, Limbus, Yakhas, Newars, Sunuwars, Tamangs, Bhujels, Jogis, Yolmus, Sherpas, Lepchas and Bhutias were broadly considered as Matwalis who were supposed to use wine and offer meat as ritual food items compulsorily. The caste like Kami, Damai and Sarki were considered as untouchables in the traditional Gorkha society. But those untouchables remained vibrant in application in Nepal till 1926 only after which the concept of untouchable castes underwent considerable changes. However, the Tagadhari group has been categorized in the present study into two sub-divisions, viz., Jharra (Pure) and Thimaha (Non-Jhara or non-pure) . The Jharra Tagadharis have to wear sacred threads of nine strings while the Thimaha Tagadharis have to wear sacred threads of six strings only. The Thimaha category is very much akin to the Matwali way of life as they sacrifice animal blood while observing their rituals. Again, Matwali category has been classified into Setho (White) and Kalo (Black) groups. The caste like Rai, Limbu, Manger, Gurung, Newar, Sherpa, Tamang, Thamı etc. are conceptualized here as Setho type as they appeared to belong to Mongoloid stock of the Himalayas. The Kamis, Damais and Sarkis, the untouchables of the past, have been categorized as Kalo type (Sharma: 2000) for they appear to have possessed Aryan like characters as of Bahuns, Chhetris and Thakuris of the Gorkha society. The clan structure of these Kalo Matwalis is same as of the Tagadharis. It is believed that once upon a time in Nepal they were converted into untouchables from the Tagadharis for their anti-social activities and violation of caste endogamy or exogamy on practice of the then Gorkha society (Sharma: 1997).

The Kalo Matwalis are part and parcel of the Matwali group as a whole as ritually they are very much akin to the Setho Matwalis. Below Matwalis, the Khampti tribe is conceptualized to have occupied the hierarchy on the ground that Khamti tribe is socio-economically as well as culturally more sophisticated than the Adivasis. So, the Adivasis come at the bottom of caste hierarchy of the plantation. Culturally, the Adivasis are conceptualized as good as untouchables by the plantation society as they still take beef or they kill cows and bulls and made shoes from the flesh of the cows and bulls. Interestingly, there is no Kami, Damai and Sarki caste of the Gorkha community at the plantation. The Sarkis used to kill cows and bulls and made shoes or they used to collect flesh of dead cattle and made shoes in the past especially in Nepal and Darjeeling-Sikkim, Himalayas. Moreover, they used to take beef along with Rai, Limbu, Gurung, Manger, Tamang, Thami etc. in Nepal (Pradhan:1991). This was one of the immediate causes for their out migration to Munglan (India) as beef easting was strictly prohibited then in Nepal by the Gorkha Government. Not a single Gorkha kills cow and bull and takes beef here at the plantation. But the Adivasis are found killing cows and bulls and taking beef. This might be the logical synthesis to put them at the lowest stratum of the plantation system of the Anula Shagun T.E.

However, living with the industrial environment of tea industry, a new social stratification has been emerged at the plantation considering the local situation of Gunnanagar. This is clear from Table 11.3 of the study. The traditional caste hierarchy of the Gorkha society got complete transformation in the Anula Shagun T.E. of Arunachal Pradesh. This is again evident from Table 11.4.

Table 11.3: Caste Hierarchy in the Anula Shagun T.E.

Sl. No.	*Caste Status*	*Caste Hierarchy*
1.	Tagadharis (Thimaha) *	Chettri
2.	Matwalis (Setho)	Manger, Gurung, Rai, Limbu, Tamang, Newar, Thami
	Matwalis (Kalo)	Kami, Adivasi

* No Jharra Tagadhari (Bahun) or priestly caste is there at the plantation.
Source: Field Work: 2003.

It is very distinct from Table 11.3 of the study that there is no Jharra Tagadhari caste in the plantation. But quite a good many Jharra Tagadhari households are there in the Satkilu Gaon (village) and other villages of Chowkham. It is because of the fact that Jharra Tagadharis being priestly caste do not want to discontinue with their priestly occupation along with the agrarian economy in the region. Thus, only Thimaha Tagadharis are there in the plantation as manual workers. Again the Matwalis have been conceptually classified in the study into Setho and Kalo types.

Table 11.4: Social Stratification in the Anula Shagun T.E.

Sl. No.	*Status*	*Caste/Tribe*
I	Tribals (Sons of the Soil)—(Backward)	Khamtis
II	Non-Tribals (Migrants) (Developed)	Gorkhas/Assamese/ Biharis/ Bengalis/ Marwaris/Adivasis etc.

Source: Field Work: 2003.

Table 11.4 of the study indicates that there is an absolute polarization of the plantation society into tribal and non-tribal groups. Such a polarization is the concomitant impact of Arunachal society as a whole which has very clearly classified the entire population of the state into tribal and non-tribal groups. However, the table also indicates that tribal Khamtis have occupied the higher position in the social structure of the plantation. They are at the higher echelons of the society while the non-tribals occupy lower positions as they are migrants and considered as developed or forward communities of the country or outside the country. Moreover, occupationally, they belong to toiling mass (class) of the plantation system.

In fact, they are looked down upon by the Khamtis on the logic that the migrants as outsiders want to exploit the innocent backward tribals of the Arunachal Pradesh. Such a polarization of the plantation society has enabled the plantation management to divide them and exploit the workers as much as they can do for the sake of so-called industrial development of Chowkham of Arunachal Pradesh.

Family

Traditionally, peasants and landless agricultural workers had joint family system in agrarian Nepal (Sharma: 2000). A family used to be the patriarchal in nature consisting of a man, his wife, sons, daughters, married sons, daughter-in-laws, grandsons and granddaughters. In the present study, the term 'family' denotes a group of persons sharing the same hearth and living together in the same house whether related or not. The workers are not allowed to build private houses in the plantation. The plantation has provided labour quarters of 80' by 100' of length and breadth respectively. Considering this, the present study has planned to classify the family into Nuclear and Joint types. The Nuclear family denotes a family which is composed of parents and unmarried children. A Joint family denotes a family consisting of parents of a couple, unmarried brothers, sisters, father, mother, father-in-law, mother-in–law, grandsons and granddaughters. The family structure of workers of the Anula Shagun T.E. will be very clear if we see Table 11.5 of the study.

It is observed from Table 11.5 that 71.3 per cent of the family is of Nuclear type while only 28.7 per cent are of Joint type. Unlike in the traditional Gorkha society, the structure of family is different in the sense that it may not always be patriarchal in nature. The percentage of Nuclear family is highest in case of the Newar and Thami castes. But these percentages of two castes do not carry any significant meaning as only one each of Newar and Thami castes are there in the plantation respectively. The 90.0 per cent of Rai, 83.3 per cent of Kami, 80.0 per cent of Gurung and Limbu castes have Nuclear family. Again, 66.7 per cent of Tamang, 60.0 per cent of Chhetri and Manger castes have Nuclear family respectively. The percentage of Joint family is highest among the Chhetri (40.0%) and

Table 11.5: Family Structure of the Workers

Sl. No.	*Caste/Community*	*Nuclear*	*Percentage*	*Joint*	*Percentage*
1.	Chhetri= 30	18	60.0	12	40.0
2.	Manger= 50	30	60.0	20	40.0
3.	Gurung= 10	08	80.0	02	20.0
4.	Kami = 12	10	83.3	02	16.7
5.	Tamang= 06	04	66.7	02	33.3
6.	Rai = 30	27	90.0	03	10.0
7.	Limbu = 10	08	80.0	02	20.0
8.	Newar = 01	01	100.0	—	—
9.	Thami = 01	01	100.0	—	—
	Total= 150	107	71.3%	43	28.7%

Source: Field Work: 2003.

Manger (40.0%) castes in the plantation. Next to them, Tamangs have 33.3 per cent of joint family. Again, Gurung (20.0%) and Limbu (20.0%) castes have Joint families. Next to them, Kamis (16.7%) and Rai (10.3%) have Joint families. Table 11.5 also indicates that the Nuclearization process of the family got complete shape in the plantation system. Socially, the separation of newly married couples from their parental home under the Ansa Banda (division of ancestral property among the sons) system of traditional Gorkha society is a driving force (Sharma: 2000) which has also gladly accepted by the plantation system of the Anula Shagun T.E. The table also portrays the fact that till today, the Joint family system is persisting in the plantation due to the widespread agrarian economy of the region under study. The agrarian economy requires more and more manpower resource in the family to pursue on the cultivation of land and thereby having bread and butter for their family while living in the North Eastern wilderness.

Changing Roles of the Family Members

The Anula Shagun T.E. is basically a patriarchal society as the main authority of the family lies in the hand of the male members. This is based on the logic that they are the recent migrants from Nepal Himalayas which is predominantly a male dominated (Bannet: 1978) society. Thus, the decision making power of the family lies with the males only. Of course, this is found a bit different in case of Tamang, Thami and Gurung castes. Among these three castes, power and authority are by and large equally shared by male and female members of the family. It is because of the fact that basically they were pro-Buddhists in Nepal Himalayas before migrating to the Anula Shagun T.E. The authority structure is more or less same among Rai, Limbu, Chhetri, Manger, Kami and Newar castes as of their places of origin. However, in regard to the traditional female liabilities especially among the Tagadharis that had to be soldiered by the parents at the time of marriage ceremony by offering Daijo (Dowry) in Nepal (Sharma: 2000) has been changed as females are also the earning members of family in the plantation. Unlike in the past, the elder sisters need not to be compulsorily respected by the younger brothers and sisters and daughter-in-laws of the family (*Ibid.*).

With the continuation of kin-based joint family (28.7%) at the plantation, the domestic role of the family members has been by and large same. The males have to do more difficult tasks involving higher level of physical or muscle power than the females who normally look after the smaller kids, cook food, collect cattle fodders etc. In the agrarian field, male plough the land and females transplant the seedlings in the prepared field. The field levelling, breaking wet mud joints etc. are to be done by the male members only. The males involving in such a job is called as Bausees in the Gorkha society.

Due to the industrial environment, female mobility is greater compared to the traditional Nepal especially in relation to attending marriage ceremonies, death rituals and shopping at Gunnanagar, Chowkham, Medo, Teju and Wakro towns. Even some of the females go to attend Bajars at Tinsukia, Doom Dooma and Dibrugargh towns. However, as Sharma (2000) observed that such openness is very much restricted among the Tagadhari women workers. The Matwalis also do not like to see their female members freely mixing with other males especially in sexual matter.

The ongoing movement for women empowerment as launched by various tribal women organizations and other non-governmental organizations in Arunachal Pradesh has made the women workers also to emancipate themselves from the clutches of their mother-in-laws, husband's brothers, female affines and kin-bonds of the family as a basic unit to sustain the traditional values of the social system (Bhadra: 1997). The Gorkha women have earned the capacity of emancipating themselves from the clutches of traditional myths and misconceptions (Bose: 1997) while living in the industrial environment. The women workers have a strong Mahila Samity at Chowkham having a Khamti woman as its president and a Gorkha woman as its secretary. The women organization is working on anti-drugs/alcohol practices at the plantation.

Marriage

Marriage as a social institution appears to be very much optional in the Gorkha society especially while selecting the marriage partners. In this context, Table 11.6 shall clearly depict the marriage patterns of the workers in the plantation.

If we analyze Table 11.6 of the study thoroughly, we will find that 63.7 per cent of marriages have taken place within the respective castes only while 36.3 per cent of their marriages have taken place among various castes and tribes of the plantation. Caste-wise, Newar (100.0%) and Thami (100.0%) have married within their own castes only. Thus, caste endogamy is very high among the Newar, Thami, Chhetri and Tamang castes in the Gorkha society of the plantation. In regard to inter-caste marriage, Limbu (66.7%), Gurung (58.3% and Rai (45.6%) is quite significant in understanding.

Table 11.6: Marriage Pattern of the Workers

Sl. No.	*Caste/ Community*	*Intra-Caste*	*Percentage*	*Inter-Caste*	*Percentage*
	Gorkhas				
1.	Chhetri = 42	39	92.8	03	7.1
2.	Manger = 70	40	57.1	30	42.9
3.	Gurung = 12	05	41.7	07	58.3
4.	Tamang = 08	07	87.5	01	12.5
5.	Rai = 33	18	54.5	15	45.6
6.	Limbu = 12	04	33.3	08	66.7
7.	Newar = 01	01	100.0	—	—
8.	Thami = 01	01	100.0	—	—
9.	Kami = 14	08	57.1	06	42.9
	Total = 193	123	63.7	70	36.3

Source: Field Work: 2003.

Table 11.6 also indicates that Kami (42.9%) and Manger (42.9%) have married with other castes and tribes of the plantation as well as Chowkham region. But the workers viewed that marriages among the Matwalis are not to be considered as inter-caste marriages due to similar ritual practices of all the Matwali castes. Many Tamangs, Rais, Limbus and others have married Khamti women in order to make sure of their identity at the plantation of the state forever. It shows that the traditional concept of Jat Bibaha (marriage within own caste), Ajat Bibaha (marriage with other lower castes) and Kujat Bibaha (marriage with the untouchables) of the past have some degree of continuity at the plantation. But in most of the cases, the marriage choice is becoming very much optional for all castes and tribes. Some castes like Newar, Kami and Chhetri appear to have been much conscious about their marriage alliances and they do the same within their own castes only. During the present situation in the plantation, most of the youngsters opt for love marriages rather than Maagi Bibaha (Arranged marriage) due to the high financial implications of arranged marriages. This has been taking place in the plantation as the dominant Khamti tribe of the region do Chori (elopement) Bibaha as per their dormitory system of the past (Mishra: 1994).

Traditionally, the Tagadharis used to maintain a gap of four generations from the mother's side and eight generations from the father's side before marrying a girl (Sharma: 2000). But since the plantation is consisting of many castes and tribes, it is really next to impossible to draw the genealogy of marrying couples. However, the clans associated with father and mother's sides have been as far as possible avoided before arranging marriages among all castes and tribes. The concept of endogamy and exogamy of the past is hardly found to have been affecting the marriage alliances in the plantation today. The Gorkha system of Satto Bibaha (marriage by bride exchanges) among the Tagadharis is not at all found today as the plantation system does not allow two wives for the same male. The concept of Jat Dandha (penalty for breach of endogamy) of the past is not at all found here in the plantation as it used to take place at their places of origin (Sharma: 1997). To marry a Khamti girl is a symbol of acquiring high dignity by the Gorkhas in order to confirm their destiny in the wilderness of the plantation situation as well as the Arunachal Pradesh as a whole especially after 1987. This fact has been nicely supplemented by the observation made by Das (1995). Marriage appears to be a strong bond or thread for restoring concrete national integration in the development process of the state of Arunachal Pradesh. Interestingly, not a single Gorkha has married Adivasi woman at the plantation. The rationale behind marrying Khamti women is to ascertain their identity through acquiring citizenship in the tribal state at least for the children borned from the Khamti women.

Very recently, the Arunachal Pradesh Government has approved such marriages if the tribal girls do willingly marry boys of other communities. Even after having children, any Gorkha or other communities males want to leave Arunachal Pradesh, they can do it at their liberty except their children who cannot be taken away as the children borned from the Khamti women are logically as well as legally considered as tribal children of the tribal state. This is because of the fact that for instance, among the Khamtis, descent genealogy or lineage is equally drawn from the female side also. This might be the obvious reason why most of the Khamti children speak Nepali/ Gorkha language fluently at par with Khamti at the Anula Shagun T.E., Chowkham, Gunnanagar, Medo, Wakro etc. In fact, as we interviewed the tribal marriageable youths about their options for marital partners, it is found that 90.0 per cent of the tribal boys and girls opt for Gorkhas and only 10.0 per cent of them opt for Khamti and other tribes of the state for the same. Again, of the 10.0 per cent tribal youths, only 2.0 per cent of them belong to Namshum clan of the Khamti society. While 8.0 per cent from other clans of Khamti youths opt for inter-tribal marriages. It indicates that Namshum as the traditional ruling clan among the Khamtis (Mishra: 1994) appears to be less conservative in selecting marriageable partners. To the Khamtis, the Gorkhas hail from the Himalayas which they considered as the abode of Lord Buddha (Bhanja: 1984). The observations show that the Himalayan culture, society and tradition have a great bearing (Haimendorf: 1966) on the tribal-Hindu relationship in North East India including the Arunachal wilderness.

The Commensal Relations

From the point of view of commensal relation, the traditional Gorkha society was divided into two broad divisions, viz., Pani-Chal-Ne-Jats (castes from whom water can be taken) and Pani-Na-Chal-Ne-Jats (castes from whom water can not be taken). This is evident from Table 11.7.

It is transparent from Table 11.7 of the study that excepting untouchable castes like Kami, Damai and Sarki, Pore, Cheme, Jyapu (Newars) etc., every caste used to accept water from every other caste in the past. This is relevant both in Nepal and the Eastern Himalayas as observed by Sharma (2003). Such commensal relation underwent a sea change aftermath of their migration to the Anula Shagun T.E. of the Arunachal Pradesh wilderness from their places of origin.

Table 11.7: Traditional Commensal Relation in regard to the Acceptance of Water

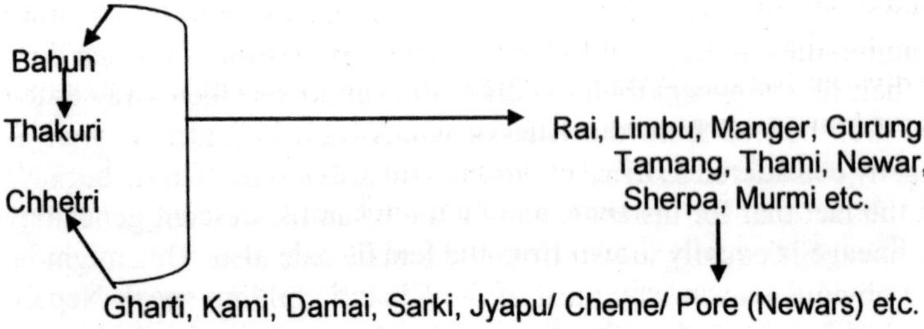

Source: Field Work: 2003.

Table 11.8: Commensal Relation of Water at the Plantation (Anula Shagun T.E.)

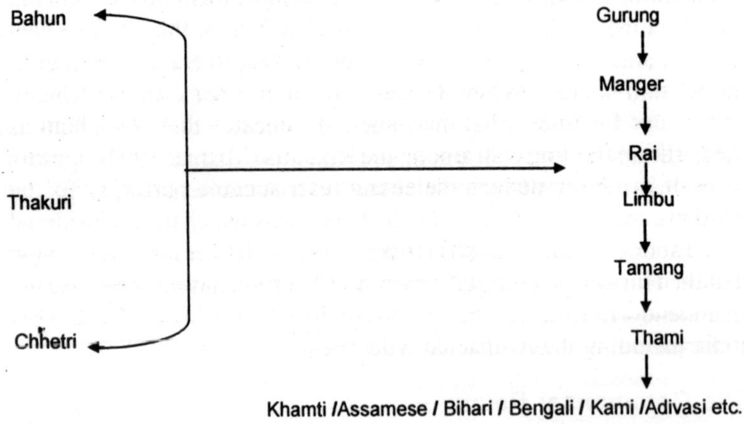

Source: Field Work: 2003.

Table 11.8 of the study indicates the fact that the commensal relation in regard to water has been drastically altered at the Anula Shagun T.E. Unlike in the past, all castes and tribes take water from each other at the plantation. It is a matter of great pleasure and vanity for the plantation workers if they are being served with water, tea and snacks by the owner's family of the plantation as well as other Khamtis of the region.

In regard to the acceptance of Kuccha food like boiled Dal (lentil) and rice, Chhetris are a bit conscious from other castes and tribes. In regard to Pucca foods like tea, snacks etc., all the castes and tribes accept the same without hesitation in day to day life at the plantation. The acceptance of Kuccha and Pucca food is open among all the castes and tribes except at the time of observing their respective caste and tribal rituals.

In Khamti Buddhist Losar or Losang festivals, all the Gorkhas, Adivasis, Biharis, Assamese, Bengalis and others of the plantation were found taking both the Kuccha and Pucca foods openly. Similarly, the Gorkha Seal Roti (cuisine) is very popular among Khamti, Assamese, Bihari and Bengali communities of the plantation as well as Gunnanagar and Chowkham areas of the region.

Religious Practices of the Workers

From the religious point of view, the Arunachal hill tribes are purely Buddhists while the tribes aboding the central territory of Arunachal Pradesh have their traditional tribal religion known as Animism and the foothill tribes of Lohit district of the Arunachal Pradesh have their original Buddhist religion being brought from their places of origin (Bose:1997). Though the religious practices of the workers are related to Hindu, Buddhist and Christain religions, the nature of performing the same is predominantly tribal (Sharma:1997). Table 11.9 of the study depicts the structure of religious practices of the workers.

Table 11.9 shows that the Anula Shagun T.E. is predominantly a Hindu industrial society with Khamti tribal core culture. Interestingly, the table also shows that Tamangs and Gurungs of the Gorkha community are purely Buddhists by religion in the plantation while they are mostly Hindus in the Eastern Himalaya (Sharma: 2000). This might be the apparent reason why Tamangs and Gurungs are very near and dear to the Khamti tea plantation owner. A Tamang Lama (priest) along with other Budhist Lamas from the Khamti community are employed at the Gunnanagar Buddhist monastery which was built by the forefathers of the present Khamti tea plantation owner. Even some Mangers are planning to revert to the Buddhist religion. In fact, they were purely Buddhists in Nepal Himalayas prior to their migration to the Anula Shagun T.E. It is observed from Table 11.9 that 10.0 per cent of Rais, 33.3 per cent of Kamis and 20.0 per cent of Limbus have been converted into Christainity. Trend towards conversion to Buddhism and Christainity is increasing by leaps and bounds in the plantation. This is due to the widespread influence of

Table 11.9: Religious Structure of the Workers

Sl. No.	*Caste/ Community*	*Hindu*	*Percentage*	*Buddhist*	*Percentage*	*Christain*	*Percentage*
	Gorkhas						
1.	Chhetri= 30	29	97.7	—	—	01	3.3
2.	Manger=50	46	92.0	—	—	04	8.0
3.	Gurung=10	—	—	10	100.0	—	—
4.	Kami= 12	08	66.7	—	—	04	33.3
5.	Tamang=06	—	—	06	100.0	—	—
6.	Limbu=10	08	80.0	—	—	02	20.0
7.	Rai= 30	27	90.0	—	—	03	10.0
8.	Newar= 01	01	100.0	—	—	—	—
9.	Thami= 01	01	100.0	—	—	—	—
	Total=150	120	80.3	16	10.7	14	9.3

Source: Field Work: 2003.

Buddhism and Christainity in tribal Arunachal Pradesh as well as Meghalaya, Nagaland and Mizoram of North East India. In fact, the population of North East India has Mongoloid characteristics having the admixture of Indian, Tibetan and Burmese cultural elements (Bose: 1997).

Traditionally, the Gorkhas, except priestly Bahuns, used to practice tribal cults in the Nepal Himalayas by inviting Jhankris (Shahmen) to perform rituals. Different castes had various types of Jhankris of their own. Animism while observing the rituals of the past has been transformed into a mixed cultural blend of Tribalism and Hinduism at the plantation. The Buddhist Losar/Losang, the Gorkha Dasai (Dashara), Tihar (Deepawali) and Christian Bara Din (X'mas) are common festivals of the workers. The Saraswati Puja, Durga Puja and Pujas at Namghars (Assamese) are equally given importance by all castes and tribes of the plantation.

The Khamti Gaon Puja (worship of village god) is equally celebrated along with Bihu (Assamese cultural festival) at the plantation. The observance of such divergent festivals of Gorkhas, Assamese, Khamtis and others do not carry any religious dogmatism or conservatism rather these festivals are observed as the common plantation festivals in which the participation of all castes, tribes and communities matters much. So, what is pertinent is participation of all castes and tribes (Sharma: 2000) that carry a sense of cultural symbiosis (Bose: 1997) in the plantation than traditional sense of religious dogmatism as such in the changing industrial environment. The tea industry has also fully recognized these festivals as the common plantation festivals (Kar: 1981) of the plantation society. Thus, a cross-cultural social environment has been emerged today at the plantation.

Health Practices of the Workers

The health practices of the workers have apparently two facets, viz., concept of diseases and measures for treatment (Sharma: 1997). The plantation workers having purely agrarian background of their past, had an ample knowledge of medicinal herbal plants to cure diseases (Baruah: 2000). This along with the invitation of Jhankris (Shamen) could give them a deep conviction (Macdonald: 1976) that the patients would be perfectly cured. By 'disease', they used to believe misfortunes that could be evaded out through the secret Mantras (prayers or counselling) by Jhankris (Barreman: 1972) at their homes (Sharma: 2003). Having sufficient forest around, the workers still use herbal medicinal plants to cure diseases. But the use of Jhankris at the plantation is day by day diminishing considerably due to non-availability of Jhankris in the plantation or Chowkham area. No more, the Jhankri system gathers much adoration from the Gorkha society. The belief in Jhankris is almost nil among the youngsters who have been exposed to modernity. Excepting a Kami Jhankri of 70 years old, there is no other Jhankri in the plantation today. The Fa-Foo (prayers) and Chinta (puja with loud voice along with the music of instruments of Jhankris) in black nights by giving or sacrificing the blood of black cocks to evil spirits as in the past is not at all prevalent at the plantation. No Jogi (ascetic) roams around the houses of the workers at black mid-nights to evade out Bhut-Pisach (evil spirits) and bless the houses with the sound of human bones for inviting favourable stars (luck) to the members of the households. On the whole, health practices of the workers are the individual concern and the management of the plantation has nothing to do about it (Bhadra: 1997; Sengupta: 1999).

The use of Adivasi Hariya and Gorkha Rakshi, Jhar etc (handmade liquors) made of fermented millet and rice by the Adivasis and Gorkhas are very popular among all castes and communities of the plantation. The Tongbas (Chyang) of Bhutias of the past is not known to the workers. There is no Bhatti (liquor furnace) at the plantation. In fact, every Matwali and Adivasi as well as Khamti family prepares the beverages at home. All the workers take drinking water from the Dhura (labour line) tube wells and almost all the plantation workers actually attend Jhoras (streams) as the places for their toilets and urinals. They go to Chowkham Government Hospital when the patients become seriously ill due to tuberculosis or other diseases (Chowkham Government Hospital: 2003). Almost 90.0 per cent of the enrolled patients of the Chowkham Government Hospital are males who are suffering from tuberculosis (disease). Normally, Dal (lentil), rice, vegetables and Chapattis are common food items of the workers. Once in a week or fortnight, they take meat or fish at homes.

XII

The Inter-ethnic Relations

In this chapter, we will try to comprehend as to how a new type of inter-ethnic relationship has been evolved at the Anula Shagun T.E. Discussing the inter-ethnic relationship among the various communities, a stress will be given to the influence of language, marriage and cultural traits of various communities of the plantation. By an "ethnic group", here we understand what Frederick Barth (1969) observed as "a population which is largely biologically self-supporting, shares fundamental cultural values, realizes in overt unity in cultural forms, makes up a field of communication and interaction, has a membership which identifies itself."

The tea plantation industry named the Anula Shagun T.E. is poly-ethnic in nature than mono-ethnic type. Interacting with various communities, every community tries to retain its distinct cultural identity (Das Gupta: 1997). A kind of cross-cultural symbiosis has emerged at the plantation. Here, we have at times inserted the term 'integration' along with 'symbiosis' considering or operationalising the government process of integration through the industrialization of Arunachal Pradesh. Again, we will see as to how the industrial environment has established a unique type of social system keeping in tact the cultural separateness of the various communities. In the process, some of the cultural traits of a community have been perfectly integrated in different forms and some other traits of the culture have been apparently diffused while interacting with other communities in day to day industrial intercourses.

Before discussing the diffusion (integration) and differentiation processes in the following section, let us first see how the inter-ethnic relationship that had taken place in the Anula Shagun T.E. (Gunnanagar), Chowkham in the light of historical background of the Arunachal Pradesh as such. The core-peripheral aspects of the plantation system call for an interesting Sociological analysis of inter-ethnic relationships.

Historically, the Arunachal Pradesh as a whole, was the dens of various ethnic trading communities which had been hailing from Assam, Myanmar (Burma), Bhutan, Tibet and Bangladesh. In fact, as it is already mentioned in the study, almost all the tribes of Arunachal Pradesh were immigrants from Myanmar (Burma),Tibet, Bhutan and Bangladesh. According to the Census of India, 1961, there were as many as 82 tribes and sub-tribes in Arunachal Pradesh. This is evident from Table 12.1.

Table 12.1: Tribe-wise Distribution of Population in Arunachal Pradesh (1961)

Sl. No.	*Name of the Tribal Group*	*Population*	*Place of Origin*	*Cultural Zone (District)*
1.	Adi	1,07,880	Tibet	West Siyang/East Siyang
2.	Aka	2,195	Tibet	East Siyang
3.	Apa Tani	10,049	Tibet	Lower Subansiri
4.	Bagni	24,822	Tibet	East Kameng
5.	Bangre	1,575	Tibet	Lower Subansiri
6.	Dafla (Bagun)	35,111	Tibet	Lower Subansiri
7.	Khoa (Bagun)	659	Myanmar	Dibang Valley
8.	Khamti	2,600	Myanmar	Lohit
9.	Khamba	1,120	Tibet	West Siyang
10.	Memba	2,497	Tibet	West Siyang
11.	Maji Dhammai	2,144	Tibet	West Kameng
12.	Mikir	564	Tibet	East Kameng
13.	Hill Miri	564	Tibet	Lohit
14.	Mishmi	5,075	Tibet	Dibang valley
15.	Monpa	20,317	Tibet	Tawang
16.	Sherdukpen	5,075	Tibet	West Kameng
17.	Singpoos	1,154	Myanmar	Changlang
18.	Solung	983	Tibet	East Kameng
19.	Tangsa	1,519	Tibet	East Kameng
20,	Wancho	10,900	Myanmar	Tirap
21.	Yobin	23,393	Myanmar	Changlang

Source: Das: 1995; Field Work: 2003.

Let us look at Table 12.1 of the study. It is observed from the table that tribes of Arunachal Pradesh had either the Tibet or Myanmar (Burma) background. They migrated to Arunachal Pradesh for their livelihood from their places of origin. The Khamtis had migrated from Myanmar to Sadiya (Assam) and then to Chowkham of Lohit district of Arunachal Pradesh in 1785 (Mishra:1984). It is explored from the field survey that Khamti tried to occupy the Bordumsa of the then Tirap and present Changlang district of Arunachal Pradesh but they were badly pushed to Chowkham by Singpoo tribe of the region. Today, there are at least sixty respective ecological zones of 82 tribes and sub-tribes (Das: 1995) in Arunachal Pradesh. The Khamti tribe had agriculture along with business on Khamti tribal arts and crafts (Bose: 1997). Besides agriculture and business, they had barter system on selected items that were to be procured from outside the Arunachal Pradesh. To sustain agriculture, animal husbandry was also done by the Khamtis. The Chowkham being nearest to Tinsukia town of Upper Assam had the influence of Assamese society since the Ahom and British days. Due to the earthquake in Dibang valley in 1950 (Das: 1995) and Chinese invasion to the soil of the country in 1962, most of the then industries of Dibang Valley had to be shifted to the foothills of Lohit district. The mono-ethnic boundary of Chowkham started slowly converting into poly-ethnic habitation, after 1962. This gave rise to the influx of Marwari entrepreneurs from Margherita, Tinsukia, Naharkatia, Sadiya and Dibrugargh of Assam to Chowkham to open up the wood based industries. Thus, the then mono-ethnic industrial (Khamti tribe) habitation had to be converted into poly-ethnic industrial environment (Bose: 1997). That continued till 1987 after which the wood based industries started closing down due to the ban for deforestation by the Government of Arunachal Pradesh. The Marwari in good number had to leave the Chowkham for elsewhere the country.

With the introduction of integrated industrial policy of tribal Arunachal Pradesh after 1987 (the year of the creation of a full-fledged state), the local tribes started tea industry in the state. In Gunnanagar (Chowkham), Mr. Chowkhamoon Gohain converted his Namshum Saw and Veneer Mills (P) Ltd. into Gunna Tea Industries (P) Ltd. in 1987. To meet the problem of labour shortage, the Gorkhas who were denied to get passes under the pretext of Inner Line Permit system of the Government of India prior to 1987 (*Ibid.*) along with Adivasis from Assam were imported from Nepal as tea plantation workers in the Anula Shagun T.E. Thus, the earlier poly-ethnic wood based entrepreneurial environment started slowly converting into labour-poly-ethnic industrial habitation. The earlier ethnic boundaries (Das Gupta: 1997) had been formed with the people of Assam and Khamtis of the region while the tea plantation environment of Anula Shagun

T.E. is much more complex than the earlier ones having Gorkha, Khamti, Adivasi, Bihari, Bengali and Marwari communities although it is purely surrounded by Khamti periphery as the core cultural niche of the region. This will be clear from Table 12.2.

Table 12.2: The poly-Ethnic Boundaries of Anula Shagun T.E.

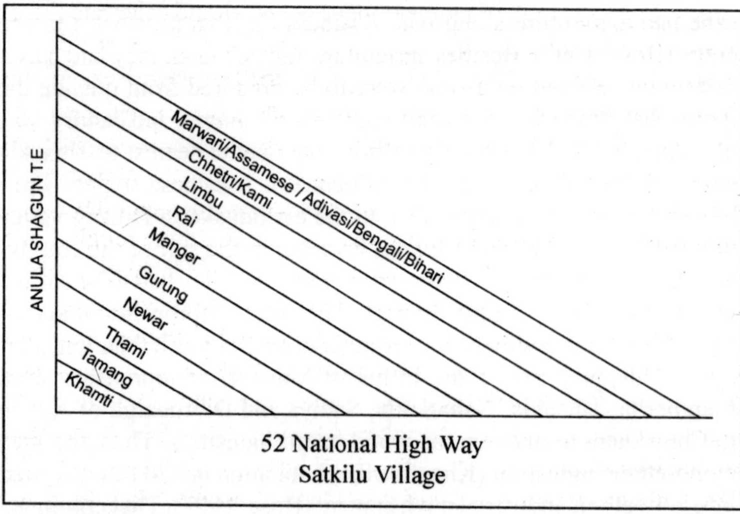

Source: Field Work: 2003.

Table 12.2 clearly indicates the fact that although Khamti villages are located at the proximity of the plantation, they form a core group having ten layers of castes and communities in the plantation. At the tength layer, there are Adivasis, Assamese, Bengalis, Biharis and Marwaris in so far as the dynamics of inter-ethnic relationship is concerned. Each layer maintains its respective boundary (identity) by diffusing certain cultural traits of the other communities. The maintenance of ethnic boundary is in respect of language and culture (Das Gupta: 1997). The Khamtis vis-a-vis the Gorkhas, Adivasis, Assamese, Bengalis, Biharis and Marwaris speak their respective languages at their homes.

Interestingly, it is clear from Table 12.2 of the study that Tamangs of the Gorkha community are much nearer to the Khamti planter's family. They openly share the worshippings at Gunnanagar Buddhist monastery. This common religious bond may have helped the Tamangs, Thamis and few Gurungs to be nearer to the Khamti tea plantation owner and his family. The common Losar and Losang festivals of the Buddhist religion have definitely pulled them together in day to day socio-cultural life with the dominant Khamtis of the region. But they have maintained their separate identity in respect of language and other cultural practices. The Gorkhas speak the Nepali/ Gorkha language as their mother tongue at homes and celebrate Dasai (Dashara) and Tihar (Deepawali) festivals which the Khamtis do not do so at their homes. This is the area of differentiation process. While the diffusion process in regard to Dasai and Tihar is that Khamtis also attend the Gorkha households if they are invited for the festival feast. Next to Gurungs, the Mangers are quite nearer or closer to the Khamtis in respect of diffusion process as the Mangers have also high tendency to convert themselves into the Buddhist religion due to their tradition that they borrowed from the Nepal Himalayas. Many Tamangs, Gurungs, Mangers and Thamis have Mit relationship with not only among themselves but also with the Khamtis. The Mit relationship is formed with the ceremony in which two concerned persons as friends exchange money, handkerchiefs, embrace each other and are friends for the whole life. The money so exchanged should be kept carefully so that it is not lost throughout the life. The Mit relationship may take place between both the sexes or sometimes with two persons of the same sex (Sharma: 2000). Again, traditionally, the Mit relationship could take place between high castes and low castes in the Gorkha society. Thus, the meaning of Mit connotes friend which has been comprehended with making the 'blood' relationship or blood brothern and sistern. Such relationship can be contacted between men and women of different castes, tribes and communities also. Once contacted, the relationship thus holds good on marriage and other ceremonial occasions. In any ritual or ceremony or festival, the Mits must be invited in the host (host's) household (*Ibid.*).

To retain the Mit relationship, the sons and daughters of two Mits are to be completely refrained from marrying. At the death of thc Mit family member, another Mit has to strictly observe the death rituals as prescribed by their tradition. Majority of Gurungs, Mangers, Tamangs and Thamis have not only interwoven in Mit relationship among themselves but also with the Khamtis of the region.

If a Mit relationship is violated in regard to marriage or sexual matter then the following customary punishment is awarded to the accused members of the Mits' families. First, a kind of social boycott is done. After paying a specific amount of fine as decided by the society (Samaj), in the form of cash or kind, the accused members of the Mits' households have to leave the plantation. Such penalty is not only accorded by the Gorkha society but also by the plantation management. The Chhetris, Kamis along with Adivasis are at the farthest end of the boundary maintenance arch amids the poly-ethnic social as well as cultural environment of the plantation.

Table 12.3: The Differentiation Process at Anula Shagun T.E.

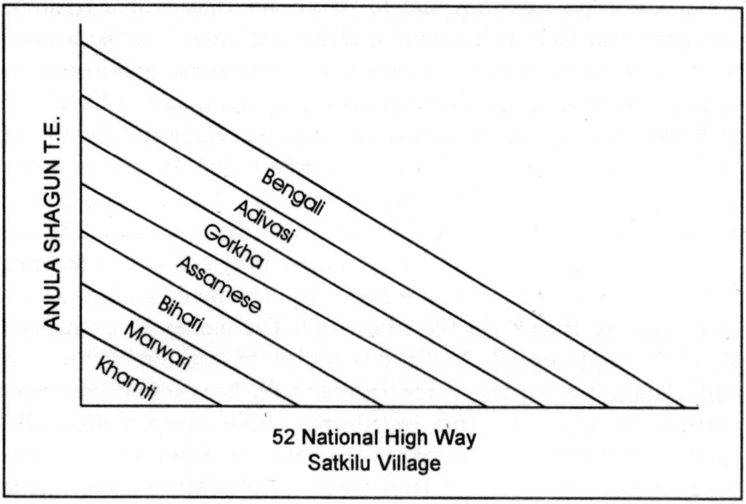

Source: Field Work: 2003.

Table 12.3 of the study shows that Marwaris are at the close contact in so far as inter-ethnic class relationship with the Khamtis of the plantation is concerned. They are the suppliers of goods and other necessary articles to the Khamti planter. Next to Marwaris, Biharis are at the desired proximity of the Khamtis. Next to Biharis, Assamese, Gorkhas, Adivasis and Bengalis are there in the inter-ethnic class relationship system (arch) of the plantation on its differentiaion process with the Khamtis.

Let us come to the question of integration and differentiation (Bhadra: 1997) process that is fastly emerging at the plantation.

It is very transparent from Table 12.4 of the study that the extent of integration is on the higher side in the plantation than the degree of differentiation. The Sociological parameters like marriage, religion, language etc. have made the plantation universe as an industrial unit.

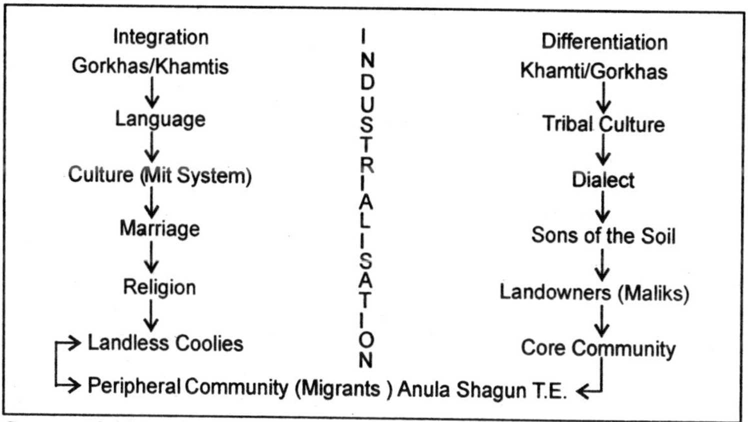

Source: Field Work : 2003.

The gap of difference between "We" and "They" brought about by the concept of ethnicity is not so much on vogue in the plantation. In simplest term, it can be safely said that all the communities as migrants are living here to earn their livelihood. Being a minor group, the Gorkhas belong to a peripheral community in the sense that the major or core community of the region (Gunnanager, Chowkham) is Khamti by tribe. The inter-mingling process at the plantation in respect of socio-economic relationship, however, at times, has reflected some differentiations between the Khamtis and Gorkhas. Such differentiation is overtly observed in two important occasions, viz., marriage and death rituals. Even if the marriages take place between the Gorkhas and Khamtis, each community celebrates the marriage ceremony in its own way at its household and such process has been completely accredited by both the communities. What is important is whether the marrying couples are fully agreed or not to such marriage. At the time of death of the household persons or marriages, each and every community or caste observes its own rituals and observance of such divergent rituals by the respective communities are uninterrupted by others including the management of the plantation.

As stated above, the emerging social stratification of the plantation has differentiated Gorkhas (migrants-landless) as share-croppers from the Khamtis who are the landowners (Maliks). It is due to the widespread impact of monetized capitalist economy (Das: 1995) of the state of Arunachal Pradesh. The tribal Khamtis bother much about the ways and means of earning money rather than the community affiliation or ethno-centrism. Similarly, although the Gorkhas have settled down here at the plantation permanently, their main intention is to earn as much money as possible and invest the same in Terai belts of Nepal. So, their way of living in the plantation is purely as landless agrarian in nature of share-croppers type. But interestingly, it is also observed that most of the Khamtis want to expose the fact that they are not the owners of land may be due to the fear of paying land revenue that is to be paid to the Government of Arunachal Pradesh after 1987. Prior to 1987, they were exempted from paying taxes to the government (Mishra: 1994). So, what they said is that entire Satkilu village is a Gorkha village (Gorkhas of Satkilu Gaon and Anula Shagun T.E.) as the land is jointly cultivated by the Gorkhas of Satkilu and the Gorkhas of the Anula Shagun tea plantation. While in reality, it is found that 90.0 per cent of the land of Satkilu Gaon is actually owned by the Khamtis. So, in very rare situations, such differentiation takes place due to ethnicity issue between the Khamtis and Gorkhas. This may be due to the industrial environment of Gunnanagar (Chowkham) and lack of communal atrocities as we found in other districts of the state. Unlike other North Eastern states, Arunachal Pradesh does not have the problem of communal riots and terrorism except in Changlang and Tirap districts, as we found in Nagaland, Manipur, Mizoram, Meghalaya, Tripura and Assam. Even the communal problems associated with the Chakmas from Bangladesh and Deoris from Assam were settled down within a short period by the Government of India (Das: 1995) in the recent past through rehabilitating them in the eastern districts or frontier wilderness of Arunachal Pradesh. A Chakma village found just near the plantation where Chakmas are the owner-cultivators of land and not a single Khamti landowner is found who has leased out his land to the Chakmas on share-cropping basis in the Chakma Gaon of Chowkham.

The above discussion makes it very distinct that the Khamtis want to lease out their land to the Gorkhas only. Even if a few Khamtis have given land on share-cropping to Adivasis in Tengapani Gaon, the nature of entire village is of dry type and hence the agrarian relationship between Khamtis and Adivasis is by and large not so vivid or as complex as of the Satkilu Gaon. This might be due to the background that Adivasis have very limited knowledge regarding land terracing and thus they are poor wet rice cultivators in Chowkham – the so-called land of Khamtis. So, the degree of differentiation between Khamtis and Gorkhas is very thin or narrow compared the same between the Khamtis and Adivasis.

At the social parlance, it is also observed from the responses of the workers in regard to marriage alliances, if take place, between the Gorkhas and Khamtis, ninety per cent of Gorkhas, excepting the Chhetris, stated that marriage is very much optional for their upbringings. It is their future so to choose marriage partners is counted upon their desire. While the differentiation between the Gorkhas and Adivasis is cent per cent because of their separate habitation, dialect, religion (most Adivasis are Hinduised Animists) and way of life. The feeling of "We" and "They" is very pronounced between these two ethnic communities at the plantation. The Gorkha differentiation with the Assamese, Bihari and Marwari communities is also not so wide compared with Adivasis as the languages of these communities are based on Devnagari script. In fact, it is also observed that Gorkha society hardly feel a gap in relationship with these communities which are basically consisting of the businessmen by profession in Chowkham region. Thus, a kind of cultural symbiosis has been evolved at the plantation due to its industrialization process. The industrialization process does not ordain prior prominence to the question of ethnicity. Everybody wants to earn something for himself or herself. Every community people except the Khamtis, know by heart and soul that they are migrants to the plantation universe and therefore their destiny being uncertain does not allow them to make the 'ethnic' issue as guiding principle for their living at the plantation. It happened at the time of closure of Namshum Saw and Veneer Mills (P) Ltd. in 1987 when almost all the Assamese workers numbering about five hundred who had been involved with ULFA activists of Assam, had to leave the Gunnanagar for elsewhere in search of their bread and butter.

The foregone contention has therefore highlighted very clearly that 'ethnicity' is just at the cultural level only as every community normally shows its identity. For instance, a Gorkha always introduces himself as a Gorkha only if anyone asks him about the ethnic group that he belongs to. The same thing is also found in case of other communities at the plantation. Here, we can say that basic differentiation is found at the identity level. This is because of the fact that even if a Gorkha wants to change his ethnic identity or ethnicity at the plantation into a Khamti, not a single Khamti accepts it overtly though it may so happen covertly due to the reason that a Gorkha guy may have a Khamti wife.

However, it is also observed that there is a difference of "We" and "They". By "We", they mean the plantation co-dwellers and by "They", they mean the people other than the plantation dwellers. Thus, the theoretical amplification as drawn by Barth (1969) has a wide application here in case of the study under reference as 'a group of population' for self-supporting industrial environment of capitalist economy (Das:1995). But the present situation of the plantation is the concomitant result of cohesion brought about by the plantation plural society (Bhadra: 1997). The plural society of Master-Servant relationship (Bhowmik: 1981) of the plantation has categorized the Gorkhas as a minority group. The inter-community boundaries among the Gorkhas, Khamtis, Bengalis, Biharis, Assamese and Marwaris are very narrow or thin in Chowkham and the Anula Shagun T.E. The segregation paradigm or theoretical sociological dimensions have of course temporal and informal effects among the communities simply on the ground that each and every community has its own feeling for community to which they belong. The segregation concept itself connotes to a solidarity but it may be in the negative form that may last long for even in the conflicting situations (Weibe and Marriappan: 1979). Such a negative solidarity appears to have been emerged at the plantation. Though every community tries to survive in better way than others, their relationship is poly-ethnic in nature because the immediate neighbouring households of a community belong to other ethnic communities.

Borrowing: Thread of Inter-ethnic Integration

At times, on emergency, each household has to depend on neighbouring households due to its isolated location. The emergency calls for borrowing and other types of supports from the immediate neighbours. Thus, borrowings have created a broader social neighbourhood. For the Anula Shagun T.E. workers, Chowkham as a whole is their immediate neighbourhood consisting of almost two thousand households. Each and every person knows others personally. So, borrowing does not count upon the community background of the persons from whom one is borrowing money or other things. So, borrowings take place with any community. What is pertinent is to solve the problem arises due to illness or Pujas, or rituals etc. The moral supports at odd times from neighbours irrespective of caste or community background has, therefore, helped to have established the cultural integration—Unity in Diversity in the Anula Shagun T.E. among all the ethnic communities.

The integrated development thesis as introduced and developed through the state industrialization process of Arunachal Pradesh calls for cultural symbiosis. It is non-conventional tea growing/producing niche (area) that appears to have been a model tea plantation for Arunachal Pradesh Government where every ethnic community is simply considered to be the means of production rather than the ultimate owner of the productive unit. This fact has been amply supplemented by the statement made by Mr. Chowkham Gohain who once said that he is, in the eyes of the government, an industrialist than a Khamti by ethnicity. He said to me also while I was conducting field survey at the plantation during 2002-2003. Further, he pointed out that he can develop the tea industry keeping aside the ethnic issues by restoring the ecology of the region at par with the Government schemes for the state. In fact, he is an ardent believer of eco-friendly industrial development of the state. Thus, the ethnicity issue of social relationship is very vague at the Anula Shagun T.E. today.

XIII

Summary and Conclusion

As the title suggests, this is a Sociological study of tea plantation workers in the enchanted but wilderness frontier of Arunachal Pradesh of North East India. Till now, not a single study has been conducted on tea plantation workers of the state. The Arunachal Pradesh along with Nagaland, Meghalaya, Manipur and Mizoram are non-conventional tea growing states (CCPA: 1996) of North East India. Prior to 1981, there was not a single tea estate in Arunachal Pradesh. By and large, tea industry had started in Arunachal Pradesh only after its formation as a full-fledged state in 1987.

The State Sponsored Industrialization

Opening the tea industry in the state of Arunachal Pradesh, was due to the concomitant outcome of the state process of industrialization in full-fledged form. Prior to 1981, the Government of Arunachal Pradesh had established the Arunachal Pradesh Forest Development Corporation Ltd. in 1977 just to streamline the process of wood cutting and continue the then forest wood-based industries of the state. However, in the meantime, the corporation introduced tea industry in the light of reports duly submitted to the government by various expert committees on tea industry appointed earlier for the purpose at Kanubari and Medo of Tirap and Lohit districts respectively. In 1991, two private tea estates were established in full-fledged form, viz., M/s Siang Tea Industries (P) Ltd. and M/s Namshum Tea Company (P) Ltd. in Changlang and Lohit districts respectively. The favourable climatic condition of these districts enabled the private tribal owners to introduce and expand the area under tea cultivation in the state. However, it is observed that tea industry had to face the problem of labour shortage as local tribes did not accept the tea plantation jobs. So, in order to meet the problem of labour shortage, outside labourers were started to import at the plantation jobs by issuing them the temporary Inner Line Permits. The Government of Arunachal Pradesh felt it much better to encourage the import of labour force rather than inviting big tea companies in the state so that the local tribal planters could be flourished with tea industry in the light of declared state sponsored process of industrialization of Arunachal Pradesh after 1987.

Accordingly, the then Jhum and Government waste lands were selected for the introduction and expansion of tea industry in the eastern frontier districts of the state to have enchanted as well as safe frontier wilderness. At least, the government of Arunachal Pradesh had a specific target of additional nine thousand hectares of land to be brought under the tea cultivation by the year, 2006 A.D. In the process, Tea Board of India had been reportedly playing a vital role by providing loans at handsome subsidy schemes. This may be the apparent reason why then there were more than twenty tea estates in the state of course of small size. Excepting two private tea estates of 300 and 500 hectares, all other tea plantations were of very small size in the state.

The Eastern Enchanted Wilderness Frontier

As mentioned above, the eastern frontiers of the state were to be made safe enclaves since the British days (Griffith: 1967) down to the post-eighties of 19th century when it emerged as a full-fledged state of Arunachal Pradesh. With the introduction of tea industry in the frontier wilderness, the eastern belts of the state became closed enclaves being barricaded by the plantation society. The enclave formation in Myanmar and Chinese borders of the state had helped the government for permanent safety of the country (Elwin: 1958). This gave ample opportunity for the tribal planters who are the elites of the society (Mishra: 1994) to earn good income. The tea industry also provides good revenue to the state exchequer. Compared to other tea plantations of Assam, Tripura, Nagaland, Mizoram, Manipur and Meghalaya, the cost of production is very low of Rs. 20 only per kilogram of made tea without providing most of the welfare benefits to the workers of the industrial society. It is found that the government bureaucrats of Arunachal Pradesh along with the management of the plantation industry belong to the sons of the soil while the workers are migrants once and for all time from Assam and Nepal Himalayas. Therefore, the migration of tea plantation labourers and local tribal owners of the tea estates have been responsible factors for the formation of enclave society in Arunachal Pradesh enchanted wilderness frontiers. Ever since the British days, the eastern districts became the focal points for administrators, explorers, tourists, academicians as well as the government bureaucrats. Thus, the frontiers are very much enchanted to all concerned. The workers have been stationed here at the plantations with temporary Inner Line Permits, the period of which in most cases have been already lapsed. If any worker challenges the plantation management for poor wages and welfare incentives as per the provisions of labour legislations of Government of India, then he will be excommunicated from the plantation with evacuation notice first. This has made the workers as good as slaves in the plantations of the state. The escalation of such enclave formation would have been plausible if the local tribes would have joined the plantation jobs.

Universe of the Study

For the sake of analytical convenience of the study on the socio-economic life of tea plantation workers in Arunachal Pradesh, the Anula Shagun T.E. of Lohit district of the state was appropriately selected. On the average, the Anula Shagun T.E. has highest number of Gorkha workers (Coolies) than other tea plantations of the state. The Gorkhas have been recruited by the Khamti owner of the plantation ever since 1987 when the plantation was established. Being an agro-based industry, the Gorkhas were recruited for possessing their agrarian expertise of the past. The pull factor for the Gorkha migration to the plantation frontier is permanent settlement with regular job and agrarian environment around the plantation that provides with ample opportunity for agriculture and animal husbandry to the agrarian Gorkha workers. The study revealed the fact that the Gorkhas are preferred for the plantation jobs as Coolies due to their perseverance, loyalty to the master, semi-tribal culture of their places of origin, friendliness, entrepreneurial characteristics and similar physical endowment (Waddel: 1978) as of the local tribes of Arunachal Pradesh. The plantation is about 106 kilometers away from the Tinsukia town of Upper Assam. The greatest caliber or expertise being possessed by the Gorkha people regarding the culture of terracing of the land in steep Himalayas has absolutely attracted the tribal planters of Arunachal Pradesh to accommodate them in the Anula Shagun T.E. in particular and the state as a whole in general. They appeared to have been possessed a kind of cosmopolitan culture (Chaube: 1985) that helped them to integrate with the core culture of the state in general and the Universe of the study in particular. About one lakh and five thousand Gorkhas are living in the state today. The cheerful nature, smiling faces and cooperative jesters of the Gorkha (Northey and Morris: 1976) Coolies (workers) have attracted the tribal planters to not only employ them in the plantations but also lease out their agrarian belts to the Gorkha workers on share-cropping.

The Hindu-Buddhist Contact Zone

The toiling Hindu workforce with Buddhist tribal ownership of the Anula Shagun T.E. appeared to have fulfilled the industrialization process of the tribal Arunachal Pradesh Government. The lower caste Hindus of the Nepal Himalayas (Bista: 1991) along with the Hinduised Adivasi Animists of Assam has made the structure of workforce a complex one in the Anula Shagun T.E. The original Buddhist tribal (Animists) background of the Gorkha castes like Tamang, Thami, Gurung, Manger, Newar etc. (Waddel: 1978) has given them stimulus to revert to their original Buddhist religion in the truest sense of the term in the plantation though prior to their migration to the plantation they were nicely tinctured to Hindu way of life in Nepal Himalayas. Migration has equipped them with easy ways and means to convert themselves into the Buddhist religion giving pretension for cultural integration with the local Khamtis who are again Buddhists by religion. It is further observed that in fact they were obsessed with the forceful Hinduisation process in Nepal mainly by the Bahun and Chhetri castes (Tagadharis). In that venture, the Tagadharis got complete patronage from the Gorkha Government (Pradhan: 1991) in Nepal.

Caste Continuities at the Anula Shagun T.E.

In spite of emerging integrated society at the plantation, each and every caste and tribe maintains respective caste/tribal inclusiveness in regard to their rituals. They have not been able to erase out their tradition completely in de novo way (Jayraman: 1975). The caste title is still followed strictly while introducing oneself in day to day social relationship. A Khamti always claims himself to be a Khamti and a Gorkha claims himself to be a Gorkha by ethnicity with his caste title along with the clan that he belongs to. The caste-tribe continuities (Srivastava: 1966) are observed in regard to marriage and death rituals because their rituals are totally based on their tradition.

Maintenance of Ethnic Boundaries

Every community of the plantation has completely retained its ethnicity in regard to language, rituals and culture. Each community observes its own rituals, maintains own culture and speak own language. The concept of "we" and "they" become very pronounced at the time of observing the marriage and death rituals of respective communities.

Emergence of Integrated Plantation Society

In spite of fully exploited society of the plantation system, an overt plurality has accommodated the divergent cultural traits of all communities. This is amply portrayed at the time of the celebration of plantation level festivals like Losar/ Losang, Dasai, Tihar, Saraswati Puja, Durga Puja, Bihu (Assamese cultural festival), Mag Sangranti etc. when all the workers are found to be freely participating with the cultural food items and jesters of high emotions (Kar: 1981). The Mit relationship has further sustained well for the emergence of an integrated society at the plantation. Inter-caste/community marriages have helped to restore the integration process among the ethnic communities. The uncertain future of the workers as migrants does hardly allow or encourages them to express anguishes for "ethnicity" issue in the plantation. Nothing except restoring the plantation solidarity (*Ibid.*) is the means of their livelihood. The plantation management also hardly bothers about the ethnicity issue as they aspire much for earning money from the plantation. Borrowing among the plantation communities is another strong thread of cultural integration in the plantation.

Stratification Over Hierarchy

Boarding at the plantation-industrial society having stratified Khamti social system (Mishra: 1994), the traditional caste hierarchy of the

Gorkhas have been fastly eroding into the plantation-industrial type. A de novo type of social stratification is emerging in which the Marwaris and Biharis are occupying the higher positions and it has been accepted by the plantation system. The plantation owner being the master of the area also prefers this new type of social stratification of the society. Communities of working class are at the bottom or they are the peripherals of the plantation system.

The Exploitation Syndrome

The organized exploitation of working class is the characteristic feature of the Anula Shagun T.E. where not a single labour legislation of Government of India has yet been implemented. The exploitation by merely providing wages of Rs. 35 per day per worker and house building materials to the workers, is an established industrial philosophy being absolutely tolerated by the Government of Arunachal Pradesh process of tribal industrialization ever since 1987. It is also observed that such exploitation is persisting well at the plantation due to the absence of trade union organization of the workers (Bhadra: 1997). Not a single trade union organization is found at tea estates of the state. There is no state mechanism for restoring harmonious industrial relations in tea estates of the state. The Department of Commerce and Industries of the state government hardly bothers about the socio-economic upliftment of tea plantation workers of the state. Therefore, the trade union movement that is most prevalent at tea industry of far and wide corners of the country (Sharma: 1991) has not yet penetrated into the tea industry of Arunachal Pradesh.

Low Level of Living of the Workers

The tea plantation workers are by and large the illiterate folks. So, their level of living is very low compared to the tea plantation workers of neighbouring Assam and West Bengal. They are hardly exposed to the industrial living outside the plantation as they feel themselves as "Sukumbasis" or recent settlers at the plantation of Chowkham area of the Lohit district. While Khamtis feel themselves as "Raithaneeys" or the early settlers. Operationally, they are as good as "unorganized" agrarian folks of the Arunachal Pradesh. The unorganizedness of the workers has nicely supplemented by the fact that most of them remain damn busy with agriculture and animal husbandry throughout the year. Such uncertain destiny has forced them to be in close touch with their places of origin. They normally invest their money in Terai belts of Nepal instead of investing the same in the Arunachal Pradesh itself.

Labour Commitment to tea Industry

In spite of uncertain future, the workers are fully committed to the plantation industry as not a single charge sheet has been issued so far to the Gorkha workers for not doing work properly in the plantation till today since its inception. Right from plucking of tea leaves to the packaging of made tea, no work remains pending or undone. This may be the apparent reason why hardly Mr. Gohain visits factory or field except once or twice in a month. The workers are given premeditated impression that the plantation is theirs' and to copy ideas like formation of trade unions from the Assamese workers means to disobey the master or God father—owner of the Anula Shagun T.E.

Future of the Anula Shagun T.E.

The organizational goal of Anula Shagun T.E. had to expand the plantation area from the then 219 hectares to 700 hectares under tea cultivation by the end of the year, 2006 A.D. with thirty lakh kilograms of made tea. The young flush along with cheap migrant Coolies (workers) can fulfil this future plan of the plantation. The absence of management hierarchy having tribal family ownership and management of the plantation may prove fulfilled the organizational goal of the plantation. This may be the reason why new tea plantations have been evolved at Medo, Bordumsa and Tengapani areas by the Khamti owner of the Anula Shagun T.E. In the process, the Gorkha agrarian people of Satkilu Gaon have given him a proactive cooperation by providing labourers to the new plantations. Almost all the responsible posts of these new tea plantations are being given to the Gorkha servants (Coolies) of the Satkilu Gaon and the Anula Shagun T.E. In fact, the Gorkhas have won the confidence of the tribal tea planter to not only initiate new projects on tea plantation morally but also to practically invest huge money or capital on these projects in various enclaves of the eastern most enchanted as well as frontier wilderness of the Arunachal Pradesh of North East India.

References

"Tribal Elites and Social Transformation" by K.K. Mishra, Inter-India Publication, New Delhi, 1994.

"Hellow Fifty" (in Nepali Gorkha) by Vir Vikram Thapa in Uttar Purwanchal Dibya Bharati, a By-Monthly Magazine, Edited by J.P. Sharma, Gangtok, Sikkim, 2008.

"Vramer" (in Napali Gorkha) by Runarayan Sinha, Varanasi, 1986.

"Khukuri" by Min Liwang, Himal (India) Publication, Kalimpong (Darjeeling), 2011.

"The Gurkhas: Settlement and Society" by Sanjay Rana, Mittal Publications, New Delhi, 2008.

"Perspective of Security and Development in North East India" by S.K. Agnihotri and B. Dutta Ray (Ed.), Concept Publishing Company Pvt. Ltd., New Delhi, 2005—an article by Meeta Deka entitled "The Stilwell Road and the China Syndrome" and the article by Shri R.P. Bhattacharjee entitled "Security and Development Perspective in Arunachal Pradesh".

"Indian Napalis: Issues and Perspectives" Edited by T.B. Subba, A.C. Sinha, G.S. Nepal and D.R. Nepal, Concept Publishing Company Pvt. Ltd., New Delhi, 2009.

Articles cited:

A. "Introduction" by A.C. Sinha.

B. "Where is Home for an Indian Nepali writen by Michael Hut.

C. "Nepali Settlement and Cattle Rearing in India's Northeast" by D. Sapkota.

D. "Trafficking of Nepali Women in India" by Shrada Chhetri.

E. "Food and Identity: A Study among the Nepalis of Sikkim and Darjeeling" by Joyti Prakash Tamang.

F. "Shared Destiny: Indians of Nepalese Origin (INO) and Nepalese of Indian Origin (NIO)" by Prof. A.C. Sinha.

G. "The Last Word So Far........" by Prof T. B. Subba.

"History of Arunachal Pradesh" by Prof. M.L. Bose, Concept Publishing Company Pvt. Ltd., New Delhi, 1997.

"Tribes of Arunachal Pradesh in Transition" by Dr. Gurudas Das, Vikas Publishing House, New Delhi,1995.

"The Nepalis in North East India: A Community in Search of Indian Identity" Edited by A.C. Sinha and T.B. Subba, Indus Publishing Company, New Delhi, 2007.

Articles Cited:

1. "The Indian North East Frontier and the Nepali Immigrants" by A. C. Sinha.
2. "The Nepalis in North East India: Political Aspirations and Ethnicity" by T.B. Subba.
3. "Soldiers and settlers: The Recruitment of Gorkhas" by Imdad Hussain.
4. "Gorkhas. Contribution to External and Internal Security in India" by K.K.Muktan.
5. "Being a Nepali in Northeast India: Predicaments of a Privileged Nation" by T.B. Subba.
6. "Conflict Afflicted Nepalis of Assam: the Reality" by Lopita Nath.
7. "Nepali Participation in the Electoral Politics of Assam" by Kripa Prasad Upadhaya.
8. "Nepali Christians in the Khasi and Jaintia Hills of Meghalaya" by Amena Nosa Passah.
9. "The Gorkhas in Mizoram" by K.L. Pradhan.
10. "The Nepalis in Manipur: Movement and Settlement" by C.K.N. Chhetry.
11. "The Quest for Ekrupta: Unity, Uniformity and Delineation of the Nepali Community in Darjeeling", Rhoderick Chalmers.
12. "The Indians of Nepali Origin and Security of North East India" by A.C. Sinha.
13. "Epilogue" by Prof. T.B. Subba.
14. Othering of "Not-So Other": A Study of the Nepalis of Assam by Anindita Dasgupta.
15. "The Myth Making Greater Nepal" by K.M. Dixit.
16. "Fei-isation of the Nepalis of North East India" by Sagal Nag.
17. "Human Movement and the Colonial State: The Nepalis of Northeast India under the British Empire" by Tejimala Gurung

18. "Contribution of the Nepalis of Northeast India to the Development of Nepali literature" by Tek Narayan Upadhaya and Roma Adhikari.
19. "Evolution and Growth of the Nepali Community in Northeast India by Purusotham L. Bhandari.

"The North East Frontier of India" by Alexander Mackenzie, Mittal Publications, New Delhi, 2011.

"Look East Policy and India's North East", Edited by Thingham Kishan Singh, Concept Publishing Company Pvt. Ltd., New Delhi, 2009.

Articles by:

1. "India's Look East Policy: Origins and Conceptualization" by T.K. Singh.
2. "Mapping India's Look East Policy: Shifting Alignments" by K. Indrakumar.
3. "Development and Discontent Meet in North East: Perspectives on India's Look East Policy" by Ajiailiu Niumai.
4. "Look East Policy: Its Gaze and Danger in the North East" by H.G. Sharma.

"Marginalization of Gorkhas in India: A Community in Quest of Indian Identity" by K.R. Sharma and T.C. Das, Abhijeet Publication, New Delhi, 2011.

"Globalization and Plantation Workers in North East India" by K.R. Sharma and T.C. Das, Kalpaz Publication, New Delhi, 2009.

"Agony of Plantation Workers in North East India" by K.R. Sharma and T.C. Das, Kalpaz Publication, New Delhi, 2008.

"Socio-economic Life of Cinchona Plantation Workers in India" by Khemraj Sharma, National Library Publication, Dibrugargh (Assam), 1997.

"Sociology of Indian Tea Industry", Mittal Publication, New Delhi, 2005 by Khemraj Sharma.

"Tea Plantation Workers in a Himalayan Region" by Khemraj Sharma, Mittal Publication, New Delhi, 2003.

"The Himalayan Tea Plantation Workers" by Khemraj Sharma, National Library Publication, Siliguri, West Bengal, 2000.

"Tea Industry in India: An Introduction" by Khemraj Sharma, National Library Publication, Siliguri (West Bengal), 1999.

"Plantation Sociology of North East India", Abhijeet Publication, New Delhi, 2010 by Khemraj Sharma.

"The Gorkhas of North Eastern Frontier of India" by Dr. Khemraj Sharma, Abhijeet Publication, New Delhi, 2012.

"Assamma Nepaliharuko Aitihasik Pristhabhumi (in Nepali/Gorkha)" by Shyamraj Jaisi, Bodha Kumari Smriti Prakashan, Digboi (Assam), 1990.

"Migration and Development: The Nepalis in North East" in *Economic and Political Weekly*, 16(24) by Drikant Dutta, Bombay, 1981.

"The History of Gorkhas Communities in North East India, Sahkahi Samiksha, Shillong, by B.D. Dungel, 1983.

"The Nepalis in Northeast India: Ethnicity and Resource Appropriation" in the *Social Tension in North East India*, Edited by J.B. Bhattacharjee, NEICSSR, Shillong, 1982.

"Nepali Community in India" by Suman Raj Timsina, Manak Publication, New Delhi, 1992.

"History of the Assam Rifles", 1977 by L.W Shakespeare, Aizwal, Mizoram.

Website, 2011, *Gorkhas in Myanmar.*

Grazing Reserves and Gorkha Grazers in Assam, in Website, 2009.

Mistaken Identity of Gorkhas in India: An Account in Assam in Website, 2009 by Nanda Kirti Dewan.

"Sadiya Ko Darpan (in Nepali/Gorkha)" by Debi Prasad Gautam, Purbodaya Sahitya Prakashan, Jagun, Tinsukia (Assam), Published by Shri Trilokya Nath Gautam, 2009.

"Sadiya Ko Jhalak (in Nepali/Gorkha)" by Trailokya Nath Gautam, Jai Bharat Printing Press, Varanasi, 1985.

"History of the Assam Rifles" by L.W. Shakespear, Spectrum Publication, Guwahati (Assam), 1924 & 1980.

"The North East Frontier of India" by K.R. Pemberton, Mittal Publication, 2011, New Delhi.

"The Mismi Hills" by T.T. Cooper, Mittal Publication, New Delhi, 2000.

"In The Abor Jungle" by H.H. Hamilton, Mittal Publication, 2001, New Delhi.

"Assam Review and Tea News", Kolkata, 1999.

Barreman, G.D. "Hindus of Himalaya: Ethnography and Change", University of California Press, Berkeley, 1972.

Barth, F. "Ethnic Groups and Boundaries: The Social Organization of Culture Difference", Allan Unwin, London, 1969.

Baruah, Tultul, "Mundas in Tea Plantation: A Study of Their Health Behaviour", N.L.Publishers, Dibrugargh, Assam, 2000.

Bennet, Synn: "The Dual Role of High Caste Women in Nepal" in James F. Fisher (Ed.) *Himalayan Anthropology*, Hague, Paris, 1978.

Bhadra, Mita: "Ethnicity and Inequality among the Workers in Tea Industry" in R. K.Bhadra *et al. Plantation Labours of North-East India*, N.L.Publishers, Dibrugargh, Assam, 1997.

Bhadra, Mita: "Women Workers in Tea Plantations in India", Heritage Publishers, New Delhi, 1992.

Bhadra, R.K.: "Social Dimension of Health of Tea Plantation Workers in India", N.L.Publishers, Dibrugargh, Assam, 1997.

Bhanja, Kamelesh, "Mystic Tibet and the Himalaya", Cultural Publishing House, Delhi, 1984.

Bhowmik, Sharit: "Class Formation in the Plantation System", People's Publishing House, New Delhi, 1981.

Bhowmik, Sharit: "Tea Plantations in West Bengal" in Sarath Davala (Ed.) *Employment and Unionization in Indian Industry*, Friederick Ebert Stiftung, New Delhi, 1995.

Bhowmik, Sharit: "Tea Plantation Labour in India", Friederick Ebert Stiftung, New Delhi, 1996.

Bhuyan, C.: "Ahom Buranji", Guwahati, Spectrum Press, 1947.

Bista, D.B.: "Fatalism and Development: Nepal's Struggle for Modernization", Orient Longman, Calcutta, 1993.

Bose, M.L.: "History of Arunachal Pradesh", Concept Publishing Company Pvt. Ltd., New Delhi, 1997.

Caplan, L.: "Land and Social Change in East Nepal: A Study of Hindu-Tribal Relations", Routeledge and Kegan Paul Publication, London, 1970.

Chakraborty, R.N.: "Socio-Economic Development of Plantation Workers in North-East India", 1997, N.L. Publishers, Dibrugargh, Assam.

Chaube, S.K.: "The Himalayas: Profiles of Modernization and Adaptation", Sterling Publishers Private Limited, New Delhi, 1985.

Chaudhury, S.S.: "Challenges of Tea Management in Twenty First Century", N.L. Publishers, Dibrugargh, Assam, 2000.

Consultative Committee of Plantation Associations, Calcutta, Tea Industry: A Report, 1996.

Das Gurudas: "Tribes of Arunachal Pradesh in Transition", Vikas Publishing House Private Limited, New Delhi, 1995.

Das Gupta, P.K.: "Maintenance of Ethnic Boundary in the Tea Plantations of North Bengal and Assam" in R.K.Bhadra, et. al

(Ed.) *Plantation Labours of North East India*, N.L.Publishers, Dibrugargh, Assam, 1997.

Devi, Uma: "Plantation Economy in the Third World", Vikas Publishing House Private Limited, New Delhi, 1989.

Directorate of Commerce and Industries, Government of Arunachal Pradesh, Itanagar, 2003.

Dozey, E.C.: "A Concise History of the Darjeeling District since 1835 with a Complete Itinerary of Tours in Sikkim and the District", Jetsun Publishing House, Calcutta, 1989.

Dubey, Rameshwar: "Privatization and Its Implications for Trade Unions" in C.S. Venkata Ratnam *et al. Labour and Union in a Period of Transition*, Friederick Ebert Stiftung, New Delhi,1994

Dubey, S.M.: "Modernization and Elites in Arunachal Pradesh", Government of India, Delhi, 1975.

Dutta, Choudhury, S.: *Arunachal Pradesh District Gazetteers*, Lohit District, Government of Arunachal Pradesh, Itanagar, 1978.

Elwin, Verrier: *A Philosophy of NEFA*, Advisor to the Government of Assam, Shillong, 1958.

Gogoi, L.: "The Tai Khamtis", Namsoom, 1971.

Government of India: "Anglo-Burmese Relations, 1771-1826", Gauhati, 1947.

Government of India: "Plantation Labour Act, 1951", New Delhi, 1951.

Griffith, P. : "The History of Indian Tea Industry", Widenfel and Nicolson, London, 1967.

Guha, A.: "Planter's Raj to Swaraj", ICHR, New Delhi, 1977.

Haimendorf, C. Von, Furer: "Anthropology of Nepal", Vikas Publishing House, New Delhi, 1966.

International Labour Organization: "Basic Problems of Plantation Workers, Geneva", 1950.

Jayraman, R.: "Caste Continuities in Ceylon: A Study of Social Structure in Three Tea Plantations", Popular Prakashan, Bombay, 1975.

Jones, W.O.: "Plantation" in David L. Sills (Ed.) *International Encyclopedia of Social Sciences*, Vol. 8, Macmillan Press, New York, 1968.

Kar, R.K., Savaras of Mancotta: "A Study on the Effects of Tea Industry of the Tribal Life", Cosmo Publication, New Delhi, 1981.

Legislative Assembly Report, Government of Arunachal Pradesh, Itanagar, 1987.

Macdonald, A.W. : "Preliminary Note on Some Jhankris of Munglan" in John T. Hitchock (Ed.) *Spirit Possession in the Nepal Himalayas*, Vikas Publishing House, New Delhi, 1976.

Mamkottam, Kuriakose: "Globalization and the Emerging Labour-Management Relations" in C.S. Venkata Ratnam (Ed.) *Labour and Unions in a Period of Transition*, Friederick Ebort Stiftung, New Delhi,1994.

Mishra, S.N.: "Arunachal's Tribal Economic Formation and their Dissolution" in *Economic and Political Weekly*, Vol. XVIII, No. 43, October, 22, 1983, New Delhi.

Myint, Hla: "Economics of Developing Countries", Hutchinson University Press, London, 1973.

Nepali, G.S.: "The Newars: An Ethno-Sociological Study of a Himalayan Community", United Asia Publication, Bombay, 1965.

Northey, W.B. and Morris, C.J.: "The Gurkhas: Their Manners, Customs and Country", Cosmo Publication, New Delhi, 1976.

Parmer, P.K.: "The Gurkhas", Deep and Deep Publications, New Delhi, 1990.

Pradhan, Kumar: "The Gorkha Conquests": Causes and Consequences of Unification of Nepal with Particular Reference to Eastern Nepal", Oxford University Press, Calcutta, 1991.

Ramaswamy, E.A.: "Introduction" in Sarath Davala (Ed.) *Employment and Unionization in Indian Industry*, Friederick Ebert Stiftung, New Delhi, 1995.

Ratnam, Venkata, C.S.: "Globalization and Labour-Management Relations: Dynamics of Change", Response Books (A Division of Sage Publications), New Delhi, 2001.

Regmi, M.C.: "A Study of Nepali Economic History (1768-1846), Manjushree Prakashan, New Delhi, 1971.

Sampath, L.M. : "Union-Management Relations in Changing Scenario" in C.S. Venkata Ratnam, *et al.*, (Ed.) *Labour and Unions in a Period of Transition*, Friederick Ebert Stiftung, New Delhi, 1994.

Sarkar, Jayanta: "Society, Culture and Ecological Adaptation among three tribes of Arunachal Pradesh", Anthropological Survey of India, Calcutta, 1987.

Sarkar, R.L. and Lama, M.P.: "Tea Plantation Workers in the Eastern Himalayas", Atmaram and Sons Publications, New Delhi, 1986.

Sengupta, Sarthak: "Preface" in Sarthak Sengupta (Ed.) *Health, Healers and Healing: Studies in Medical Anthropology*, N.L. Publishers, Dibrugargh, Assam, 1999.

Seth, N.R.: "Labour Relations in New Economic Environment" in C.S. Venkata Ratnam *et al.* Labour and Unions in a Period of Transition, Friederick Ebert Stiftung, New Delhi, 1994.

Sinha, Pravin: "Union in a Period of Transition in C.S. Venkata Ratnam et al. *Labour and Unions in a Period of Transition*, Friederick Ebert Stiftung, New Delhi, 1994.

Srivastava, R.P. : "Caste-Tribe Mobility in India and the Case of Kumaon Bhutias" in C. Von Furer Haimendorf (Ed.) *Caste and Kin in Nepal, India and Ceylon*, Asia Publishing House, Bombay, 1966.

Subba, Tanka B.: "Ethnicity, State and Development: A study on Gorkhaland Movement in Darjeeling", Har-Anand Publication, New Delhi, 1990.

Waddel, L.A : "Among the Himalayas", Ratna Pustak Bhandar, Kathmandu, Nepal, 1978.

Weibe, D. Paul and Marriapan, S.: "Indian Malaysians: The View from the Plantation", Manohar Publications, New Delhi, 1979.

Wolf, Eric: "Specific Aspects of the Plantation System in the New World" in Eric Wolf (Ed.) *The Plantation System in the New World*, University of Washington Press, 1959.

Xaxa, V.: "Economic Dualism and Structure of Class: A study in Plantation and Peasant Settings in North Bengal" Cosmo Publications, New Delhi, 1997.

Index